Who's Your Mama?

Who's Your Mama?

The Unsung Voices of Women and Mothers

edited by
YVONNE BYNOE

with a Foreword by Rebecca Walker

Soft Skull

"An Unnatural Woman" was first published in *Rise Up Singing: Black Women
Writers on Motherhood*. Edited by Cecelie S. Berry (Doubleday: New York, 2004)

"Sounds Like a Plan" was first published in *Brain, Child* in December, 2006.

Library of Congress Cataloging-in-Publication Data is available upon
request.

ISBN: 978-1-59376-239-1

Cover design by Amy Woloszyn
Interior design by Beth Kessler, Neuwirth and Associates, Inc.
Printed in the United States of America

Soft Skull Press
New York, NY

www.softskull.com

★ contents ★

"If we stand tall, it is because we stand on the backs of those who came before us."

—Yoruba proverb

★

in rememberance of

CORALEE EVANS BYNOE
MARGARET CLARKE BYNOE
NELLIE WHITE EVANS

★ foreword ★

Parenthood is complex. As mothers, we have to wade through conflicting ideas about the benefits of motherhood itself, the various myths and methodologies of giving birth, and the varied schools of parenting, from attachment theory to timed feedings and effective discipline techniques. No matter how much (or how little) money we have, we rarely feel financially ready to have a child. And because there are so many unwanted children in the world, we sometimes feel we should redirect our energies. If we really cared about saving the world, we think to ourselves, we would forgo our own offspring, and adopt another mother's child.

It's hard to fight the realities of modern life. There are a few positive signs, but the world seems to be falling apart as fast as we put it back together. The predictions of one hundred year wars, multigenerational economic instability, and an onslaught of incurable diseases are overwhelming. One article about children kidnapped and sold into slavery can put even the most certain mom-to-be on the path of ambivalence. The mention of two million men of color languishing in American prisons is reason enough for a woman of color to stock up on birth control pills. Add a few GMOs and IEDs, a memo on global debt from the IMF, and one late night encounter with the INS and it's a miracle anyone chooses to have a child at all.

But we do, which means we have to do more than affirm our choice to become mothers. We have to demonstrate how and why we moved forward; we have to prove we are worthy and, in the face of all other indicators, that we have made a good decision. Which, of course, is impossible. I've yet to meet a woman who can logically explain her longing to have a child. Looking down at the flesh of our flesh, blood of our blood, most of us have to shake our heads. Our decision to get on the roller coaster is totally, completely, one hundred percent irrational. It's physical, spiritual, and psychobiological. It is beyond this world.

We want to have a baby, but it is more than that. Consciously or not, we want to let go of who we are now, our own random conglomeration of cells and carefully orchestrated lived experience, and see who we can become. We want to fire up the catalytic converter, the human spaceship, and change! It's a shame, a missed opportunity, that giving birth and having children is considered so ordinary, so normal in our culture. Because when we acknowledge what a huge, ginormous deal it is, a world opens. Inexplicably powerful, irrevocably altering, to become a mother is to step into the mystery. It is to acknowledge there is something else going on beneath the surface of everyday existence.

In our drive to make life better for our babies, we touch the superhuman. In the unconditional love we feel for our children, we get a grip on what life is all about. Invested in our future like never before, and with the ability now to see the past, present, and future as one continuous stream, we become, in a sense, immortal. And in our sudden recognition that motherhood has been happening since the dawn of time, we develop a profound respect for every mother who offers so much of her life's energy, and so doing, ensures the survival of our species.

Are you with me? Forget six hundred dollar strollers and ten thousand dollar a year nursery schools. Forget food stamps and emergency-room-only health care. Forget LSD and UFOs. When motherhood is a choice (and sometimes even when it isn't), crossing over is powerful.

Motherhood is the real deal.

And like all supernatural experiences, the mystical ride of motherhood seeks corroboration. Am I insane, one mother asks another, speaking of the range of feelings that come up in the course of an ordinary day. The guilt, bliss, exasperation, love, terror, is this normal? Insulated in our domestic spheres, we long to know we are not alone in the intensity of our feelings, and especially, in the depth of our struggle to keep it all together. Our struggle to bring home the bacon, fry it up in a pan, and make sure our children know why Mama can't stop everything to build a car wash out of a box of Legos.

That's usually where extended family comes in. And the gaggle of moms spreading their blankets and breaking out the rice crackers at the playground. And the long trips down mommy-portals on the internet. It's also where writers come in, and books. Disembodied voices and tactile, reassuring objects keep us company and give us room for reflection. We see ourselves in the pages we choose, and feel less alone. Somebody gets it, gets us. But what if your extended family isn't supportive of your partner's gender, or all the moms at the playground are richer or poorer or speak a different language? What if all the books about motherhood are written for mothers with whom you have very little in common?

That's when you have to intensify your search, and if you're lucky, find a book like this one.

I'm thrilled to join Yvonne Bynoe and the talented essayists included in this illuminating collection about contemporary motherhood. I'm thrilled because this book is so necessary, and because it is also so good. I'm thrilled because any woman who has birthed, lost, wants, or vehemently decided against having a child will find herself sensitively represented in these pages. And every woman, regardless of race, class, sexuality, or religion, will find some place, some literary nook, that completely affirms her choices.

Unlike many popular books on motherhood, this collection doesn't shy away from mothers who have temporarily "abandoned" their children while they try to better themselves, or who try hard to keep their families together only to be hit with economic devastation and unanticipated divorce. *Who's Your Mama* doesn't sugar coat or whitewash the realities of contemporary motherhood. Bynoe is not afraid to say that we miscarry, worry about our children's racial identity, give up on breastfeeding because the office is not conducive to pumping. She gets that a whole lot of women swallow middle class assumptions and make our way to the AFDC office for food stamps.

And she also gets that, in the midst of calamity, we show up every day to be the best mothers we can. Over and over again, the essayists in the book break it down: at the end of the day, it's about our kids. They take so much from us—energy, freedom, money—but they give so much, too. They demand honesty, tenderness, emotional competency, and sound financial planning. Let's face it. If we're awake to what's really going on in this human experience called motherhood, raising a child is the ultimate finishing school. If we let them, our kids can make us so much better.

Which is not to say that women who choose (joyfully!) not to have children are "less." They actually may be more enlightened than the rest of us, because they don't need to have a child to become more selfless. But guess what? Even the judgment projected onto women who don't want to have children isn't in this book. It's just not. In this book you can be free to, well, be.

And not just you, but me, too. Because right up front, in her introduction, Bynoe generously acknowledges the role my memoir, *Baby Love*, played in the gestation and birth of *Who's Your Mama*. She read my journey to biological motherhood, including my hunt for fabulous maternity clothes, perilous negotiation with Western medicine and midwifery, and brutal reckoning with my relationship with my own mother, and saw parts of herself she hadn't seen in the public discussion of motherhood. Like every good editor, she realized she couldn't possibly be alone. There must be thousands of women coming up short in the maternity section at Barnes and Noble and on Amazon, and Bynoe determined to do something about it.

It means a lot to me that *Baby Love*, a book, as Bynoe accurately notes in her introduction, that is equally revered and rejected, inspired this work and led Bynoe to find stories that are real, brave, and true. Stories that speak to who we are now. Many women of our generation are not wealthy, sustainably partnered, or advanced in their profession of choice, but they are claiming their motherhood fiercely. They may challenge the cost of childcare and food, realize later than they ought that they need more support, or have to buy their sperm from the sperm bank, but they are answering the call to procreate with passion and vigor. They choose to follow their longing, and even though there are larger issues, they have no intention of, yes, throwing the baby out with the bathwater.

After reading the essays here, I realize that I can't ask for more. Writers sit down and spill blood and open a portal and if that portal rips a hole in the fabric called conventional thinking and facilitates the rise of voices ordinarily silenced, then our job is complete. Without that response, our call is pointless. And so I want to thank Bynoe personally here, in print. This book not only lessens the invisibility of unsung mothers, but it lessens my own feelings of marginalization. My voice, too, has been silenced and judged. Bynoe is not the only one who sees herself in *Baby Love*, but she's one of the few who has claimed it unequivocally as a signpost in a larger territory, an indicator of a rich and fertile parallel world.

This is the kind of recognition that can only come from another mother, and it is the kind of recognition that means the most. It is also the kind of recognition this book is all about. *Who's Your Mama* recognizes your motherhood may be complicated, but that doesn't mean it isn't true.

So here we are, my friends. I stand with you as new women on old ground. In the spirit of *Who's Your Mama* I promise to celebrate you in all your diversity, to believe in the absolute necessity of each and every voice, and to work as hard as I can in my corner of the world to make life better for all of us. That's what mothers do, right?

foreword

We do it for our children, and hopefully, more and more, through simple acts of generosity and complex acts of legislature, we do it for one another.

Because all mothers deserve the best—including you.

—Rebecca Walker

Who's Your Mama?

Introduction

YVONNE BYNOE

I wasn't one of these women who ever had a jones to become a mother. When my friends started having children, I politely gazed on their babies from afar, not wanting their spit-up, pee, or poop to damage my designer outfit. Yes, I was that woman—childless and loving it. Throughout my life I knew that I would become a mother one day, I just couldn't pin down when that day would be. In the meantime, I felt that I had more important things to do than worry about "birthing babies." I had to go to law school, establish my career, visit the Motherland, and write a book—then I could think about being a mother. I also had to find someone who I wanted to have children with; someone with whom I could see myself intertwined for the rest of my life. Easier said than done.

I suppose that I got my laissez-faire attitude from my mother. She never pushed me or my sister to get married, nor did she express any overwhelming need to become a grandmother. She had been a stay-at-home mother for years, but she had made getting an education and becoming financially independent a priority over marriage and motherhood. Perhaps she had regrets about her own choices, or maybe she just wanted to prepare my sister and me for the broadening horizons that awaited us. I don't really know the answer but I thank my mother for giving me options. I am equally equipped to be a domestic goddess or a corporate executive—I can literally bring home the bacon and fry it up in the pan. My grandmother however didn't encourage the idea of waiting to get married or to have children. Regarding the latter she used to say that there was never a right time to have a baby, you just did it. For her generation that advice made sense, but I knew that it wasn't appropriate for me. I had to live a life, achieve some personal goals, and figure out who I was before I'd be ready, willing, or wanting to devote myself to a child.

I became a mother in 2004. As the oracle at Delphi counseled, "Know thyself." I always assumed that when the time was right, everything would fall into place. For me, the "right timing" had to do with my feeling that I needed not only love, but also some measure of knowledge to pass on to my child. Moreover, I felt that I needed to have the ability to make sound judgments for my child, and that required having some experience with both the charms and disappointments of the world. The practical side of me also demanded some other prerequisites such as financial stability, work that allowed me to stay home, and a partner willing to help out with the child. I had a problem-free pregnancy and an absurdly easy birth, which I attribute to being on my "right path." For me, the "right timing" to becoming a mother was after I finished the items on my then life list. I also married a man who was willing to support me on every step of the journey from pregnancy to motherhood.

Women have been having children for a millennia; I knew however that my expression of motherhood would be personal and unique. My decisions about how I would raise, interact with, and educate my son would not only be informed by my personality, values, beliefs, and background, but also by the music, icons, politics, and events that shaped my generation. I am part of a multiracial cohort of women born between 1965 and 1981, whether you call it the hip-hop generation or Gen X. As preteens we read Judy Blume novels. We grew up in the age of MTV and BET. Women such as

Madonna, Queen Latifah, Pat Benatar, Blondie, MC Lyte, Joan Jett, The Bangles, Mary J. Blige, TLC, Lauryn Hill, and Alanis Morissette provided my generation of women with lyrics to sing as well as fashions to copy and female identity models to preview and try on. Our politics were shaped by Reaganomics and the comparatively halcyon Clinton years. In the shadows of our collective conscious-ness was feminism. Not the strident, Helen Reddy "We are Woman" rendition, but a more subtle knowing. Unlike our mothers, we took it as a given that we were equal to men. We also took it for granted that we should control our own bodies and the course of our own lives. What escaped us is how to actually "have it all." Besides Claire Huxtable on the television program *The Cosby Show*, there were very few examples of successful career women who also had happy mar-riages and healthy children. Oprah Winfrey was single and childless; so was the title character on *Murphy Brown* (1988–1998), a high pro-file news reporter. Murphy Brown, an affluent, middle aged White woman, ignited a national debate about single mothers when she became pregnant. As far back as *Julia* (1968–1971), *Alice* (1976–1985), or *One Day at a Time* (1975–1984), however, working mothers were portrayed as widowed or divorced. The underlying message from Hollywood was that mothers work only out of financial neces-sity (i.e., there's no husband), not because they were quenching their own professional ambitions nor because they had a desire to participate in the world. I don't think that it's a far stretch to say that Hollywood helped many young women to internalize the idea that they can't be the best career woman and the best mother at the same time.

It is clear that some women of my generation hewed more closely to the conventional ideals of motherhood. Buoyed by their husband's considerable incomes, they stopped working once they became mothers. In a radical shift away from second-wave femi-nism, many Gen-X women privileged motherhood over their careers. For years critics have scoffed that these women have opted out of the corporate world and leadership positions. They've opined that in spite of their elite educations they have chosen to mimic the suburban housewives who were presented on 1950s television shows such as *Father Knows Best* or *Leave It to Beaver*. In truth some Gen-X women have concluded that they can best impact society by staying home and raising loving, responsible, and sane children. Other women however are less sanguine about domestic relationships and the prospect of finding a man who's positioned to be the sole financial provider. This group generally views marriage and motherhood as à la carte options, rather than part of a prix fixe menu. Consequently these women, some married, others single, continue to work outside the home after having children. I, like a host of women, fall somewhere in the middle.

I wanted the financial freedom and personal satisfaction of working, yet I wanted to be my son's primary caretaker. It was hugely important to me that I had firsthand knowledge of how my son was growing and developing. I just couldn't stomach the idea of someone else telling me about his first steps and first words. I also wanted to be there for him when he needed me. If he was sick, had a school holiday, or just woke up scared one morning, I didn't want to have to haggle and justify with my employer to spend time with him. Moreover, I knew that in that eventuality there would be no contest—my son would win every time. In order to accomplish this, however, I have a partner who can shoulder the finances when mommyhood temporarily impacts my income. I've come to see that regardless of the path women of my generation have taken, motherhood, like our other identities, is a *remix*. As the rap music term implies, we are taking the original motherhood narrative, combining it with some contemporary elements, and creating a new, remixed motherhood that speaks to our personas, needs, desires, and the times we live in.

In the earliest days of my motherhood, I searched for role models, women who had transitioned into motherhood to whom I could relate. Unfortunately I often left the bookstore disappointed. So much of the literature on motherhood did not speak to me. A large percentage of the books published annually on motherhood focus on affluent, married White women and their experiences as combatants in the "mommy wars." The "mommy wars" is a ferocious and ongoing debate about whether mothers should work outside the home or not. I personally found the topic rather strange since I thought that the underlying principle of feminism was a woman's right to choose. I simply wasn't comfortable reading books where women bashed other women over decisions they've made about child-rearing and work. Within the rubric of feminism, I did not believe that "choice" ended with the decision to have a child or not. I believed that feminism extended a mother's choice to decide the framework in which she would parent. From my vantage point a woman who consciously decides not to work and stay home with her children is no less empowered than the mother who is employed outside the home. Each choice has its benefits and its liabilities, and it's each woman's responsibility to weigh the sides and make a decision that works with her values and beliefs. Also these stark poles leave little room to explore the true dynamism of women's lives. In the eighteen years spanning from a child's birth to their legal maturity, a woman can actually make several different work/family decisions. So, I wasn't feeling the "mommy wars" books.

Many of these mommy-war books also made me uncomfortable because they presumed that going to work was an option for most American women. The only way that going to work can be a lifestyle choice is if the mother is connected to a man who has the ability (and desire) to wholly financially support her and their children. In reality, few American women have the luxury of deciding whether or not to work. A majority of women work outside the home either full- or part-time and have done so for decades. The increasingly volatile nature of the U.S. economy almost requires that each household have two wage earners. Simultaneously there are more single mothers in the country because divorce rates continue to hover at about 50 percent, and there are more unmarried parents living together. Thus despite all of the ink that is devoted to the White, married, stay-at-home mother, this group is a minority both racially and economically. The fact that this small demographic is represented in the media as the motherhood norm instantly obscures and marginalizes the voices and stories of the majority of mothers in the United States. The true majority of American mothers includes women of color, White women, low- and middle-income women, affluent women, single heterosexual women, lesbians, married heterosexual women, women living with a partner, women who are employed, and stay-at-home mothers.

From a more personal perspective I'm dismayed that little attention is given to hip-hop generation musical artists such as Salt-N-Pepa, Monie Love, or singers T-Boz and Chilli from TLC, Lauryn Hill, or Angie Stone, a member of the Old School rap group Sequence, in their roles as mothers. At least in the rock and pop worlds you see pregnancy and "mommy" shots of performers such as Madonna, Gwen Stefani, Christina Aguilera, and Sheryl Crow. Aside from Baby Phat CEO, Kimora Lee Simmons, who is frequently seen with her two daughters, Ming and Aoki Lee, however, and an occasional sighting of Jada Pinkett Smith, it is as if there are no celebrity Hip Hop moms. I must confess that I love Kimora. The brash, blingy, ex-Mrs. Russell Simmons is a Hip Hop fashion icon, a shrewd businesswoman, and a proud mother of two seemingly well-adjusted daughters. The absence of these women in the media is a little strange, since over the years an array of male rap artists have created sentimental odes to their mothers. The list includes songs such as Talib Kweli's "Mama Can You Hear Me?," Ghostface Killah's "All That I Got Is You," Snoop Dogg's, "I Love My Momma," Kanye West's "Hey Mama," and of course Tupac's classic "Dear Mama," but everyday representations of hip-hop mothers are virtually nonexistent. As in the greater society, hip-hop likes its women young and sexy—mothers, regardless of how fit or hot they are, just don't fit that bill.

It's not surprising that *American Idol* contestant Fantasia Barrino created an uproar with her song "Baby Mama" from her 2004 debut album, *Free Yourself*. The twenty-something Fantasia, a single mother, was roundly accused of promoting promiscuity and "celebrating" single motherhood. In her own defense, Barrino countered that she used her music to highlight the challenges of being a young, single Black mother. Statistics show that Black women are more likely than other groups to be single mothers. While some Black women (like other women) never marry, married Black women are more likely than others to become single parents through separation and divorce. Despite these facts, Fantasia was effectively silenced for publicly discussing her motherhood experience. I began to wonder how many other women and their motherhood stories were being relegated to oblivion because neither they nor their perspectives jived with the approved maternal image.

Under the radar of the media and politicians, the American family has changed. According to the U.S. Census, 2000 marked the first time that less than a quarter (23.5 percent) of American households were comprised of a married woman and man and one or more of their children, a decline from 45 percent in 1960. By 2010 the figure is expected to drop to 20 percent. Given these shifting realities, I also wondered how our society and public policy could be enriched by learning about the diversity of ways that real American women—women of every hue and social strata—experience motherhood.

I felt that it was critical that women who are not mothers also be included in this dialogue. Within our society there still exists the notion that every woman should be a mother. What space then does a woman occupy in our culture if medically she cannot bear children, she is not partnered, or simply has no interest in motherhood? I have come to realize that motherhood is a very important part of who I am. Instead of perhaps running away from it because I saw it as an assigned role, I now embrace it as my personal choice. I don't prioritize motherhood as my core female identity however. To do so would mean accepting the idea that my life had no merit prior to the birth of my son and ceases to be important when I can no longer conceive. I would like to use this work as a way to reposition motherhood within a spectrum of female identities. I am hoping that we can begin to have greater respect for all of the phases of a woman's life and for the individual decisions women make about motherhood, whether the choice is yes, no, or maybe.

The origins of this anthology began in San Miguel, Mexico. I was on vacation and had taken along Rebecca Walker's latest book, *Baby Love: Choosing Motherhood After a Lifetime of Ambivalence*. Although I was familiar with Rebecca Walker, I didn't purchase her book because I was looking for a third-wave feminist text. Frankly I bought the book because I was curious. After reading several book reviews and a slew of online comments that ran the gamut from enthusiastic to caustic, I wanted to see firsthand what the uproar was about. What had Rebecca Walker said about motherhood that had roiled so many people? *Baby Love* turned out to be an honest account from a woman of color about her winding path into mommydom. I realized that her candor was at the heart of the controversy. So many books about motherhood smugly assert that motherhood is a woman's true calling. I was relieved that Rebecca allowed her skepticism and concerns to pierce the veil of maternal inevitability.

I felt represented in Rebecca's book. On numerous occasions while reading *Baby Love* I howled laughing (remembering a similar thought or incident) or gently nodded my head in agreement. Finally another independent, college-educated woman of color in her mid-thirties was trying to negotiate not only a partnered relationship but also impending motherhood. Rather than trying to transform herself into some camera-ready version of the all-knowing mother, Rebecca exposed her doubts, her insecurities—her humanness. Rebecca fretted about her son's health and the cost of healthcare. She wondered about what it will cost to educate her little boy. She sought out a doula to help with her birth (as I had) as well as alternative medical professionals. She didn't want to become a hausfrau and shopped for cute maternity clothes and got a pedicure. I was awed as she discussed the sensuality and sexuality that she experienced during her pregnancy. Unfortunately, I couldn't relate to that portion of the book. The most relevant message that I received from *Baby Love* is that it is possible for a woman to integrate her old self-identity with her new, maternal one. Rebecca Walker, the feminist activist, author, and fashion-aware woman, didn't fade out because she became pregnant. In turn, the Yvonne Bynoe whom I knew so well did not have to disappear now that a little person calls her "mommy."

I immediately saw the benefit of more women publicly telling their motherhood stories, so that other women could read and engage their ideas and perspectives. I mused that perhaps women's harsh criticisms about each other could be softened by learning about the other's reality. I also thought about the possibility that highlighting representative twenty-first-century mothers could be a catalyst to reforming antiquated public policies concerning them and their families. We've developed a niche culture that sanctions people exploring only the narrowest range of information and ideas. The concept of stretching beyond one's comfort zone has become passé, and consequently our democracy has been diminished. I've found that people tend to retreat into their own like-minded camps. Subsequently these physically and/or intellectually isolated groups are resolute in their vacuum-formed convictions. They frequently are also all too ready to demonize people who espouse opinions different than their own. I am hoping that this anthology is a microstep toward building new bridges between communities.

The initial outline for this anthology was written on my plane ride back from Mexico. The only prerequisites were that essays had to be personal narratives and they had to be interesting. I also wanted to include the work of women who were not professional writers, average Janes who would not otherwise have a platform for their views. On another level, I wanted to be sure that there was a cross section of women in the United States. I didn't social-engineer the anthology, however, since I was not attempting to make any particular political statement. Among the hundreds of submissions, women of a variety of races, socioeconomic levels, and sexualities shared their stories. The contributors in this anthology had stories that I personally found the most compelling. In this century our nation's social and political progress is really dependent on us humanizing more mothers and their families. I hope that by reading about the life and motherhood experiences of this group of American women, readers will be encouraged to mentally transfer people whom they perceive to be unlike themselves from the margins to the center of their realities.

August 2008

Living in the Third Sphere

MARLA TEYOLIA

My name is Marla and I am a *stay-at-home mom*.

The realization of this fact would have had me reeling to the floor if I had not already been sitting in an armchair, weighted down by pillows, breastfeeding my two-month-old twins . . . at the same time. A laptop computer was teetering on two pillows in the tiny space between my children's heads so I could search cyberspace looking for sites that would give me some sort of road map, a you-can-do-it-too semblance of support as to how I was going to remember who I was (activist, leader, actor) with the new mother I had become.

I read the question posed by the Mocha Moms, Inc. website, "Are you a stay at home mom looking for others like you? Consider becoming a Mocha Moms member" with complete and utter shock. My husband walked in at precisely the same moment my face went white and asked, "Are you okay?" (he's met with a nod) "No, really, are you okay? You look like you just read something really disturbing." He was right. I was disturbed. I was completely thrown by this persona—*stay-at-home mom*. It didn't seem to fit with the image I had of myself—an empowered woman with dreams, ambitions, a *life*. How could I now be a stay-at-home mom? It may have seemed an obvious transition to him and to others around me, considering that I hadn't been working, had let go of my artist management company two years earlier to pursue an acting career, and was doing a *tiny* bit of consulting during my pregnancy. But to me, it came as a slap in the face. Is this who I had become? A stay-at-home mom? My body responded viscerally, throwing my already-emotional state a little bit more off-center.

The road to pregnancy had not been an easy one for us. We didn't just fall into pregnancy or parenthood the way so many of our peers had. For us, parenthood was a very conscious choice—one fraught with an in vitro procedure and daily progesterone shots for twelve weeks. The decision to undertake this process and to put my body and spirit through an array of tests and shots, doubts and fears, made the prize of two little embryos that much sweeter. I was still riding this high when it came time for me to venture out into the world with my little bundles of love and connect with other moms. A solid month of feeling too weak to leave the bedroom for anything more than a "night out"—which consisted of watching a movie downstairs with my husband while grandma watched the babies upstairs—can make you feel like a prisoner in your own home. The urge to connect to the outside world quickly turned from that proud new mama let-me-show-off-my-children glow into a I-*need*-to-meet-more-moms jonesing frenzy.

And so out I went. To the playground. To the café. To our local farm. Any place where I felt that I could meet moms. And yes, I met them, the urban-hipsters-turned-stay-at-home-moms that moved upstate from Brooklyn. They were welcoming, funky, supportive, mostly White women who offered advice, camaraderie, or to hold one of the twins while I breastfed the other. But the more I ventured out, the more I realized something was missing. It was my sisters. My lovely brown, Black, and Asian sisters. It is difficult and tiring to be someone else's diversity. I missed being surrounded by our flyness, by our shared histories, by the way in which we walk in the world. Most of the women of color I knew were working or single with no children, and when they left the community during the day, I was left feeling isolated, alone. Yet the urge to connect with like-minded women brewed stronger every day. Sometimes at the playground I'd meet other moms of color who were staying at home, but there seemed to be a divide that I was afraid to cross. It was carved out of classism, perceived socioeconomic and parenting style differences. I remember seeing an indigenous Latina with two children. We kept on playing eye tag, not sure if the other person wanted to connect solely based on our appearances. In the Latino community, racism runs rampant towards indigenous, dark-skinned people. All of my red flags went up around being too Americanized and not "brown enough." But we took a leap, meeting somewhere in between. And sitting there on the Teflon grass in the park, we connected in our native tongue, and it felt good, really good. It became clear that the stay-at-home moms in my community are not just the white, Ivy League–educated women described by the *New York Times*. We are also mothers of color, who may or may not be traditionally educated, who may or may not speak English, who may or may not be in this country legally, who may or may not have the financial means to comfortably stay at home with our children. Yet we do. We do it because we believe in raising our children ourselves. We do it because the jobs we had before our children weren't fulfilling us emotionally or spiritually. We do it because we don't feel skilled enough, competent enough, supported enough to really find our strengths, to uncover our passions, and to cultivate our capabilities in areas that only seem like pipe dreams to those around us.

In a society that values money over fulfillment and has a legacy of disenfranchisement for people of color, the hurdles we must overcome internally to view living a purpose-driven life as our birthright cannot be understated. Many times it feels like family members look at me cross-eyed for demanding that my life outside of my children be fulfilling. They think I should get a job and use my degree to help my husband pay the mortgage. And yet for each woman, the role of activist, community organizer, and leader ultimately begins as a selfish, purposeful act—to better our own lives and the lives of our children. It is interesting to be a woman of color who is perceived as hip or funky by the progressive White community. You have the ability to gain access and acceptance in a way that is easier for you than it may be for others from your culture. I do not hold this responsibility lightly. Instead, I utilize it to create bridges among the different communities to which I belong. For example, one of my passions is organic, healthy food. The Latino community has a legacy of decadent cuisine that is high in fat and rich in taste. Organic foods are seen as too expensive and hippie to be culturally relevant. My solution was to join the board of our local CSA, the Common Ground Farm. It is a nine-acre farm that provides local, pesticide-free fruits, vegetables, herbs, and flowers on a weekly basis to its members from the months of May through October. I love this place. Seeing where my food comes from and being a part of the process has been transformative for me.

The membership however was very homogenous, and did not reflect the diversity of our town. My solution was to create a program called the Family Wellness Fund, in which I raised funds to subsidize shares for families of color, single-headed households, and families of limited financial means so that they too could benefit from produce that is produced locally and without harmful chemicals. In this way I created a community that I wanted to be a part of, one that is rich in cultural and economic diversity, one in which my children would not feel like the only children of color among a sea of whiteness.

Most of us question the notion that stay-at-home mothers and the term "leadership" belong in the same sentence. If each of us were honest with ourselves—men and women, working outside the home or not—we would most likely find a part of us that either currently or has in the past looked down on stay-at-home moms. This is the legacy that patriarchy and first-wave feminist ideology have imprinted on our psyche. I admit, I was one of those people. When someone told me she was a stay-at-home mom I had an immediate visceral reaction, silent thoughts of *Oh, God, how boring*, or *What a waste, she was such a powerful, intelligent, (fill in the blank) person before she had kids.* Being a part of this community now, however, I realize that we, stay–at-home mothers, have the yearnings not to be the same people we were before we had children, but rather super-improved versions of ourselves where our past lives, our present realities, and future ambitions synthesize to create a balanced whole. And from this balanced place we can begin to contribute to our families, to our communities, and ultimately to ourselves.

In her book *Closing the Leadership Gap: Why Women Can and Must Help Run the World*, Marie C. Wilson discusses how women who engage in community-altering and community-defining work are overlapping the spheres of work and home, of private and professional, creating what she calls a "third sphere." I want to live in that third sphere. I see the potential lurking in our homes, apartment complexes, and projects. As of 2006, there are 5.6 million stay-at-home moms in the United States. If each of us took it upon ourselves to find our passion, our unique calling, and direct that toward creating and changing the communities in which we live, the United States would be a totally transformed place. Yet we must start with ourselves. We must *engage* with our children, our families, and our surroundings from a healed place. I urge us to embark on the spiritual, emotional work that healing the soul requires. It is scary terrain. But we must make the journey.

It is time for the mothers to lead.

Consciously or unconsciously we know that society cannot continue down this course of mass consumption, of global bullying, of oil-driven wars, and of apathy among its citizens. We know that something must change.

It is *us*.

We must change to be the leaders that this world needs.

It is time for a societal paradigm shift and a broadening of that third sphere so that *all* stay-at-home moms can see their potential when they look in the mirror. That is my goal; that is my purpose. Through being a stay-at-home mom, I've found it now. And my world is becoming a better place.

★ **MARLA TEYOLIA** is an emerging writer who is currently working on a book regarding stay-at-home mothers and leadership titled *Empowered Mama: A Modern Stay-at-Home Mom's Guide to Activism, Leadership, and Living a Passion-Filled Life*. She has also been published as part of the anthology *We Got Isues! A Young Woman's Guide to a Bold, Courageous, and Empowered Life* (New World Library, 2006), edited by Rha Goddess and JLove Calderón, both featured in this anthology. Marla is a certified Empowerment Workshop trainer and is part of a woman's art and civic engagement project called We Got Issues! She is also a seasoned leader in the area of women's empowerment and has organized and facilitated countless events as varied as local women's circles, community workshops, national theatrical tours, and countless activist events. Marla lives in upstate New York with her husband, two children, and her dog, Dancer. For more information, please visit www.empowered-mama.com.

To My Unborn Children

JASMINE DAWSON

I knew where my husband, Korey, was most of the time. When someone saw me they asked, "Where is Korey?" and "How is he doing?" They were as programmed to ask as I was programmed to respond with "He's at work," "He's at home watching the game," or "He's out fishing." It took months after his passing for me to understand that no one would ever ask me these questions again.

Korey and I met nine years earlier while working nights at a carrier service. We were both attending college during the day. I was preparing for my senior year and Korey attended a local junior college after having attended a four-year university. We had both transferred from other colleges and were living at home with our parents. Korey was two years older than me, the same height as me, and cherished the ground that I walked on. We were one. It hadn't been that way at first. It took him about one hundred times to ask me on a date before I finally said yes.

I hadn't been attracted to him initially. He was too short. While I used to think I needed to look into a man's eyes to tell if he was lying, it seemed ridiculous to *always* stand eye-to-eye. We had a mutual friend whom I thought of as a player, but for Korey the guy was just one of his boys. I initially assumed Korey was a player—guilty by association. Many of the guys I dated were not worthy of introductions to my parents.

A good friend told me that I should stick with Korey because he was a good dude. I didn't need to be convinced. We shared many similarities. We lived around the corner from each other for six years and had never seen each other. We both attended colleges that were about thirty miles from each other and could remember times when both of us had been on each other's campuses. But we never met. After the first date we moved fast. We were together every day, studying and working. We moved into our own apartment in just a few months.

Korey had to do everything quick. We were talking about marriage early on. He made a habit of proposing when standing at the checkout counter at the grocery store or while we were in the car. Each time he would say, "I just want to know what you would say." He feared I would say no. I was the practical one, the skeptic. Were we ready for marriage? I had just gotten my degree and had taken on a full-time and part-time job so that he could continue to work part-time and earn his degree. We made good money but were living in a one-bedroom apartment. Both of our parents had been married and remarried several times. What did we know about marriage? After Korey passed, his mother told me he had always wanted a wife, even as a young man.

We finally got engaged after an over-the-top weekend in a tourist town in the Bay Area. His surprise proposal, with a pianist that played our song in a restaurant, more than a dozen red roses, and the reservations at a breakfast inn, was beyond romantic. We read poetry to each other and called family to share the news. Every moment had been magical, but I felt ashamed. None of my friends had experienced anything like this; this was the stuff we read about or saw on TV. But it was Korey's way; he knew what he wanted. We paid off our wedding by working several jobs. We were determined to have the wedding of our dreams without having to owe anything afterwards. But as Korey would have it, we were buying our first home at the same time. My income paid for the wedding; anything extra we earned went towards bills and getting the down payment for our first home. Korey wanted to leave his wedding and walk into his own home. I thought it was too ambitious; "Let's just wait a year after the marriage and recoup," I complained.

While finances were tighter than they had ever been, we continued as we had always done, being everywhere we could together. When we attended parties together or hosted barbecues at our home, friends and family were overjoyed. We were the poster children for young couples who worked hard to get their degrees, buy their home, and make a marriage work. We lovingly told friends that the keys to our magic had been the friendship, the desire to want to see each other succeed. You had to not only be lovers but business partners as well. Financial responsibility at times felt like the cornerstone of our marriage.

Still, something was missing. We had always noticed it and soon after the marriage everyone seemed to notice. "When are you two having kids?" they asked. Over and over the questions would come our way. We teased that we needed to make more money first, then we said whenever we wanted kids we would just baby-sit our niece and nephew. But behind closed doors our marriage and faith were being tested every night. We were infertile and Korey refused to believe it. I hated seeing Korey's spirit beaten down after he realized month after month that I was not pregnant. He felt it was a stain on his manhood. His friends had children. Couples that had gotten married around the same time as us were having kids. Korey would say, "I just want to get you pregnant."

Korey was from the old school where a man gets married, buys a house, and has some kids. He hated guys who didn't take care of their kids. For me to begin the conversation of seeing a fertility doctor was very tricky. I would clip articles about infertility and statistics. But I needed a man's perspective to convince Korey. He didn't want to hear it, and for several months I continued to press that we needed to get real answers. It eventually took us three teams of doctors at three different hospitals before we found the right specialist.

The doctor had been featured in an article that we read and reread more than a year before. The urologist was world renowned for developing a diagnostic technique for mapping sperm to determine if a couple could become candidates for in vitro fertilization (IVF). The procedure involved using a fine needle to go inside the testicles to locate and retrieve sperm.

After sperm was found, candidates began the IVF and intra-cytoplasmic sperm injection (ICSI) process, where fresh sperm is retrieved, guided by the map findings, and then injected into several eggs in order to fertilize the embryos.

It had not only been our only solution to have our own children, but was very expensive as well. We were struggling to pay our monthly mortgage despite both having good jobs. I was in graduate school and wanted Korey to enter graduate school after I graduated. We wanted to move from the suburbs to cut down on high gas costs. We wanted to upgrade our cars and take more vacations. Never before had we needed to take out a loan to do something; whenever we wanted something out of our means we used the envelope system and bought groceries with quarters, nickels, and dimes. We ate tuna fish sandwiches for dinner, spaghetti for a week, and egg sandwiches. We knew how to sacrifice for the little things, but were simply unprepared for this almost-$20,000 procedure. The only way was to take out a loan. Korey was determined. There was no turning back. After several appointments with the urologist, Korey's sperm was mapped and eventually retrieved. We became IVF candidates, and Korey read all the literature and did the research.

He worked overtime shifts at his job and carpooled to save on gas. We ate dinners at our parents' houses instead of cooking when we didn't have enough food in the refrigerator. We cut back on gifts to our families during holidays and birthdays. We were working on our baby.

After paying for the procedures, we were so excited to know that we would soon become pregnant. We were closer and closer to our goal, and it hadn't taken long for me to begin dreaming about how our lives were going to change with a baby. I saw a girl in my dreams. My mother saw a boy in hers, and Korey's mom saw twin girls. She was so convinced that it had caused Korey to panic. Not only had he feared girls but he also knew that with IVF at my age there was almost a 30 percent chance of multiple births, and he knew the risks. With multiples we could have a higher risk of pregnancy loss, premature delivery, infant abnormalities, handicap due to consequences of very premature delivery, pregnancy-induced hypertension, hemorrhaging, and other significant maternal complications. Korey knew the problems. Because he was born a premature baby and stayed in and out of the hospital as a child, he simply wanted a healthy baby, and most important, a healthy wife.

Our team of doctors prepared me for the IVF procedure, and I began ordering all the medications that came in several boxes and special packaging. Korey's mapping procedure was a success, and our team of doctors loved him.

His doctor was so smitten with Korey that they were making plans to go deep-sea fishing. I was nervous about the IVF process but overjoyed that we had found sperm in Korey. His mother recalls the day the procedure was done and how he had called her law office while she was in with a client. He said, "Mom, I got sperm!"

Every day Korey and I talked about how we would raise our kids, which sports they could play given their inherited "short" gene. We talked about child abuse and what kind of harm we would inflict on anyone who harmed our children. We talked about childcare, preschool, and dating. We talked about how we would be as grandparents and what we wanted to leave behind for each child after we passed on. We wanted three or four kids but would be content with any number God gave us. We had come this far.

The IVF process wasn't easy on me. The medications were difficult. I had just taken a new, high-demanding job that required constant commuting and meetings. The job was extremely stressful each day. Still, we were determined to begin our family—it had taken all of our years to get to this point. As I took the injected hormones and prescribed medicines, I became weary. The hormones were causing my skin to break out and the injection sites were sore and swollen.

There were three shots each day and sets of pills including prenatal pills. I was tired many nights and sluggish, but we were determined. Korey had gotten me flowers and a card, his normal thing, just a year before. We were preparing for the big day of the embryo transfer. We told family and close friends that their Christmas present would be an announcement. Korey had had unbelievable support from close friends—which had been something he feared being without.

Finally the day arrived and we were going in for the transfer, a light procedure. That day Korey, in his excitement, lost his wedding ring. Our mothers were concerned because it was the diamond-encrusted upgraded ring that I gave him as we renewed our wedding vows just two years after we married. "It's okay, I can get another one," he said. Nothing could spoil his joy. We were going to be parents.

After waiting two weeks, we were pregnant. I had taken a pregnancy kit at work and called him the day we learned. I called him on his cell phone as he headed to work and said, "Hi Daddy." He shouted. I had wanted to tell him to his face but couldn't wait. We were really parents. He was really a father now and we had proof. I know that after years of frustration and anger, he had to have cried and thanked God for that moment.

In those few weeks before Christmas we bought diapers and began practicing diaper changing with my stuffed Elmo. I had started crocheting baby booties, hats, and a blanket. Korey began laying out his plans to convert his beloved Oakland Raiders paraphernalia room to the baby nursery. But still Korey was worried. I had to sit down and let him do things. He didn't want me lifting boxes or anything heavier than my purse. He definitely wanted me to quit my job and just take care of the baby and myself. He wanted a healthy child.

As Korey went to work on New Year's Day, I started cramping and spotting. I was losing the baby and everyone knew it. I foolishly worried that Korey would leave me because I could not carry this baby to term. The days that followed the miscarriage were the hardest test of our marriage. I was angry that my body had defied me and still fearful that I could not give my husband what he desperately wanted, a child.

The night of January 30, Korey told me for the final time that he would never leave me just because I couldn't have his baby. He didn't care that I miscarried and he would love me forever even if I never had his child. Sure, I had known this, but I was vulnerable and truly felt he would leave me even after everything we went through. That night he kissed my entire face the way he had done many times before when I was I was sick and wanted him to tell me a bedtime story.

The next morning, after having missed several days of work, Korey begged me to let him go fishing, his favorite pasttime. He knew I worried about him fishing in remote areas that he claimed were better for real fisherman. I never shared with him how I was frightened when he had fallen into the water while fishing on a riverbank months before. He never admitted it to me; another fisherman's wife had shared the story with me in secrecy. He passed my concerns off as worrying for nothing. In an odd way he knew the more I worried, the safer he would be. He had no fears.

The day was perfect, he assured me. No clouds in the sky and the fish were biting, he was sure of it. He hadn't caught a fish in months and was eager to get out there. Sure, I said, as he cooked me breakfast, which he hadn't done in months. He made me breakfast because he wanted me to have a good day, he said. We had always taken time to eat breakfast, and I had only recently been unable to eat properly given my commute schedule. For Korey it was a new day. He could not have been more loving and sincere in that moment as he begged me to go fishing.

Later that day, after my lunch, I had taken a call from him, and he told me that he had finally caught a fish and would be heading home to cook it for our dinner. I was so happy for him, and even happier that we had reached our highest point—a deeper understanding that while we both wanted a child so badly, nothing would ever change between us. We had each other.

Our last call hadn't felt like the last time I would speak to him. It was like any other call we shared. Brief and sweet and to the point and with an "I love you" at the end. In that conversation we must have expressed how much the night before had meant and we must have talked about how excited we were to try and get pregnant again. We knew we were back to where we were before we talked about the baby constantly.

About an hour after our call, Korey passed away. He was in an auto accident while going to get more bait after catching his prized fish. He had misguided a turn on the uneven graveled road. He was only thirty-two years old.

I am certain that Korey would want me to try again for our baby. We still have frozen embryos and extra sperm stored. He would want me to raise our children the way we often discussed. He would want me to tell our daughter that he wanted the world for her. That he would have worked until his muscles ached and his feet were swollen to make sure she had shoes on her feet, clothes on her back, and most important, food in her belly. He would want her to not accept the hand of any boys that would not love her the way he did. He would tell our son to always leave the toilet seat down and open the door for any woman, especially his mother. He would tell our son that he would always be at every sports game he ever played no matter the time and that he would personally train him every day to be tougher and stronger on the field or basketball court. Korey would tell our son to always respect women. Most important, Korey would expect this because our kids would watch how he treated me.

After losing Korey I reasoned that this was what we started and what I had to finish. Korey passed away intending to someday become a father. Even though he told me it didn't matter if I never had our child, to me it does. There are days that I feel obligated because we spent thousands of dollars to pay for the IVF procedure. Then there are days that I feel our child would hate me for having them though knowing they would never meet him. There are days when I worry that people will ask why I would name our son Korey Jr. if Korey Sr. passed years before. Would any of my explanations make sense to anyone?

I know that no matter what I decide tomorrow or in three months or even a year, I have nine embryos waiting for me. I know that I'm not driven by feelings of obligation but of desire to tell them why they were conceived, how they came from the two of us—a mommy who's willing to give them the stars and moon with a village of family and friends awaiting their arrival and a daddy who is in Heaven making sure that they make the right decisions. I will tell them how their paternal grandmother told me that if you are quiet and just listen, Korey will come to you and tell you what to do. I will tell them, like my mother tells me, that if I am a good person on earth, then when I get to Heaven I will see him again. But the most important thing I would tell them is that I chose to bring them here because of the love Korey and I had for them years before they were born.

And when they are much older I will tell them that I chose to be a single mother because they deserved to be born and deserved to live each day like their father had, with joy, wonder, and love.

I know that I will question my actions each day that I get closer to beginning the IVF process a second time. I pray that someday my unborn children understand the amazing sacrifices it took to give them life.

★ **JASMINE DAWSON** was born in 1976 in Oakland, California. She has been in school from preschool to graduate school. She's tired of school but glad to have been at it so long. She writes because she has been inspired by family life and love. She has a bachelor's degree from San Francisco State University and a MFA from Mills College. She has written and published book reviews, essays, and research. She writes now from having experienced a deeper pain than most could imagine and many may never experience. She lost her husband, Korey M. Dawson, of four years in a car accident just before she finished her first novel. She is currently working for the City of Oakland and coordinating a scholarship award in her husband's name.

Starter Child

AMY KALISHER

As Dylan lumbers out from his elementary school and into my life—eleven years old, pear-shaped, moon-faced, and grinning, backpack slung over one shoulder, glasses slipping down the bridge of his nose—Robert smiles through the windshield at his approaching boy, and I brace myself for a challenge. If Dylan treats me as the enemy, I won't take it personally. If he tests me with hostile behavior or unpleasant questions, I'll be respectful, calm but firm. If there are awkward silences, I'll relax into them; I will breathe.

The boy throws his backpack onto the backseat, clambering in after it. "So," he chirps, once his father has made introductions, "is there anything you'd like to know about me?"I look to Robert, but he is distracted, busy maneuvering out from behind a row of yellow school buses. "Whatever you want to tell me," I manage, after a moment's struggle to find my voice.

"Well, I don't like George Bush," Dylan begins, launching into a cheerful stream-of-consciousness soliloquy on politics, baseball, and video games, peppered with movie quotes. "It's like Dick Cheney saying to George Bush," he declares at one point, in his best James Earl Jones, "'George, I am your father . . . 's brother's nephew's cousin's former roommate . . . '" He then performs several pages of the script to the *Star Wars* parody, *Space Balls*, verbatim.

At first I twist in my seat to meet his gaze, but Dylan isn't looking at me, so I turn back, watching Robert's broad hands on the wheel instead, steadily circling through the turns. At a red light, he drops them to his lap, and I look at his face. It is the first time I've seen him in profile, and I am disconcerted by this fact, by the oblong stretch of his skull, and how plainly I can see through his thinning hair.

It is February, a Tuesday. Exactly a month ago, on the heels of two consecutive miscarriages and the cusp of a third attempt, my husband and partner of twelve years admitted he was having an affair. Within twenty-four hours, he had moved out of our Providence, Rhode Island apartment. The pain still doubles me over: nausea, heartache, anger, shame. I barely eat, rarely sleep; I've dropped fifteen pounds in three weeks. Halfway through my menstrual cycle, I began to bleed, and the blood was black. I am not myself.

Robert is in similar straights. His spouse, Dylan's mother, took off a week before mine, also for another, after months—years, it eventually emerged—of tumult and dishonesty. Thanks to my brother, Robert's friend and co-worker, we've had each other as a support group, meeting nightly via telephone from our respective bedrooms, fifty miles apart. This Tuesday hooky is our second date.

"May the Schwartz be with you," Dylan is saying in the backseat. I smile at Robert and he smiles too, more tenderly than I have ever seen, into the rearview mirror.

Daily life is full of landmines for me, painful, unexpected reminders of what I've lost. Just the other day I wept in a doctor's waiting room, sideswiped by grief by the innocuous but suddenly impossible task on the clipboard in front of me. *Emergency contact:* _____, the intake form demanded. Robert's profile and fatherly gaze serve as further reminders of my unfilled blanks. Where do I fit in his world?

More important, where do I fit in my own? I never expected to be single again, let alone dating, let alone married or contemplating parenthood in the first place. Financial and emotional security are relatively new concepts for me, and still precarious. As of just two years ago, at age thirty-four, I finally have my bachelor's degree, a marketable skill (I design websites), and enough of a solid footing to think maybe I am capable of a stable life after all.

For many years, my life simply wasn't solid or secure enough to support a family, so I told myself I didn't want one. I saw how children limited the independence of the women around me, how society treated them as less intelligent—or at least less interesting—than their childless counterparts. I remember my own mother's angst and despair, her admission, when I was fourteen and her marriage was disintegrating, that she wished sometimes my brothers and I had never been born. It wouldn't have been a stretch to say that I believed that it took a smarter, stronger woman to not fall into the same trap.

In recent years, however, my biological clock had become a time bomb, ticking ominously in my ear. Suddenly the thought of forgoing motherhood *hurt*. A *lot*. So I pushed aside my fears, dismissed my prejudices, muscled past my husband's reluctance, and strained toward a moment when a family of my own seemed, finally, within reach, only to watch it shatter in my hands.

As devastated as I am, I'm also relieved to be off the babies-or-not roller coaster, at least temporarily. But I'm also terrified. Loneliness and despair seem just around the corner. Sitting in the passenger seat of this unfamiliar car, a new man to my left and his unfamiliar boy jabbering away behind me, I grip the door handle and once again remind myself to breathe.

Dylan talks throughout the drive home, through the bulk of the afternoon, through dinner and an hour or so after dinner, and finally, unbelievably, through twenty minutes alone upstairs, pacing in front of the bathroom mirror when he is supposed to be brushing his teeth.

There are a few breaks in the action: ten minutes of homework, for instance, and a short barrage of questions during dinner, when Robert coaches his son to shift from monologue to dialogue. "What's your favorite sport?" Dylan asks me. "Did you vote for George Bush?" "Do you have any kids?" "Do you *want* to have kids?"

Robert interjects reprimands, a spectrum of stern-to-plaintive variations on "Dylan!" as the boy sweeps his arm through the air, almost toppling his glass and mine, when he eats with his fingers straight from the serving platter, and tries to steal food from his father's plate. After Robert sends him upstairs to get ready for bed, we two adults move to the living room. I loosen my expression of delighted surprise the way a businessman, toward the end of a long day—but not quite home yet—ever so slightly loosens his tie. I am exhausted.

"He likes you," Robert nods, smiling, and then shouts upstairs, where his son is now droning through a series of Darth Vader speeches and light-saber sound effects. "Dylan! Brush. Your. Teeth!" When the fourth prodding renders no result, Robert tromps upstairs.

I try to relax, to dispel the guilty thought that all my efforts thus far have been less an attempt to win over the child than to impress the man. But I can't see past Dylan's obesity, can't fathom Robert's fatherly devotion, and worry that if this truth were known, it would expose me as the selfish, immature, deeply ambivalent not-yet-mother that I am.

Finally, all is quiet, and my man (*My* man? Could that be where we're headed?) returns with the verdict. He is grinning as he comes down the stairs, and I am struck by his lively dark eyes, high cheekbones, lanky frame—nothing like his son's pale, blue-eyed roundness. "It's official," Robert reports. *I think she's great*, Dylan has said. *If you want to marry her, it's all right with me.*

Despite my best efforts to the contrary, it isn't long before I find it undeniable: Robert and I are falling in love. By springtime, we are talking about marriage, fantasizing about having a child together. He is unequivocal. I am elated, but cautious. It is my life that will change most drastically, perhaps not entirely for the better.

Ah, but the sex! The first time is so intense, so astonishing, that afterward we both weep. The same happens again, and again. Together, we attribute this to three factors: mutual vulnerability, the novelty of reciprocal passion, and, perhaps most of all, biological tension. Although longing to conceive a child together, we feel compelled to wait. In the heat of the moment, however, in spite of my underground ambivalence, this resolution sometimes falls to the wayside.

In other words, we don't wait long.

Dylan's affection for me is also growing. He sidles in for hugs, leans against me on the couch, even turns his moony face up toward mine on occasion, lips puckered for a kiss. (I give him my cheek.) I find his attention gratifying and unnerving. When I see Dylan with his mother for the first time, it clicks. Dylan's mother showers him with affection, tells him over and over that she loves him, that he is handsome and smart and hilarious. Visits with her are rare. It isn't uncommon for her to back out at the last minute, to postpone seeing her son for weeks on end.

As Robert and I explore a potential future together, I put my cards on the table, one at a time, admitting that I'm troubled by Dylan, his weight, his physical awkwardness, his nonstop talking and scatter-mindedness. I am also disconcerted by Robert's habit of exasperated nagging without clear expectations that his son eat right, take on household chores, or put himself through the paces of homework and bedtime without constant oversight. Though time spent alone with Robert is increasingly wonderful, time with Dylan, I admit, requires a great deal of restraint.

"From what you are saying," Robert remarks on more than one occasion, "It sounds like you don't think I'm a good parent. And that you don't really like my son."

"I don't think you're a bad parent," I assure him each time. "You are dependable and devoted and committed. You obviously love Dylan and he clearly knows it. That, in and of itself, is *huge*. But you've said it yourself: you have blind spots. I'm just telling you what I see." I make suggestions for reform, and Robert takes all of it, amazingly, gracefully, in stride.

So much so that I finally lay down my last card, the uncomfortable truth I can no longer ignore or deny. Robert has a right to know, even if it spells the end of our romance. "You're right," I confess—because as much as I care that his son's life go well, that Dylan receive all the attention and guidance he deserves, I don't love the boy with anywhere near the ferocity befitting a parent. And, to be perfectly honest, especially around the time each month when it becomes apparent that, once again, I'm not pregnant—"I do find myself thinking I don't like your son." I cry admitting this, admitting my frustration and revulsion when Dylan sneezes salad all over the bathroom, when he spits into his water glass or farts at the dinner table and thinks it's funny, or lies, or sneaks food, or requires one too many reminders to trim his toenails or clean his room or quit saying "turd." True to form, Robert recognizes me for the sacrifice I am contemplating: giving up my newfound freedom as a single woman in the city, self-employed, beholden to none, in order to come into his home and help parent his child, to take second place in line for his attention, to make his house, his family, his world, my own. He encourages me to speak up when Dylan annoys me, to correct and redirect, and to note the changes that have already taken place since I came along: The boy eats salad! And broccoli! He wipes his pee off the toilet seat!

It is true, I tell Robert, I must recognize that though I literally broke into a cold sweat the first time I dared ask Dylan to close the screen door, fearing the stereotypical retaliatory zinger—"I don't have to listen to you. *You're not my mother!*"—no such statement has yet been uttered. In fact, Dylan has twice proclaimed me awesome and cool and good to have around; first, when I cooked his new-favorite chicken dinner, and again, after I made the mistake of renting *Austin Powers.* "You look like you need a hug," he has taken to saying, in the insipid nasal drone of Dr. Evil.

Robert concedes that Dylan can be annoying. "He's not an easy kid. It makes sense that you would struggle. *I've* lived with him for twelve years. I can still feel what it was like to hold him on his very first day on the planet. He's . . . he feels like . . ." Robert struggles for words, his voice almost breaking, "a part of me."

Which catapults me straight into the core of my sadness: This boy, with his walrusy body and talonlike toenails, toward whom I feel more aversion than I do affinity, might be the closest I ever come to having a child of my own.

But this man, *this man!* He might just be the love of my life.

Over the course of the summer, I toss out the ex-wife's abandoned magazines and cosmetics, strip wallpaper, rearrange furniture, dig a garden, and lug in carloads of clothes and books and art supplies. In September I rent a moving truck and give up my apartment. Dylan, hearing the news, pronounces it "cool."

I'm well settled by Halloween, when Robert and I drop Dylan off with friends for trick-or-treating on our way to town hall so I can register to vote. While we're at it, we get married.

Autumn becomes winter. In seventh grade now, Dylan arrives home earlier. Robert, newly promoted, works late. What was once an after-school hour on his own for Dylan is now three or four, with me. I come to dread three o'clock, when the door flies open and the boy bursts in, never failing to shout, "Lucy, I'm home!" before flinging his backpack and beelining for the bathroom.

"Close the door!" I shout back, buttoning my sweater, hunching more tightly over my work for one last minute, because very soon, concentration will be impossible. "Much better!" Dylan inevitably sighs, as he emerges from the bathroom to hover over my desk, detailing the latest unfairness of his teachers, trying out jokes and impressions, the same ones he's belabored for months, and asking in a singsong, when all else fails to engage my attention, "What'cha doing?" It is up to me to steer him away from video games, the Internet, hours-long fantasy play, the telephone, and never-ending slices of cheese.

"How about an apple?" I suggest, knowing he'll balk unless I add, "I'll cut it up for you. Why don't you get started on your homework?" Dylan sets up at the desk across from mine. I try again to work, but find myself leaning over to decipher his math assignments, nodding distractedly as he rants about how stupid and boring school is, how much he hates textbooks and standardized testing, "pointless information," and George Bush. It always comes back to George Bush. "I'm the decider," Dylan sneers, in a pinched Texas accent. "I'm the commander guy."

Before long, he is pacing the floors on his usual rants, announcing, at intervals, "I definitely do not like girls," then several days later, "I don't get girls at all," then, "All the girls at my school think they're Paris Hilton," and finally, "Okay, I admit it. I like girls."

It dawns on me, the third time I stand cringing at the bathroom door, playing coach while Dylan grapples with the plunger after yet another low-fiber, high-paper fiasco, that I spend more one-on-one time with this child than either of his natural parents do. I want to resent it, but Robert insists that Dylan is okay on his own, that he can pick up any slack I leave. Dylan himself is heartbreakingly appreciative. "You really help me get focused, Amy. I think you're awesome and I love you."

Dylan raises the subject of a potential half-sibling often, requesting a boy and that we name it Luke. Or better yet, Anakin. I tell him the truth about my history, and that yes, we do want a baby, of either gender. But, "No promises on the name."

Robert and I do our best to grant Dylan's wish. We try. Month after month, however, no such luck. We take our vitamins, chart my cycles, see the acupuncturist, and make doctor's appointments. Another birthday passes me by. At age thirty-seven, the clock is not ticking in my favor. Robert's semen analysis comes back with borderline morphology issues. The urologist recommends a surgical procedure that might improve his sperm count. Robert is willing, but I am having second thoughts. What if we have a child like Dylan? Aren't all children, on some level, like Dylan? And what about me—balking whenever he says he loves me, offering only a lame "Thanks, Dylan," because I can't bring myself to say I love him too? Perhaps I'm not truly cut out for parenthood.

And then I'm pregnant.

We are all standing in the upstairs bathroom when Robert tells Dylan, and Dylan, distracted by the mirror, comments, "My hair is really getting long." He rotates his head slowly, trying to see himself in profile. In a year, all at once, it seems, the boy has grown five inches. Chubby yet, but no longer obese, his face is longer, with a hint of cheekbone. For the first time, I can see resemblance to his father. He's calmer, too. Our dinner conversations have become actual "How was your day?" "Did you hear the news?" dialogue. He still farts at the table, but now he says, "Excuse me."

"He's underwhelmed," I mutter, and Robert laughs.

His attention duly redirected, Dylan shrugs. "I'm not surprised. I sort of expected this. Congratulations," he nods at each of us, "Congratulations." He is solemn, but at the same time, purposefully shaking hair onto his face. I remind him not to get his hopes up, and Dylan promptly kisses me three times, on alternating cheeks.

For several days I can't stop smiling. I imagine a beautiful newborn, a robust, smiling toddler, a graceful, pensive, big-eyed child. Girl or boy, I don't care. It will be part of me, and then its own person, and I will teach it everything I know. Robert and I laugh whenever we look at each other. Concerns for my autonomy, fear of household drudgery, sleep deprivation, a lack of engagement in work and the larger world flash though my mind, but these seem suddenly temporary and surmountable. *Ambivalence be damned*, I think, *I am pregnant!* Even Dylan seems suddenly less troublesome. I imagine a new orientation to three o'clock, when his return from school might be a welcome respite after a day alone with baby. I could shower, get some exercise, let the boy bond with his sibling and earn a little spending loot in the process. I might even allow him to call the kid "Anakin."

The miscarriage comes in August, while Dylan is in Vermont, visiting his mother. Thirteen weeks this time—a record for me. Robert tells him over the phone, and Dylan asks to speak to me. I've been refusing calls from friends and family, but Robert implores me with his eyes, and I don't mind.

"I'm really sorry you have to go through this," Dylan says.

I mumble a thank you.

"How do you feel?

"I'm okay. A little sad, but I'm okay. I'll be okay."

He switches into his Dr. Evil voice. "You could probably use a hug."

I laugh. "You can give me one when you get home." For the first time, I can imagine the feel of his body in my arms. For the first time, I find myself looking forward to it.

I do love Dylan, I suddenly understand, though imperfectly. But what mother doesn't love imperfectly? There are blanks we will never be able to fill for each other. In spite of that, in spite of all my failings, Dylan loves me too.

When Robert takes the phone into the next room, I sit for a long moment, staring off into the future. Maybe one day there will be a baby, maybe not. For now, I'm back to dreading the three o'clock debriefing hour. But it won't be as bad this year. I've moved my desk to the spare bedroom upstairs. That will help. And Dylan is maturing. In his emerging resemblance to his dad, I see a glimmer of the man he might become, and imagine a time when I can genuinely feel glad to have him in my life.

In the meantime, Dylan can cut his own apples.

Names have been changed to protect the individuals' privacy.

A Shade Called Mama

KELLY JESKE

Often I feel like I'm searching for something—a landing place, a home that nourishes the many disparate pieces of myself. I dream of when I'll feel wholly satisfied and grounded in my life. I try on identities and paths like new shoes, discarding those that squeeze my baby toes or that won't look good with a pair of striped knee socks. My restlessness urges me to endlessly imagine myself remade: as a sociology professor, a kindergarten teacher, a working writer, a radical social worker. I wonder with nostalgia what would have happened if I'd gotten a master's degree in social work instead of in sociology, if I'd moved to San Francisco instead of to Portland, if I'd continued dancing, if I'd never gotten sick when I was eighteen. I agonize over the crossroads of ten and fifteen years ago and overwhelm myself with longings for what I might create in the coming years. Even as I imagine myself doing so many different things and being so many different people, I choose discreet labels to describe and situate myself: queer, femme, fat, feminist, poly. And while my aspirations and dreams have shifted continuously throughout my life, there is one dream that has remained solid. For as long as I can remember, I've longed to be a parent. Weaving through my uncertainties and fears, my wonderings and my wanderings, has been a strong, silky thread in a shade called mama.

Several years ago I was (ultimately falsely) diagnosed with kidney disease that could progress quickly and—worst-case scenario—could be fatal. I panicked over the possibility that one of my worst fears might come true: I might die before I found my way in this world. In the midst of crisis, I went to the Oregon coast with my dear friend Sage. We walked slowly along the beach, heels sinking in sand, wind playing at our clothes and hair. I watched the waves rise and fall as sea spray mixed with tears to wet my cheeks. Sage asked me to think about what I wanted, to name my intentions for living this life that might have its edges more defined. With a heart-swelling certainty, I knew. *A mama,* I said, *I want to be a mama.* She wrote my intentions into a list that I could carry with me, *mama* at the top. I looked at that list hourly at first, daily later on, then only here and there after the misdiagnosis was confirmed. Each time I read it, I felt the ache and clarity I'd experienced before: *A mama, I want to be a mama.*

In my early twenties, I met my partner Meg and we quickly began to put down roots. From the beginning of our relationship, we dreamed about being mamas together. We imagined a little one in our lives, each of us being fed and stretched and inspired by our spunky, loving family. We'd be creative, radical mamas who encouraged our child to explore, discover and become. We'd nurture our little one with expansive ideas about gender, social justice, family, love, and possibility. With our spirits ignited by our shared dreams, Meg and I turned to the pragmatic work of growing our family. We devised a plan for when we'd be ready to bring a babe into our lives—a lengthy and ambitious list, fueled largely by my fears about financial security. I had grown up in a working class family and had most recently been living on a low-paying group home job and food stamps. I wanted to feel like we had some cushion before we had a baby. I'd finish my undergraduate and master's degrees (so that I could teach sociology), we'd pay off my student loans and our credit card debt, we'd put some money into savings, and we'd own a house. Then we'd be ready.

I felt secure in the values and dreams Meg and I shared about being mamas together, but now we were checking off the tangible pieces that I associated with our readiness to become parents. Meg had a well-paying job and we started budgeting carefully so that we could chip away at our debt and start a savings account. We researched home ownership and found a program that would allow us to put nothing down and still have a mortgage payment just a bit higher than our rent. I got loads of student aid for my undergraduate degree and landed an assistantship that would almost entirely pay for my master's degree. I found myself focusing on these steps because they were things that we could measure and assess—unlike the uncertainties and insecurities about parenting, which seemed endless.

As we worked on our list, we talked more about how we'd have a baby. Clearly, we couldn't just stop using birth control. Even as a kid, I knew I wanted to become a parent through adoption. I never dreamed of walking down the aisle in a white dress, or of becoming pregnant and birthing babies. My mom and dad were foster parents, and as I grew up our family was home to babies, toddlers, older kids, and one teen. My analysis was simple—I understood that there are children in the world who don't grow up with their birthparents, and that some kids were in the system waiting for an adoptive family. It made sense to me that I'd pursue adoption when I was ready to become a parent. I talked up adoption as my favorite option for becoming mamas. Meg agreed that she felt good about this idea, but she was becoming more and more certain that she wanted to birth a baby. She was drawn towards the enormity of pregnancy and birth, dreaming of her body transforming and her spirit stretching. At first, it was hard for me to imagine us choosing this. I was tied to my idea of becoming a family for a little one who needed a home, mothering an existing child instead of creating a new one. But I watched Meg's eyes sparkle as she talked about getting pregnant, and I tried on the idea of this new way to become a mama.

Despite my pull towards adoption, I was also fearful of the process. I imagined home visits and social workers, I worried over how we'd be able to afford the costs, and I doubted my ability to maintain my emotional wellness while we waited for a child. It scared me to think that if we pursued adoption, then we'd be opening ourselves to other people declaring our worth to parent. Someone else would peer into our lives and decide whether we were fit to raise a child. On the other hand, if we chose pregnancy, we could get semen from a friend, inseminate at home, and virtually control our entire process. There'd be no one else granting us permission and Meg's health insurance would cover the prenatal and birthing expenses. Even without a whole lot of money or external approval, we could grow a child all on our own!

The more we explored the possibility of pregnancy, the more excited we became. Meg and I swept each other away with discussions of prenatal nutrition, birthing with a midwife, and breastfeeding. I blended fertility-enhancing herbal teas; Meg began a rigorous acupuncture regimen. We reveled in giddy elation over being two dykes queering family and creating a child on our own. Our excitement carried us through the process of researching DIY pregnancy and birth, choosing a sperm donor, charting ovulation and—finally—inseminating. It was an exhilarating two years of learning and reaching. We inseminated five times—two on our own and three with the assistance of a reproductive endocrinologist and a fertility drug—but Meg did not get pregnant. I was surprised by the force of my grief; I'd attached so deeply to the possibility of her pregnancy. As we moved through our regret and sadness, I reconnected with my original desire to adopt. Packing up our syringes, sperm donor contract, and pregnancy books, we turned our faces towards the adoption process.

As a not-wealthy queer couple, Meg and I found that our options for adopting were restricted. Many countries and agencies set standards for adoptive parents that include things like marital status (no singles or queers), income and occupation (no poor or chronically unemployed folks), health status (no chronic physical or mental illness), and other markers of worthiness such as body mass index (no fatties). Most straight, White, Christian, upper-middle-class couples have a wide range of choices: domestic, international, state-based, faith-based, and private agency adoptions. Wading through Internet searches, we looked for the few adoption agencies that were explicitly welcoming of gay, lesbian, and queer couples. We found a homogenous portrait of adoptive families that illustrated how White privilege, heterosexism, classism, and other forms of oppression shape adoption. At this point in our process, I also began to feel a nagging discomfort when I thought about birth parents and adoption situated within our stratified society. I began taking baby steps towards a consciousness that rejects simple analyses of adoption.

Even with my enthusiasm for this means of becoming a parent, I only had a cursory understanding of a very specific form of adoption. What I'd gleaned as I grew up simplified the players and outcomes: There were those poor children who needed homes and the valiant foster and adoptive parents who took them in. When birth parents came into the picture at all, they were transient and either demonized or pitied. I knew about birth parents who had children taken away from them and about newborns who were left at the hospital, picked up by my parents and cared for until they were placed with adoptive families. My family cared for twenty-some foster children, and only one sibling group was consistently in contact with their birth family. From my experience, it seemed that birth families faded into the background as soon as the state or an adoption counselor entered the picture. I didn't think much about it as a kid, but as I began to consider myself a prospective adoptive parent, I cringed at the brutality of this severance. What happened to the birth families? Did they fade away by choice or were they actually pushed out? As Meg and I searched for queer-friendly adoption possibilities, we found an open adoption agency in our hometown. Reading their website, I was intrigued by this new way of building families.

The agency held an introductory meeting at our local library where we dove headlong into learning about open adoption. Even at this initial contact, my insecurity was evident—I worried over how we dressed, how we'd be perceived: Would we seem like the kind of people who became adoptive parents? As we listened to the counselors talk about child-centered adoption, birth parent empowerment, and options counseling, my fears softened a bit. I shifted my focus outside of myself as I leaned in to absorb the words, images, and ideas being presented. In contrast to my experience of disappearing birth families and martyred adoptive parents, open adoption offers a way to focus on connection and, I thought, on integrity. I was especially captured by the way this agency focuses on options counseling for birth parents. Counselors described their work of meeting birth parents and deeply exploring the options of parenting, abortion, and adoption. I didn't expect this from an adoption agency—I'd imagined a stronger push towards adoption, but I learned that the counselors spend lots of time working with families who would not choose to place their children. In a society where women are routinely sorted by external assumptions (Too young? Well, clearly, you can't parent! Christian? Well, you mustn't have an abortion!), this practice is revolutionary.

Open adoption provides a model for building a child's family with honesty, respect for history, and courage for openhearted relationships. If we decided to work with this agency, we'd create a profile of ourselves, and a birth family would choose us to parent their child. Contact between birth and adoptive families is encouraged and supported throughout the adoption process and the child's life. I imagined our child surrounded by family: Meg and I as mamas, birth and chosen families all around. I was caught up in the possibility that adoption can occur as both an empowered choice and as a template for expansive constructions of family. This appealed to me on many levels. As a queer woman, I appreciated the opportunity to further expand my understanding of family. Meg and I live our relationship so that each of us is supported in deepening intimate connections with loved ones. We believe in nourishing our partnership and our heart connections with others. We nurture a large chosen family and we loved the idea of expanding that to include our child and his or her birth family. From the perspective of my little girl self, I yearned to give our child the chance to know her or his birth family.

My birth parents divorced when I was young, and I felt the absence of my birth father throughout my childhood. He wasn't there to tell me otherwise, so I made up stories about why he had disappeared. I figured it was all about me—I decided that I must have been a pretty horrible kid if my own father wanted nothing to do with me. As an adult, it seemed to me that open adoption could spare a child the pain that comes from not knowing.

Open adoption resonated so deeply with Meg and I that we decided to sell our house (to finance the adoption) and enter into the agency's pool of waiting families. We had individual and shared interviews, health reports from doctors, and a home study. We wrote a "Dear birth parent" letter and personal biographies. We created a photo collage. At home we set up an altar for our mama intentions and we started collecting tiny outfits. During our time preparing, we dreamed. We imagined ourselves meeting a birth mom, getting to know her and building a relationship. I hoped for phone calls and emails, letters and visits, long talks about this family we'd create together. We dreamed about being there to see the baby born, taking our little one home to nest. We researched adoptive breastfeeding, glass baby bottles, and organic infant formula. After we'd submitted our paperwork and were officially in the waiting pool, we had a party to celebrate. Surrounded by our family and friends, I filled up with hope and joy—finally, finally I was going to be a mama.

More quickly than I'd anticipated, my joy deflated into despair. As month after month went by, I flattened under the fear that we'd never be chosen. Our agency's newsletter announced when adoptive and birth parents were in mediation and when babies were born; I agonized over how quickly others were chosen and took this as evidence of our deficiencies. I read other "Dear birth parent" letters and saw enormous homes, lucrative careers, fancy vacations, and designer nurseries. I didn't really aspire to these ways of living, but I feared that birth parents would want these things for their children. We lived in a one-bedroom apartment without a yard or a washing machine. We planned on sleeping with our baby in our bedroom, cutting our meager income into even less so that one of us could stay home. When we met with other waiting families at agency events, I felt sorely out of place. Whether they were or not, I saw the others as more financially stable, more centered, more grown-up. It was like the worst junior high gym class ever—I was sure that we'd never get picked for the team. I found that in order to deal with the wait, I had to strictly compartmentalize my life. Sure, becoming a mama was the thing I'd wanted forever, but I had to pack it away on the highest shelf of my deepest, darkest closet. Other families were going to baby care classes, but I was close to tears whenever a mama and baby came through my line at the co-op. I was a fragile mess, hoping against hope and hiding my hope away.

During this painful time of waiting, I also began to connect—with horror—to the brutal grief of adoption. I'd been so focused on the aspect of empowerment in open adoption that I hadn't allowed myself to see the sadness. I started to think about the moment when a birth mom would place her child in our arms, the moment when we'd drive away with her baby. I wondered how she'd gather her things, her now empty body, and leave the hospital alone. I thought about how our most intense joy might be her most consuming grief. I felt shaken by the realization that I'd be benefiting from another person's loss. I struggled with intensely conflicted feelings because while it seems that open adoption offers more justice for birth parents than closed adoption, it still exists within the inequality of a stratified society. In particular, poverty and racism limit access to the resources and opportunities necessary for building and maintaining a comfortable standard of living. Was it wrong to placate myself with the knowledge of birth parents choosing adoptive parents? What kind of choice exists when opportunity is given or withheld based on things like race/ethnicity, class, and ability? The adoption process raised so many complicated questions. All at once, I felt strongly about adopting a child and critical of the existence of adoption in our society.

Part of the preparation for entering the pool was filling out a document called a "screening tool." The screening tool asked prospective adoptive parents to define our openness to several things including race, sex, age, exposure to drugs and alcohol, and health of the baby. The agency counselors used screening tools to sort adoptive parents before presenting profiles to birth families. That way a birth family would only see profiles of the families who were open to their unique circumstances—eliminating the needless heartbreak of birth families attaching to adoptive parents who wouldn't consider adopting their baby. While I appreciated the logic of the tool, I had a really hard time completing it. I felt like I was sorting human beings into yes, no, and maybe piles. I imagined all of these affluent White people having discussions about their openness and I felt ashamed of my privilege. I kept thinking that this was so unnatural—when women get pregnant and birth babies, they don't get to predetermine the genitalia and health of the child. Meg and I were working with a wonderful counselor who did an amazing job of hearing our concerns and responding with thoughtful support. After several conversations with her, I was able to frame the screening tool as a way of learning more about ourselves as parents while keeping the best interests of the baby and her or his birth parents in mind. It would serve no one if adoptive parents weren't clear about their comfort, skills, and resources. There is a family for every baby, our counselor assured us. It was our job to honestly determine where we stood. Most of these questions were things we didn't consider when Meg was trying to get pregnant—yet another way of stretching ourselves into mamahood through adoption.

Meg and I took our time with the screening tool, answering as best we could the first time around and revising our answers as we learned more about these complex issues and ourselves. Sex was the one category that we answered easily. We don't confuse sex and gender, nor do we see either attribute as fixed. To us, a baby's sex is one piece of herself or himself and may not predict anything at all about that child's gender. So, we were open to any sex. Age seemed easy at first—we really wanted the experience of parenting a newborn baby, so we said that we were open to babies up to six months old. But then we read a book about adopting toddlers and realized that we felt able to respond to an older baby's feelings of loss and awareness about the adoption. We found the drug and alcohol exposure question most difficult. When we combed through the research, we found it overwhelmingly inconclusive.

Most of the literature seemed intent on scaring pregnant women away from substance use. It told of worst-case scenarios, ripe with scare tactics about media-inflated "crack babies." We struggled to understand which outcomes were statistically significant and how much these could be attributed to growing up with users, instead of just to prenatal exposure. We wrestled with the image of the "perfect baby" and challenged ourselves to consider whether we were equipped to parent a child with special needs. As much as I wanted us to be realistic, I also wanted us to be aware that even the "perfect" child might develop health problems or learning disabilities or psychological issues. Signing on to parent any child—adopted or not—means accepting some amount of mystery. But becoming an adoptive parent throws open the curtains to illuminate risks and possibilities in ways that don't happen so often in pregnancy.

When Meg and I considered race/ethnicity, we knew that we were open to adopting a baby of any background. But this shade of mama comes only in white. As a White couple with a largely White community in a predominantly White city, we grappled with whether we'd be the best parents for a child of color. If we adopted transracially, how would we help our child develop their identity as a person of color? Is it enough to be aware of White privilege and to align ourselves as antiracist allies? As queer parents, could we find a place for our family in communities of color and with other multiracial families? Thinking about adopting transracially also brought me back to my questions about systems of inequality in society and about choice for birth parents. In our adoption agency's pool of waiting families, almost everyone was White. And by looking at so many adoption agencies online and in print, it seemed that there are many children of color waiting for adoptive families. Apparently lots of White folks want White kids. But what if a birth parent of color wants to place their child with adoptive parents of color? These were unsettling questions and I felt like I was on tenuous ground asking them. While this critical analysis of adoption is important, I also wanted to place my trust in the birth parents making these choices—maybe these were my own academically-informed musings and I would be making a caricature of real people by fixating on these questions. After much deliberation, Meg and I returned to our original feeling of openness about adopting transracially. We were planning an open adoption, after all, and if we were chosen by birth parents of color, we hoped to develop a relationship that would support our child.

After thirteen months of waiting for a child, we finally received the call that would turn us into mamas. A woman had given birth that morning, she'd read our letter, and she wanted to meet us. We were thrilled, amazed, and terrified as we packed our things and made our way to her hospital room. Meg and I had six hours in the car to swallow our excitement, diffuse our anxieties, and imagine how our lives might be on the verge of transformation. When we arrived at the birthing center, our adoption counselors met us with information about the birth mom and the baby. We had mere moments to digest before being led to the bedside of this amazing woman, tiny bundle of baby asleep in a bassinet nearby. She told us about the birth and how surprised she'd been that the baby looked so white. She talked and talked, patting her daughter's back every so often, responding to the baby's cries with "It's okay, sweetie, Mommy's here." I was distracted by the fact that she was in a hospital gown while we got to be dressed in our own clothes. I wondered if she felt vulnerable and exposed. We were surprised at how little she asked us, how even at the end of this first meeting we had no idea whether she liked us. We left her room certain that we'd be driving home with the car seat empty.

A few hours later, we returned for another meeting. This time she was holding the baby tenderly, talking gently to her. We talked more—small talk infused with stories about the birth—and then a nurse came in to ask a question. "Don't ask me," she replied. "Ask them—they're the parents." My eyes filled with tears and it was all I could do to hold it together. She asked if we wanted to hold her daughter. We took turns, cradling the impossibly tiny body in our hands, choking back tears at her beauty. She talked more about how she couldn't believe that this White baby had come out of her. She told us that we were going to have to learn to do something with her hair. "She's gonna have some black hair, you know?" We smiled and I told her that we hoped she'd be able to help us find our way.

We slept fitfully that night in a hotel room close to the hospital. I couldn't stop thinking about how small the baby's head was, wrapped in a soft cotton hat. I was filled with a delirious longing to hold her, to take her home. I was overwhelmed with dread at the thought of the separation that would take place. The next morning was a blur of paperwork—the termination of parental rights, the adoption placement papers. It was so stark, all in writing, all in orderly lines. She wanted only letters and pictures for now, only four times a year, and we wouldn't have her contact information.

Our time together was so brief, so much business crammed into a space filled with so much emotion. I found myself struggling to stay present with all of the tasks we had to complete. I wanted to hear her voice, see her holding her baby. But she wanted the babe out of the room while we finished the placement. The agency had called this last step an entrustment ceremony—we might prepare some things to say and have a gift, the counselors suggested. Meg had made a small quilt for her out of fabric we picked out together. We told her that we planned on making one for the baby, too. They'd each have one, cut from the same cloth, just as they were. Her eyes brightened at this and she said she'd hang it on her wall. I imagined the baby as a toddler, pointing at the shapes and colors on her quilt. Too soon, it was over. She was packing up her things and then we waited for her cab together in the lobby. We took a photo of her before she left, beautiful smile shining. As she walked out of the hospital, Meg and I were born as mamas.

We've told Quincy LaTasha the story of her birth over and over again since she was two days old. We tell her how tender and strong her birth mom was when we met her, how she loves her so much. We'll continue to do this as she grows. Recently we had a conversation with Quincy LaTasha's birth mom and she told us that she couldn't have picked better parents for her daughter. She marveled at how happy this baby looks, told us how much she enjoys the pictures and hearing about our life. She wants to visit this year, she says, she's ready. We're imagining our time together, looking forward to seeing her holding her daughter. I am so thankful for this amazing gift, for the realization of my deepest dream, for the opportunity to grow into this connection. Finally, finally, I am a mama. A mama stretching to hold loss and jubilation, reaching to construct expansive family without a manual, and learning to do my biracial daughter's hair. Mama in my own shade, a shade called mama.

★ **KELLY JESKE** reads, writes, and chases her toddler, Quincy LaTasha, in Portland, Oregon. After a year of full-time work with no sleep, she's spending time at home as a full-time mama. Her first published work was her master's thesis: *Genderqueer Meets the Doc: Masculine-Identified Transgender Individuals and Health Care.*

Growing Pains

MARCELLA RUNELL HALL

New Year's Eve 2006 was a perfectly divine evening. Despite frosty New York weather I attended an early church service in Brooklyn with my then boyfriend of three years and my best girlfriend, Keisha. The sermon was a prophetic word on how 2007 would be a year of completion and preparation in anticipation of 2008, which promised to be the year of new beginnings. Later we attended a swanky Brooklyn party where, Dave, my boyfriend, was spinning. It was a lovely and fulfilling night: a perfect way to end 2006, which had been full of transitions, many of them difficult to manage.

Early into 2007 I realized big things were starting to happen for me. In February I called my mom nearly every week, starting our conversations with basically the same question, "Hey, Mom, do I sound different now that I have been *promoted*?" "Hey, Mom, do I sound different now that I am *a published author*?" or the best one, "Hey, Mom! Guess what—do I sound different now that I am *engaged*?" (Yes, my thoughtful and loving boyfriend proposed on Valentine's Day, making the beginning of 2007 one of the most special times in my life.)

All things work-related continued to improve while I enjoyed my job directing a blossoming education and training program at a small nonprofit; in March I found out that my "dream job" was unexpectedly opening at NYU—my former alma mater and first place of official employment. I ended up getting the job offer the evening before my very blessed May wedding. During the special ceremony, which was family-only in my parents' home, there were many *amens* and *hallelujahs* from both sides of the family as the pastor (and father of my best friend, Keisha) asked everyone to pray for all of the future children he knew we were going to have. I was overjoyed, although I wondered how I was going to squeeze it all in with a new job and so much still to do. The book I had coedited, *The Hip-Hop Education Guidebook*, was doing very well and was leading me to many more writing projects and speaking engagements. My wedding, however, was intimate and romantic, and I was poised to start my dream job over the summer. I only had one other major issue to contend with—finishing my dissertation so I could complete my doctorate. Life was amazing, but I was silently wondering how I was going to in fact "have it all." My mom had warned me for a long time that early menopause runs in our family (she started at thirty-six!) so I was doing the math trying to figure when we could start on the baby making. I was thirty-two at the time . . .

In July of my amazing year, my husband and I attended the wedding of a college friend. We came home and had a romantic evening celebrating the newness of attending our first major event as husband and wife. The next day I left for Florida to complete a much-needed writing retreat to get a head start on dissertation work before my new job started. While I was in Florida, I came down with lingering flulike symptoms and was having some of the worst cramps of my life. I persevered and kept on working, however, taking borrowed antibiotics (my health insurance hadn't kicked in yet) and popping Aleve for the cramps—coupled with plenty of coffee to keep me up to write.

When I returned home, I hit the ground running at work, coming early and staying late to show my enthusiasm and gratitude. In addition I was also hanging out with friends quite a bit, celebrating all the blessings that had come to me in 2007. After a few weeks I suddenly had a startling thought. My cramps had gone away, but my period never came. I was in denial about what that might mean, because in the twenty years of getting my period, I had never been late—and I had also never been pregnant. I finally brought myself to buy a test.

I fumbled with the box, reading the simple directions over and over again, looking for the words of reassurance that might say something like, *Don't worry you probably aren't pregnant, you weren't even trying. And you used birth control, so take it easy.* But I didn't see those words, so I peed on the stick, and within five seconds it turned blue—both lines! I wasn't only pregnant, I was *very* pregnant, if that was possible. So I did it again just to make sure. And the same result remained. I, I mean *we*, were having a baby.

I came out the bathroom in awe of what I had just witnessed. I walked into my husband's music room, and said something to the effect of, "So honey, I just took a pregnancy test 'cause I was late, and it was positive, so I don't know what that means." Yes, with all my education and experience, I still couldn't bring myself to believe that I knew what it meant. My husband looked like he had seen a ghost, and maybe he did—the ghost of independence past . . . or something comparable—flashing before his eyes. He gave me a hug and I said we couldn't really confirm until I saw a doctor anyway. I went to sleep shortly after because I was nauseous and tired, and ended up waking up to pee at least twice. The writing seemed to be on the wall: I was pregnant.

The next day I handled the news by doing what I do best: marching myself to the closest bookstore and buying as many pregnancy books as I could afford. Then I made a doctor's appointment to confirm what the home pregnancy test had already told me twice. And I didn't tell another living soul, even after the doctor confirmed it.

I was having very mixed emotions. I was frantically searching the Internet to see if the bootleg antibiotics I had borrowed from an aunt in Florida were dangerous to my unborn child. When I was convinced that they were okay, I moved on to panic about the Aleve, then the possible fetal alcohol syndrome from the after-work celebratory cocktails, and eventually about the extra caffeine I had drunk during my writing retreat. I was a nervous wreck. I had been waiting to be a mother my entire life—I took care of my multiracial Cabbage Patch Kid collection as if they were living children. I babysat and shamelessly "flirted" with babies everywhere just to see them smile or laugh. I had dreamed of this moment for my entire life. And yet all I felt were mixed emotions. I felt regretful for my unmotherly discretions, I felt scared that I would look unprofessional at my new (old) job by recklessly miscalculating my birth control situation, and on some level I felt like I just wasn't ready yet.

Then the unthinkable happened. A good friend and mentor who is an NYU professor went through the most unimaginable tragedy. Her beautiful young daughter was murdered just a few short blocks from my office and in the same apartment complex I had lived in as a graduate student. Her death made the front page of every newspaper. I was devastated. And then all of a sudden I felt like a fool. I was feeling mixed emotions about this life growing inside of me, this miracle, and my friend had just lost her own precious gift.

I snapped out of it. My mixed feelings dissipated on the spot, and after a week of post-pregnancy-test brooding, I, I mean we, finally started to get excited—really excited. I shopped around for the perfect ob-gyn. And like everything else in Manhattan, I had to get on a waiting list and plead my case. I finally settled/was selected for an all-woman practice right between my office and my husband's office—perfect for midday ultrasounds. We told our parents, who were overjoyed, to put it mildly. Dave's mother remarked, "Oh what a big year this has been for me! Oh . . . er . . . I mean for you!" Both of our mothers were thrilled. I was estimated to be about eight weeks pregnant at this time, with a projected due date sometime in March.

I took the day after Labor Day off from work and went for my first ultrasound appointment. Dave and I were so excited. The first one is a vaginal ultrasound, so I told Dave he didn't need to come for this one, a mistake I would soon come to regret. My doctor was a young woman about my age, very helpful and excited, as was I . . . until she did the actual ultrasound and found that my baby did not have a heartbeat. In fact it seemed as though the baby had stopped developing about two weeks earlier. I immediately thought of how selfish I had been, and wondered if the baby could sense my ambiguity. Then I thought, *why couldn't I tell that she had died?* All the while my doctor was trying to tell me how common miscarriages are and that there probably wasn't anything I could have done. I felt like the whole scene was unfolding in slow motion. And then I felt a wave of dizziness like I might faint right there.

Somehow I pulled myself together to hear that I had two options for getting rid of the fetus. I could take a drug called Misoprostol and insert it inside my vaginal wall. I would have cramps and some pain, but it would cause my body to expel the fetus over several days of bleeding. Sounded pretty awful. The second option was to go to an abortion clinic recommended by my doctor and have a D&C procedure, which frankly also sounded pretty awful. I opted for the drug since I could at least be at home. And then I called Dave. I couldn't even get the words out, I just burst into tears. He left work and came to get me in a few short minutes (turns out the central location was very beneficial). We stood on the bustling SoHo street on the perfect early sunny September day, and I cried like a baby—and for the baby that wasn't coming anymore.

Later on, after a few drinks—the necessary liquid courage—I went home and administered the drug. I later found out it is used to terminate pregnancies in developing countries. Scary thought, because I soon found out that it doesn't always work. In fact I tried it twice, staying up all night sweating and cramping, so scared of what was happening to my body.

After two unsuccessful tries, I had another appointment and the fetus was still there, not budging. I reluctantly agreed to make the D&C appointment. Then a few days later the roller coaster continued: I started to bleed on my own and realized my body was naturally handling the situation. My husband and my doctor were happy.

I finally (after three weeks) was starting to feel better. I waited two more weeks and went back to the doctor for my checkup. And, alas, more bad news: There was still too much tissue in my uterus, and now my health was of great concern. The D&C was back on, and I needed to go the very next day.

Ironically, my talented DJ husband had just been asked to DJ on a major NYC radio show with millions of listeners—a huge break—but the same day as the procedure was scheduled.

Early on the morning of October 6, we drove into midtown Manhattan and made our way into the clinic. It was very unassuming; I kept imagining there would be protesters or some other obvious sign of what was about to go down. When we walked in the waiting room, there appeared to be at least fifty young women waiting, some with male partners, but many solo. I was pretty sure I was the oldest person in the room at thirty-two.

Fortunately, my doctor had called and arranged for one of the private outpatient waiting rooms, so we only had to wait two hours, as opposed to however long the other young women were waiting. As I went in for the procedure I was terrified and sad. I was literally on the table with my legs spread, getting the IV of anesthesia, when the doctor performing the surgery said two things to me. First, he said, "Don't worry, you are young, you can have another baby later. How old are you?" I replied, "Thanks. I am thirty-two." He said, "Oh, well, in that case you should have one really soon and then another one right away; you really need to have two before thirty-five." I said, "Um, okay, thanks." And then he said, "And you should probably lose twenty-five pounds too." I was mortified. I couldn't have been in a more vulnerable position, literally and metaphorically. As I was passing out and the anesthesia was kicking in, I was thinking, *this is the worst day of my life*.

When I awoke half an hour later, I was in a room with many other women at various stages of recovering from their procedures. People were being offered cookies and juice, since we couldn't eat for many hours leading up to the surgery. One young woman remarked that she wanted the same cookies "as before." I was dumbfounded in that moment. I was in excruciating pain, trying to process all that was going on. Then "Dr. Tactless" came out and said I would be in more pain than everyone else because the tissue had connected to my uterus and was more painful to remove. *Perfect,* I thought.

Later on, after I was safely home, Dave was able to leave me alone long enough to do his thing on the radio, and by the next day I was physically feeling better.

It would be nearly three months before my period returned and my body finally healed from the trauma. Every website said it would be back after four to six weeks, but that wasn't my experience. Having a miscarriage is a painful and often taboo conversation topic, and yet is eerily common, especially in women over thirty. I found out that most doctors won't even start to run tests until it happens three times. And what I have discovered, once I tell my story, is that many other women have had similar experiences or are close to women who have had them. While I was only a mother for a few short weeks, I now know it is possible. And I believe that my experience, albeit painful, contributed to my year of preparation.

I am no longer worried about my job security, as my probation period is over and it truly is my dream job—I even got promoted. Recently my husband and I were finally able to take and enjoy our belated honeymoon—pregnancy free—which has some benefits. I have been faithfully taking prenatal vitamins, exercising, and eating much better. I am much closer to completing my dissertation and looking to graduate this year. We have paid off our debt and are saving to buy our first home. And we are making plans to try again soon. In retrospect, if I had known what was going to happen, I probably would have been terrified and certain that I couldn't handle it. But I have once again learned that a crisis is only a crisis when you don't have the knowledge and skills to deal with it. This will not be my crisis again. I am looking forward to being a mother when the time is right.

★ **MARCELLA RUNELL HALL** is the Associate Director of the Center for Multicultural Education and Programs at New York University. She is also a freelance writer for the *New York Times* Learning Network and *VIBE*, and is the author of *The Hip-Hop Education Guidebook Volume 1* with Martha Diaz (Hip-Hop Association, 2007), *The 10 Most Influential Hip-Hop Artists* (Scholastic/Rubicon, 2008), and *Conscious Women Rock the Page: Using Hip-Hop Fiction to Incite Social Change* (Sister Outsider Entertainment, 2008) with JLove Calderón (also featured in this book), Black Artemis, and E-Fierce. She lives in Brooklyn with her husband, David Hall, a.k.a. DJ Trends.

Namaste Revisited

SONALI S. BALAJEE

As my heart froze, the waves began to pull me under again, and I didn't put up a fight. First my toes, then my heels, the crease between my upper thighs and hips, my soft belly, my armpits. I sighed deeply and took in a great amount of air before my chin, the tops of my ears, and my hair followed suit.

Once under, I opened my eyes and tilted my head to the surface to see the faces before me begin to blur and wash away. The light and sound from the outside world continued to mute as I let myself go deeper and deeper. I allowed the weight of the tragic and breaking situation above the waves carry me closer to a darkness that would, ironically, end up sustaining me again through trying times.

The journey itself appeared more treacherous than the reality of actually reaching the dark, murky depths, as I had to break through one painful emotion after another to get to my destination. I wasn't sinking to a terrifying place, but rather to a place of safety. Once I felt I had arrived, it was always just a matter of patiently listening and waiting for the cues to know what to do next.

"She must marry him immediately, before she is showing. Within the next month should do it. That is our wish."

Above water, the most tender parts of my soul had felt attacked by these words that pummeled towards me like spears just released in battle. But I did not let them see their words pierce me. I put up a strong wall for them to watch, a rather false fortress of mind and body, as I quietly left the scene, spears slowly sinking in, and slipped into the beckoning waters.

This time, the grave sadness oozing from the piercings could not be slowed nor stopped due to my already weakened condition. I sat in the still of the deepest waters, as my frenetic and frightened thoughts clung for dear life to my heart, waiting . . . and waiting . . . for something. Anything. Just a few guiding words would have done it. My heart was trained to listen acutely, but suffered in the moment from immense exhaustion, slowing down the ability to complete its current task. *Yes, this is when my life actually stops*, I mused bitterly. *There's no way out of this one.*

And then in the midst of the panic, the bottomless blue, the heaviness . . . the sudden, unexpected, strange little cramps in my stomach. Peculiarly sharp waves within deeper, achy undulations. Heart-rate quickened out of surprise, palms sweaty. My hands clutched at my belly. In the depths, or recently, above the waters, the presence of these sensations was new. As one of my yoga teachers had suggested, I took a deep breath into the brief spasms of pain, trying to feel them out. But they just didn't make sense. These spine-bracing, stick-it-to-ya, bind-your-emotion-to-the-universe-type cramps couldn't be compared to anything I'd ever felt before. Later my midwife would inform me that these intense pangs signaled the beginnings of a pregnancy taking hold. For now, they brought nothing but discomfort and agitation. My fists and teeth clenched in frustration; I couldn't hear the guidance I desperately needed with this much distraction.

The pain came on again. I clamped down on my anxiety, determined to see it through. Again I breathed deeply into the source of my pain, my lower abdomen, this time imagining sending peace to that part of my body on my exhale, as I was trained to do. After several rounds of this, the pain had subsided, and my heart firmly grounded itself in my surroundings. I strained to listen again. From within the spellbinding silence and darkness came a familiar showering of gentle yet powerful words.

It's just their pain talking. Listen, but don't take it on. You've got a being inside you that's trying to grow. Listen to understand.

In more tender years, staying in the depths was the safest thing to do, and provided me with needed protection from sharp tongues, painful hands, stinging slaps. I didn't know back then how to come back up, and why it was important to do so. But with thirty-one years now behind me, I had learned that the gift was about facing what was in front of you, going deep to access inner guidance, and then resurfacing to apply what you had found in your day-to-day life. As I witnessed members of my family and other teachers throughout the years, I learned that there were many ways to access this serene wisdom. Upon hearing that I was pregnant, I had revived other practices taught to me by my father's family and my Buddhist relatives on my mother's side. I often chanted and meditated, two, maybe three times a day, in prayer in front of a makeshift altar (an old forest green saucer holding important, symbolic objects), my candle, and the sandalwood beads my father had bought me from the oldest Hindu temple in India.

Without the beads and my altar, all I had was my breath and focus. I began to concentrate again, taking a long inhale, allowing the words I had just heard to make sense and take hold. Looking up towards the surface, I half hoped that the upcoming dialogue would actually heal the pain, and simultaneously half feared the possible irreparable damage. I placed my hands protectively on the new, soft bulge in my abdomen, and floated slowly back up to the live scene.

As the water became more transparent, and the faces less blurry, I could hear the family counselor for that session say, "Sonali, Sonali . . . do you have an answer to your father's statement? Sonali? I'm sorry, sweetheart. It seems like you're so far away."

I surfaced with a jolt, my journal immediately jumping from my lap to the floor. My eyes then followed three pink and peach pamphlets as they flew out of the journal midair and fell lazily to the floor with ironically weighty titles like, "Open Adoption: The Choice Is up to You," "Eat Right Now! Making It through Your First Trimester," and "The Facts about Compassionate Abortion." As the last one on abortion hit the ground, I realized four pairs of eyes were focused on its title. I seized the moment of distraction to slowly follow the lines of sight from the pamphlet to each pair of eyes, trying to gauge the place the others in the room had been occupying while I was briefly away.

First, my brother. My dear, one-and-only brother. He had traveled to Portland, Oregon, from California just to be here with our family, in our first-ever family counseling session about this new arrival. He sat calmly with brow furrowed, and awkwardly wore a sideways, closed smile. His observant, dark eyes sat far away from the lens of his glasses, glancing once in a while at our father, who was seated right next to him.

I glanced back down to the pamphlet and then followed the imaginary line of view to my father's eyes. With roots in the City of Oranges, Nagpur, India, this aging, esteemed Hindu in our community and a member of the highest caste, the Brahmins, appeared nervous and depressed in spirit, with an outward, angry body scowl. I had just written in my journal moments before about how this type of mixed-up, disturbing countenance my father exhibited was, unfortunately, not unusual to me; throughout my life I received the award for being the object of my parents' gravest dissatisfactions due to not doing things in ways that "agreed" with them. This particular day, however, was the first time an absolute fragility was appearing in his usually rock-solid, angry stance. It was as if at any moment a deluge of tears and wails from this lion of a father might shatter the dam and drown us all. His eyelids clamped severely over his black ocean eyes of sorrow as a measure of protection, guarding his view of things that were too terrible to see and bear.

This daughter's view of her father's soul breaking right in front of her would forever remain a sharp, painful frame in her mind. An unkind-to-the-heart snapshot of a devastating moment, created by this daughter's choice to go through an unplanned pregnancy in an unmarried situation at age thirty-one as the eldest offspring on both sides of traditional Indian and Sri Lankan immigrant families. Thankfully, the large hand that was her soft, wide, velvety, jade colored couch caught her before she could melt into complete despair.

Don't take it on, the voice in the waters had calmly suggested. I listened and straightened the small curve of my lower spine and tried to get a grip before viewing my mother and her evolving complexity in this longest scene of my life.

The scattered pastel pamphlets that had landed on the floor in a small, messy pile served as a momentary oasis for all our eyes, which were exhausted from connecting with each other and our emotions. My mother's actions, however, were baffling to me in that very moment. She had suddenly chosen to gaze directly at the counselor, her mouth beginning to move without the usual deluge of words streaming forth, as her mind tried to find a place to land and as her voice gathered strength.

"I . . . I am concerned with my health over this," she whispered. "Very concerned. And I don't know how to be in the community. How do we say, 'We are going to be grandparents'?"

The counselor uncrossed her legs and then crossed them again, searching for a comfortable position. "I hear you about your health . . . and it seems as if you're looking for a way to reframe the situation to make it better for you to talk about. Let me ask you this: If she were to marry and divorce, would that be less heartbreaking?" I almost let out a full-throttled, deep belly laugh. The thought of that was beyond absurd.

To my surprise, given how much they cringe at even hearing the utterance of the first syllable of the word *divorce*, my mother and father both nodded their heads vehemently in the affirmative. Yes, they'd like me to marry and then divorce, to save the family face. To avoid shame. Yes, absolutely!

What was I hearing?

My father leaned forward in his chair and cleared his throat, signaling the usual arrival of important information or mandates. My mother and brother straightened their spines, and sat upright and motionless in their seats, a subconscious gesture of deferment and respect. My body also followed, but more like a limp cloth doll being forced to look like it was standing up.

"Ah, gee. This is the worst thing to happen to this family. But it is what it is. We must move on from here. I would like her to marry him immediately, but, ahh, she will do what she wants, as she always does. We will support her as we can. But we ask her to keep this quiet. To not tell anyone in our family, save her two aunts and cousin on my wife's side who already know. For this is *our* right to decide what happens with this . . . with this . . . *information*. Not hers. It is traditionally the eldest male, myself, who will tell everyone when he is ready."

The oceans arose underneath me, this time not to beckon me to the depths to listen and recharge, but to provide me with enough strength to greet the situation with as much grace as could possibly flow through me given the circumstances. My hand snuck underneath my knee and dug into the couch, looking for any grounding possible to withstand the rough verbal road ahead.

"I understand, father, how painful this is for you. I do not know, however, how I am to keep this from my cousins who keep calling me. From other family who check in on me. You are lucky all of those people live on the East Coast, and I'm here in Portland! And I ne-need f-family right now!" My fist had been raised during these words where I gave him back tight, and everyone watched as the quick, sharp, emphatic gesture softened and crumpled back into my lap, awaiting his response.

My brother's eyes widened, and his smile genuinely opened up just a little, showing a half-line of teeth. As he caught the growing discontent in my father's eyes, however, he immediately resumed his previous posture. My father was tearing up. He tried to straighten himself in his chair, but slightly faltered as he struggled to gather his emotions.

"This is our wish. We cannot handle anymore of this. This has put us through too much, and you must understand this is what we need."

He weakly put his hands on his knees, and his chin softly met his chest, showing the rest of us a brief glimpse of how quickly he had been graying through the years. He felt so old to me in that moment, and yet the look on his face was the same one I'd seen of him as a boy in an old black-and-white photograph with yellowed, tattered edges taken in southern India in 1950 during some of the poorest, toughest years of his life in his village. I could also see my Pati, his mother, my only living grandmother, when I looked at him. He was the spitting image of her.

Pati didn't know a thing about the news of this baby, this first great-grandchild of hers. She was in her early eighties and very sick. Surely this would be a great joy to her, even though I wasn't married? No, no . . . I was foolish to think so. She was several times stricter in her religious and cultural beliefs than my father. This could actually be quite devastating to her. I began to feel the weight of the world on my father's shoulders. There was nothing he hated more than disappointing and disrespecting his mother.

The counselor sensed the gravity in my father's emotions. She took some time to empathize even more with my parents, and gave them a few tips for how to best deal with this incredibly trying situation. My father then asked a few questions about what more he and my mother could do for their daughter. Basic answers were provided: Love her, don't judge, realize you're mourning a dream. The smooth back-and-forth of these brief discussions between my parents and the counselor brought some normalcy and steady flow to the session. Yet I knew my parents were waiting for my response to their request to be the sole communicators about this issue to our family.

I took a moment to still my thoughts and to wait for the best answer. Although most of my life my parents and I had been on different tracks, to put it mildly, I still respected aspects of who they were and loved them tremendously. And, since being pregnant, I had observed in myself this strange, almost obsessive desire to be around family as much as possible, even if I didn't quite get along with them. The answer from deep within for my most immediate next step was to take a moment to connect with how they were being affected by all this, and really think about the consequences of my desire to share the news with everyone as soon as possible.

"I just need to take a short break before I respond to something as big as that. Can we do this?" Everyone nodded tiredly. I opened my journal and began to quickly put my thoughts on paper:

I had sex in an unmarried situation. *Against my parents' wishes.*

In one situation recently, I became pregnant. *Against my parents' wishes.*

After checking into my options to not have a child, I decided not to have an abortion. *Against my parents' wishes.*

I will not get married to the father of this child within the next month, before I'm showing. Maybe I'll never be married to him. *Against my parents' wishes.*

I will "inform" whomever I want to inform of this newest family member: my immediate aunts, uncles, cousins, and most importantly, my only living grandmother, Pati. *Against my parents' wishes.*

I will be conscious of my birth choices. I'm enrolled to birth at a hospital in my HMO—free insurance. But I will remain open to what unfolds. *Against my parents' wishes. Note to self: They believe in only hospital births, although most of their family and ancestors were delivered without anesthetics, surgeries, and/or were delivered at home-based sites.*

I studied the list. I felt, after tallying it up, that I should be given the most flexibility in this situation and the most leeway. Even with my strong beliefs for what was the best next step in this situation, however, something still didn't feel right. Old, sacred phrases and words began to flood my heart: *It is your duty to listen to your parents. Family first, everything else second. Respect and listen to your elders.*

I looked up and saw my mother and father speaking in hushed tones. My brother was writing in his journal as well. I took the opportunity to meditate briefly and find the stillness needed for support. The query in front of me began to feel hazy and blurry as I entered deep waters once again. These meditative trips were not dramatic or unusual to me after all these years. They were a poetic part of the way I functioned in the world. Often these journeys were short, and what seemed like lifetimes of journeying and listening happened in minutes.

This time, the nature of the weight that was bringing me to the depths was less from a place of sadness and more from a place of confusion over which answer to give my parents. There were no huge emotional barriers to break through on the way down, which made getting to the destination a little bit easier.

Once in the stillness, I put out the question, *Given what I'm going through and what my parents are going through, do I not tell my family members myself?* I waited patiently. Slowly something was coming back. But this time, no words. Just pictures and moving frames. I first saw a snapshot of my brother's *punal* ceremony, a rite of passage from boyhood to manhood. I remembered he had not been into traveling to the high hills of Pennsylvania to go to a particular Hindu temple to get this done. But he decided to go and complete the rite when he saw how much pride it brought my father and his family.

That faded, and up came an image of myself sleeping on my grandmother's bed in her house in Nagpur, India. I was twenty-two at the time and on a family trip. During the traditional after-noon nap, I had awoken to the sound of warm feet slapping the cool cement floor in my room. Six pairs of feet, to be exact. I focused on the first person to enter the room and sit on the bed in front of me, my Pati. Then my aunt and uncle sidled up to her on both sides, followed by my two cousins, flanking their parents. The old servant also participated as part of whatever this family thing was by hov-ering tentatively in the door without locking eyes with anyone, as she was trained to do. My grandfather, my Tha-Tha, also seemed to grace our presence from beyond the living. Just to the left of my grandmother's head, I could see a life-size black-and-white portrait of his face on the wall surrounded by sandalwood beads and a gar-land of small geraniums. Just when I began to question if I was having some sort of surreal nightmare, my grandmother opened her mouth, and everyone's spines straightened. She cleared her throat.

"You! Marry. Soon, you marry, ahh?" In strong support of her statement, her right hand sprung up from her lap, and she flipped her wrist in a gesture of somewhat playful annoyance. Perhaps it was the afternoon heat and the absolute insanity I was feeling in the moment, but it seemed as if she was unknowingly tickling Tha-Tha's chin in the picture behind her. I thought I saw his mouth turn up slightly in a smile. The rest of her entourage sat quietly, also staring at me, acting as if they went through this sort of thing every day.

"Pati, I'm still sleeping," I whined quietly, knowing full well that she spoke only a few words in English.

"You! Marry. Now! No matter Indian or White. You, marry! Please??? For Pati." At the end of this serious, ritualistic, elder-given mandate, my little ten-year-old cousin absentmindedly wiped a piece of *burfi*, one of my favorite coconut and butter sweets, from the side of his mouth.

I silently asked myself, *My god, was none of this funny to you all?* I hid my breaking smile in my pillow. Pati stood up, threw the end of her sari over her shoulder, and stumbled towards me. She put both hands on my head, said a prayer, and brought her soft, wrinkled hands together at her heart in *namaste*, a gesture meaning "May the wisest in me meet the wisest in you." She gave me a quick full smile showing scattered, hanging teeth and slowly shuffled away. My aunt and uncle followed, then my two cousins, and last, the servant. In the depths, these moving frames, almost like a short film, left me with a last shot of myself half sleeping on her bed, pondering this mandate that, I was sure, had been given from mother to daughter or grandmother to granddaughter for thousands of years in almost exactly the same fashion.

What were these images and stories trying to tell me about this whole communication issue? "May the wisest in me meet the wisest in you," my beloved Pati had said. I decided to figure it all out on the way back to the tense scene that would soon come to a close with some relief . . . at least for the moment.

"*AAAmmmmmaaaaaa!* Amma, come here! Now, Ammmmiii. Please, Amma? I can't sleep by myself." My hands and body froze over the keyboard. It was useless, actually. It wasn't as if I could sneak my way out of my daughter knowing that I was here. I sighed and let my chin float down and rest on my chest. I replied to her request in a louder voice than normal so she could hear me in the other room.

"Yes, my child! What is happening? You are supposed to be sleeping by now."

"Aaaaammmma, I caaan't sleep. I need you here. Come."

I massaged my hands and took a quick look at the last line I had typed: "I decided to figure it all out on the way back up to the tense scene that would soon come to a close . . ." "Tense" was an understatement. In the end, I had not told my family anything about the pregnancy and her birth for a whole ten months following this conversation with this counselor. My cousin still remembers my odd response to her when she had asked me over the phone in my sixth month why I hadn't called her in a while. "Oh, Shalu, I'm going through a lot of . . . changes. Lots of intense movement in my life. I've just been *so* busy. But I'm eating well, so don't worry." My daughter would be three months old when my father would tell my cousin, our dear friends, and the rest of the entire family of her arrival. Well, *almost* the entire family would know.

I saved my document. It was 9:30 PM. It would be another late night of trying to complete this submission before the deadline in a few days. For a moment, I became annoyed with my parenting situation, and wished there was someone near to give me a soft kiss on the head and say, "Sweetheart, you continue writing. I'll go put her to sleep this time." But I was of a different breed of mothers who learned not to live on such basic expectations and assumptions. I was a single parent. Her father and I were co-parenting well now, which was much better than our situation in her early years. But in times like this, I desperately longed for a loving partner who could support my creative efforts and vice versa, and help me parent my daughter in real time, alongside me.

The trip from my laptop to the room where she was sleeping was short. The one-bedroom apartment I had occupied since I was five months pregnant was small, cozy, and easy for the little girl to navigate. During that initial period of shock in my pregnancy, which involved so much family adjustment, this apartment had not yet found me, this gorgeous space that would also eventually be the place of birth for my daughter.

Moving-in happened five years ago. *Five* years ago. I put my hands up to my face to feel my new wrinkles. Damn it, I earned them.

"Child. Here I am. What is happening?"

"Amma, I'm scared. Maybe I'll have nightmares and you won't be here."

"Child, let's just say you'll dream about good things. The turtles and rainbows will guide your way tonight. Nnnn-kay?"

"Amma, can we do 'om' tonight?"

"Sure, little girl."

I grabbed for the faded green saucer, the pictures of Pati, the candle, and the sandalwood beads. Writing my essay brought up so many thoughts of Pati and my other grandparents who never met Shanthi, my daughter. The emotions brought up around the memory of Pati specifically were the most painful, for she was alive when my baby was born, and lived a whole year and three months more without knowing about her before she died.

After lighting the candle, we chanted "om" seven times, prayed and meditated on all the sacred objects on the altar, and clasped our hands in *namaste*. Shanthi always recited our last prayer of Buddhist verses by heart; she had heard it twice or thrice a day throughout her time being in the womb. She took the sandalwood beads and placed them around her neck, and cleared her throat ever so slightly:

"May we be filled with loving kindness. May we be well.

May we be peaceful and at ease. May we be happy."

Small tears found their way down my cheeks as I looked at this beautiful, precious little girl of mine with hands clasped in front of her heart. There was so much strength in this lovely child! I smiled as a basic thought came to mind: I had done a few things right. Yes, I had.

"Amma, are Nanna and Tha-Tha coming this weekend for my birthday?"

"Yes, child. I know Nanna is coming, and Tha-Tha will definitely call. That way the two of you can wish each other a happy birthday!" As much as my decisions to have the baby, not get married, and to have a home birth angered him and made him move further away from all of us as a family, ironically his and my daughter's birthdays ended up being one day apart, and every time he would look at her in her early life, he would feel like he was looking at himself—her resemblance to him was uncanny.

The candle cast a warm light onto Pati's picture and the altar. In the long run, I think she'd be proud of me. Although in our family, perhaps for generations, I had singularly broken the mold the most times, going against several cultural conventions, I had followed my heart and accessed guidance from the spiritual practice of visiting the depths in much the same way my Pati and my family had for thousands of years.

A few years past the birth, I had come to peace about compromising the announcement of Shanthi's arrival, for it was the best thing for our family's mental and cultural survival that my father and mother follow at least one convention, do something at their own pace. Although many of my friends didn't understand how I could "give up" such a basic component of becoming pregnant, compromising on this one piece and considering my family's health and well-being *as well as* my personal autonomy was the right thing to do. Approaching the issue of my pregnancy with openness, compassion, and compromise continued to be in line with the myriad of cultural and spiritual values that guide my life. A little bit of an amended view of female empowerment and feminism than what I had subscribed to in the past.

Shanthi blew out the candle on the altar, and let out a long, sleepy sigh. I wrapped my arms around her and lay down next to her on the bed that she had been birthed on nearly five years prior. Finishing the submission would have to wait for the following morning. As my body relaxed, I allowed myself, on my inhales and exhales, to slip into the beckoning waters. No particular weight of the world propelled me closer to the depths, just my desire to feel the stillness around me and say thanks. When I arrived, I began to pull the blankets of sleep around me as I simply looked into the blue, rolling darkness, and said, "Thank you. May the wisest in me continue to meet the wisest in you."

★ **SONALI S. BALAJEE** is an independent consultant living in Portland, Oregon. Her primary professional and personal passions include cultural sustainability, yoga and naturopathy, empowerment through storytelling, and birth activism. She defines her "homes" as India, Sri Lanka, and the United States, and is the proud co-parent of a beautiful little girl.

In the Absence of Blood

KIM GREEN

I simply birthed a vision. There was no panting, sweating, grunting, or ripping out of what was hidden deep within. There was no physical pain associated with becoming my son's mother. My soul never thought it was necessary.

I am a woman who laughs at mothers who don the war stories of their child's labor like a badge of honor. I shy away from the tellers of these tales at baby showers. That is when I go get more punch. I listen with horror when I hear mothers even suggest that their physical torture made them stronger, more legitimate, or better mothers. I fault our society, so obsessed with biology, for brainwashing women to believe that childbirth gives mothers extra credit in heaven. Pain and blood do not a mother make. Mothering is a transformative dance. Mothering is soul work.

To birth my son, my loins were never split. Lust had nothing to do with it. My vision stayed inside me until it was fully formed. My vision was to breathe life into a child in the form of strength, wisdom, and a warrior's grit. I envisioned giving all of that while staying intact. I stayed intact and blossomed into a mother. I beam with pride at the thought.

Since I was a little girl I have always known how it would be. I would become a mother by adoption. I spoke this vision to all my puzzled, ponytailed, preteen friends. At the time I couldn't explain the whys and the hows of my future adoption, but I just knew what would be, would be.

Perhaps it was my rugged childhood landscape that shriveled my desire for biological motherhood. I grew up with a family of women. Their men had either left, died, or disappeared. My grandmother, aunties, and female cousins were all single women with too many babies to tend to.

The women in my landscape never seemed to have enough: enough money, enough time, enough food, or enough energy. My cousins, my motherguides, had all gained too much "baby weight," did away with their vanity, and silently mourned a lost part of themselves that neither I, nor they, could put a finger on. It was just evident that there was a hole in them, somewhere. My few male cousins were all absentminded, troubled, irresponsible, and had left their own mates to raise their own fatherless seeds.

Frankly, childbirth and pregnancy never looked appealing. "Makin' babies," as it was called in the Cincinnati projects of my childhood, gave me the idea that baby makin' was like "takin' drugs," something to be avoided, a "no-no." From where I stood, baby makin' was always done in dark, forbidden places where no one was supposed to be. It was what my cousins did when no one was around, in places they should not have gone. The elders in the community would shudder upon hearing the news. They would cry, mourning another young woman's lost dreams.

As a thoughtful child, I yearned for a more cheerful example of baby makin,' and none ever came. I hoped for a more thoughtful demonstration than what was being shown by those who were above me. As I looked up to them, my older cousins, I looked down on them at the same time.

My own gestation period was much more significant than nine months. It took me thirty-eight years to prepare for my son. The canvas of a human life takes more than nine months to paint. I wanted everything to be perfect for him. I wanted to experience a lot so that I could impart a lot. Bringing my son to life took a lifetime of forming the life that I had experienced and the life that I was committed to give. I had a lifetime to brace myself for a monstrous love that has shaken me to the core and made me a mystic. As a mother, I have become a woman of unlikely strength and unusual power. My son's very existence has forced me to compromise in ways with which my feminist training would be in constant conflict. Mothering knocks you off the pedestal on which feminism placed you. It's almost never about me, anymore.

This love for my child is excessive, dramatic, and grotesque in nature. It causes me to be demanding, unreasonable, and irrational. My vision remains that of a perfectionist. I am a sculptor who has set out to create the next *David*. I owe it to my angel to at least try for perfection on his behalf. This unwieldy love makes others judge me, envy me, or even hate me. I no longer care how I appear. *I have become child-centric.*

My son was not born of my stomach; rather he comes from my soul. I am trying to get accustomed to the strangeness of having my most vital organ walking around outside of myself, in the shape of an angel. My body functions normally only when he is in my sight. I struggle daily with the conflict of wanting to smother him with my love and needing to push him away for his own development. It has taken me over three decades to receive the electric power of his tiny grip, which has illuminated my very core, forever.

I had been married for six years when we finally decided that the time was right to start a family. I was thirty-eight. I buried the secret that I had no intention of having a child biologically. After all, it was a secret between me and myself. It was an issue of privacy. I went along with the "baby talks," partially hoping that my body would "go normal" and produce an embryo in my stomach, so that my beaming young husband and my enthusiastic in-laws would see me in a different light. They had always distrusted my selfish, eccentric, New-Yorkerish ways. I felt that having a baby would finally allow them to trust me, think that I was "normal," no longer a freak. Perhaps finally they would think that I was a good pick for their son.

After two years of trying to conceive, with no success, I realized my body was in support of my soul, holding me accountable to the promise that I had made as a little girl: *the absence of blood*.

The troubling flashbacks of the Cincinnati projects continued to haunt my mind. My visions reminded me that being in a relationship with a man was a transient state, but having a child was permanent and lonely. As the feminist that I was, adoption was my way of taking a stand for my very being. I was resisting the ultimate sacrifice of my body, my vanity, and my heart for one who may, would, could, probably . . . leave. I wanted to be one less woman with a hole in herself.

That was the dreadful look on the motherguides' faces.

After much prodding and prayer on my husband's part, he finally agreed that we would have a child by adoption. *Hallelujah.* As my husband and I were filling out our adoption applications, I was radiant with the glow of birth. My husband was torn between feeling like his manhood was in question and trying to be as excited as I. We attended countless classes, wrote too many essays and applications, got fingerprinted, assessed, visited, scrutinized, and finally accepted into the program. We were told that all that was left to do was "wait."

As I waited, I thought to myself that my son's arrival would be the biggest commitment I would ever make. I also remember thinking that if anything went wrong with my marriage, it would be me, not we. My pen quaked with anticipation of the new reality that this child would create for me. I would represent a newfangled individuality called "we," meaning me and my child. The singular "me" was about to be dead. I was signing my life away and stepping into a new life, walking onto the canvas that I started to paint as a child. This was going to be the one commitment that I could never walk away from. I would be bound.

A biological mother anticipates her child for nine months. I envisioned my motherhood for nearly twenty years. I waited for almost two years for the phone to ring. When the phone finally rang, they said, "A birth mother has chosen you." A few days later, we met her. She gave us her blessing with a hug. We hugged her back and promised that she would not be sorry.

A week later, she gave us her son. Our son. My son.

I blame my inherent cynicism for what was to become a self-fulfilling prophecy. Life's inevitably winding road manifested in troubles for our young family within six months of our son's birth. All within a whirlwind twenty months, a faulty business venture caused us to suddenly make a lot of money and lose a lot of money, which created the debilitating chronic illness with which I was diagnosed. Our seemingly idyllic Black family was crushed by the pressure and we were suddenly a family in crisis. My son was barely crawling on the tile floor and above us the devilish *d*-word was floating like a mischievous ghost.

My husband used the word first.

I cried. I yelled. I pouted. I begged, pleaded, and finally drained the water out of the pool that was once my self-esteem. Then, there was silence. I quieted and let him have what he wanted: a divorce. It was to be my last act of generosity.

The superwoman that I had become gave me the strength to rise from my sickbed, take my son, my music, and my clothes, and leave the state. I needed a distant place where I could lament in peace about what this would mean to my newly fatherless son and my ever-failing body. My divorce didn't knock me down. It built me up.

I can count my blessings now. I have met an unreasonable number of single mothers whose children have never even laid eyes on their fathers. I am blessed that my son has a father to call and a father who desperately wants to be involved in his life. My son's father didn't leave us. *He left me*. And because I am supernaturally evolved, it is my son's feeling loved which matters most, not mine. Not anymore.

My vision of motherhood is almost how I imagined it, but more mind-blowing. My son is pure light, joy, and wonder on two miniature legs. When he looks at me with his miraculous mothergaze,

I am weakened and fortified at the same time. Every day I sadly watch him grow and struggle with the hard lessons that the world has to offer him. I look at him with the agony of a mother's eyes. I am angry at the notion that reality awaits this preciously unreal innocent. I lament that his mere five little years already bring profound burdens for him to bear.

His burdens thrash around in my head while my heart plots to destroy them one by one. But I know these are his battles and his life will be built by how he handles them. My only work is to be there to catch him, if and when he falls . . .

A list of his burdens:

He is biracial. *Where will he fit into a world that divides twice: on color and then on shade? I wonder who will cast the first stone?*

He is beautiful. *Will he be judged as too pretty by boys, or will he become prey to a precocious womanchild who is looking for love? Will she seduce him with her own fatherless tales?*

He is the child of divorce. *Will the other kids judge him? Whom will he ultimately blame?*

He is the child of an artist. *Will he embrace the unusual? Will he grow to admire my eccentricity, or start to hate me because I am different than other mothers with perfectly coiffed hair?*

His father lives in a different state. *Will his father distance himself over the years, blaming the high cost of air travel?*

His mother is dark and she has dreadlocks. *Will he judge me? Will his friends tease him? Or will he seek a woman in my image, me becoming his "norm?"*

He has light skin. *Will he hate himself amongst our brown family? Or will he see himself as superior because that is what the world told him to think?*

He is partially White. *Will he hate them or yearn to be them?*

He is smart. He is funny and charming. *Will this be an asset or a hindrance?*

He is sensitive. *How deeply will he be hurt? And when?*

He is artistic. *Will they think that he is weak because he doesn't play sports?*

And, he is adopted. *Will he cling to me like I cling to him? Or will he run in search of his other mother? The birth mother. Will he too be brain-washed to worship biology, leaving me, the adoptive mother, out in the cold?*

I stay awake at night trying to figure out how to tell my angel the only secret I have. Otherwise I am his open book. How do I tell him this news that could be potentially life altering? It could alter his life or waft over his head with the lightness of a feather. It could be all or nothing. I'm a self-proclaimed weaver of words, but once again, being the mother of an angel leaves me without words and without breath.

Soul work is constant labor. Bringing him home was easy. Building, creating, sculpting him to be a young man of depth, soul, and greatness in the midst of life's cruelties is a staggering feat that only his mother can handle. That is *me*.

I am sweating, panting, grunting, and ripping away the layers to show the world that there is blood.

★ **KIM GREEN** has been a writer in the music industry for nearly two decades. As a copy director at Sony Music, Kim was the first African American copywriter in the department, writing award-winning Black History and Black Music month campaigns. Kim's work has appeared in many national and international magazines including *Essence*, the *Source, Mode, American Baby*, as well as the *Philadelphia Tribune* and *Philadelphia Pape*r. Internationally, Kim's work has appeared in *i-D* and *Wire*, both London-based publications. Kim has interviewed countless entertainers, among them Patti LaBelle, Queen Latifah, George Clinton, Tupac Shakur, and Me'shell NdegéOcello.

Kim was a featured author in the African American serial novel *When Butterflies Kiss* (Silver Lion Press, 2001) and *Proverbs for the People* (Dafina Books, 2004). Kim co-wrote the Last Poets tome, *On a Mission: Selected Poems and a History of the Last Poets* (Henry Holt,

1996). Kim is also the writer of Fantasia Barrino's *Life Is Not a Fairy Tale*. The book was listed on both the *New York Times* and *Wall Street Journal*'s best sellers lists. In addition, Kim has completed her first novel, *Hallucination,* and is in the process of compiling a collection of short stories entitled *The Helplessness of Snow.*

A True Testimony

TANIKA L. FEASTER

I had to write this story, my testimony, about one of the hardest decisions I ever had to make in my entire life. I gave temporary custody of my baby boy to a relative on his father's side of the family. I then had to go through a terrible custody battle to get him back.

When I was twenty-three, almost twenty-four, I gave birth to a beautiful baby boy. I named him Michael Jamal Feaster. He was a beautiful child, and everyone thought he was a little girl because he had so much hair. It had been a rough pregnancy; I had morning sickness up until my seventh month, but I enjoyed being pregnant. I knew I was carrying a boy the whole time, because I could feel it, I knew it! When I told Michael's father that I was pregnant, he told me to have an abortion. The evening of that conversation, tears stung my eyes as he walked down the stairs of my apartment building. I felt rejected because I actually thought he was a good guy. I later found out however that not only was he irresponsible, but he had also married an illegal alien for money—a woman of Jamaican descent. He was also on the verge of getting kicked out of the Navy. He and I knew each other nine months before I found out that I was pregnant.

When I met Michael's father and got pregnant, I was still married but my husband and I were already in the process of getting a divorce. He was going to prison and had also cheated on me during our marriage. I told my soon-to-be ex-husband that Michael's father wanted me to have an abortion. He told me to keep the baby, saying, "I know it's gonna be the boy you want." I didn't believe in abortion, and his words made me more determined to keep my child. I admit however that I did hesitate about the decision. Michael's father told me to come to the military base to get the money for the abortion. I had even made a call to the clinic and set up an appointment to get the procedure, but God was there and was not gonna let me lose the child He had blessed me with.

Three to four months after I decided not to have the abortion, Darryl, Michael's father, outright started denying he was the father. It hurt me, and in my mind I was wondering, *why would you actually try to pay for an abortion of a child that you say is not yours?* Anyway, towards the end of my pregnancy, his sister Tasha reached out to me. At the time she was the only person in his family that was trying to see about this baby. In the meantime my son was growing full speed in my belly. We thought at first that he was going to be an eight-pound, six-ounce baby, but when he was born on January 10, 2003, he was only seven pounds, fifteen ounces. Maybe he knew what mayhem was coming because my labor had to be induced to get him out of the womb.

The first three months of Michael's life were so fun and loving, but I was feeling empty. Was it postpartum depression, or just knowing that I had another child whose father was a "was-not?" At this time Michael's father's shipmates were making degrading remarks about my character. A few said that they had slept with me and that I was "a lying whore." Even worse, his family was steadily claiming he was sterile and couldn't be my child's father. It all became too overwhelming for me, so I contemplated putting Michael up for adoption. The adoption agency I was considering would still let me have some contact with my child. It was at this point that Tasha came into the picture.

We had spoken cordially on several occasions when I called her to ask of Darryl's whereabouts. As we talked more that day, I told her that I was thinking of giving Michael up for adoption. It was at this time that she and I both agreed that, instead, she would take temporary custody of Michael while I got on my feet. At the time I was on welfare and I already had a two-year-old daughter with my soon-to-be ex-husband. He was serving time in Fort Knox prison for selling drugs while in the U.S. Army. I was actively pursuing my college degree but I had no income. I needed help and my immediate family couldn't help me. Some of my other relatives wouldn't help me even if they had known what was going on. They probably would have just talked about me—I would have been the topic of gossip at the family reunion.

In May 2004, when my precious baby boy was only four months old, I went down to the juvenile intake office and said it was okay for Tasha to have temporary custody of Michael. Michael's father also came down and signed off on the paperwork. This decision hurt and pained me to no end. I prayed and prayed. I talked. I cried and honestly believed I did the right thing for my baby. Initially I saw and talked to my baby boy. He was precious and growing to be a big, healthy boy. In the same month I got a job at Wal-Mart and tried to see him whenever I could, when my work schedule wasn't crazy. During this whole time, Michael's father did not talk to me or care about what was going on with me. It was not until Tasha and Darryl paid the $500 for a paternity test that he even started taking care of his son. I figure that if he had been a true father and helped me out, Tasha would have never gotten my child, and things would not have spun out of control like they eventually did.

During the first several months that Tasha had my son, my family saw her for who she really was. She acted as if we knew nothing about child-rearing, despite the fact I had an older child that I was still caring for. She was also dishonest. Things would happen, and she would not contact me about it—like her moving in with another man. Whether or not my son was around, she just let people talk dirt about me, saying things like how I "abandoned him," and that really sunk into my skin. At the time, unlike my family, I only saw that she had done me a great favor by taking care of my son for me when I couldn't and no one else offered. I loved her and told her so. I also told her how appreciative I was for her concern and for the care that she gave to my little man.

That summer things took a little different turn. I went to go pick up my baby, and Tasha's boyfriend came outside and said he had to speak with me. He told me that Tasha was being treated for high blood pressure and that she got it from taking care of me and Darryl's responsibility—our son. He did not know me, but nevertheless questioned me about why I gave up my child. He said that I was a bad parent and that I spent more time with men than with my son. He got in my face and tried to hit me. My three-year-old daughter was in the car screaming and crying, and he had me in tears. Tasha was cowering in the house and then eventually came out and tried to comfort me and back him off. He went back in the house and looked out of his bedroom window at me. At that point, I knew I had to do whatever I needed to do to get my son back quickly. She said, "Don't take the baby because of this," and I said, "why not this?" I found out that my baby was sleeping in a playpen in her boyfriend's one-bedroom apartment. This meant all three of them in one room.

One record that I need to set straight: I have never forsaken my children for any man. I will admit there was a time when as a mother I did not have my priorities straight, but I never put a man over my children. I know I have inconvenienced my children a time or two, but I never put them in harm's way. I did what I thought was best for my children, and no one can tell me differently. Before people throw stones, they should ask what would they have done in my situation.

In June 2004 I got a better job and I even completed my associate's degree in acquisition and contract management—praise God! I was now able to spend more time with my son and buy him more things. I loved my son, so the day came when I told Tasha that I wanted him back. Tasha knew that this day was coming; she had gotten into the habit of saying that she was not gonna be ready to let him go back with me. I knew that she had become attached to Michael, but I didn't take her statements seriously—that was a big mistake.

In October 2004 I asked her for her brother's address so I could send him a copy of the court order that I was putting in to amend the order of custody. Tasha caught an attitude and would not give me his address. She said that I would have to have both him and her served with papers. She went on to tell me I wasn't stable enough to care for Michael. She said that I couldn't love him like she did or provide him with the care and time that she did. On the court order, for Michael's father's address, I put down Tasha's mom's address, since he used to live there. On October 6, 2004, I amended the order of custody, called legal aid for assistance, and got approved to receive free help. This is when I began documenting the communication that I had with Tasha. I wrote down when I called her, when I texted her, when I emailed or instant-messaged her, and when I visited. I began to see the side of Tasha that my immediate family and friends had seen early on.

Tasha was really good at playing both sides—with me, she was talking about Darryl and Darryl's mother, and with them she was talking about me and my family. Her behavior is evidence that the devil thrives in people. I never disrespected her or allowed others to disrespect her. I tried to give her a chance and to do the Christian thing, but she made it damn hard. I saw Michael growing up to be smart and handsome. She was enrolling him in speech therapy and all kinds of things without telling me. I disapproved of the speech therapy because he wasn't even two years old, and I believed that if he was around other children or had people talking to him at home that he would learn to speak. Since his grandmother paid for every-thing, she would say what she wanted to see happen, and Tasha did it. They did not tell me the name of Michael's doctor. I knew he had a doctor, however, because he has chronic asthma and eczema. They also never told me about his medical appointments until after they had already happened. They even changed my child's last name—giving him Darryl's last name.

I will never forget how I found out. I went to the Social Security Administration office to get a copy of his social security card so I could have an extra one for my records. It was then that the clerk told me his name had been changed. I thought, *how? Why? By whom?* I was hurt and didn't know what to do. I called my stepdad, my best friend, my mom, my sister, and my cousin—what could have happened? The next day or so, my good friend Ruffie and I went up to Richmond, Virginia, to get a copy of Michael's birth certificate, and I found out that his name had been changed on it too. Later I actually got to see the paperwork for the name changes and saw that my signature had been forged. I started an investigation into the matter, but I was told by the clerk that I couldn't change it back without a court order. I was crying and I immediately called my legal-aid lawyer. I told him how offended I was and that I couldn't believe that my son's name had been changed. It had taken time for me to find a name that I liked for my son to have, and then they changed the spelling of his first name and changed his last name completely.

Can you imagine what it was like having to talk to Tasha—someone who I knew had betrayed me? When I dealt with her, I had to pray so hard my head would hurt before I was done. It wasn't one of those situations where I could avoid her or not talk to her again because she had my child, so I just wrote everything down and tried to contain myself. By this time I had gotten my court dates and Tasha and I had both been ordered to take parenting classes and to go to mediation before the trial. The parenting class was very informative. Although a lot of it concerned divorcing couples with custody issues, the class touched on all types of custody cases. It even ended up helping me cope with my own parent's divorce—can you believe it?

After all of that the holidays came around, and I didn't get to see Michael for Christmas. His grandmother Joann got him and took him to South Carolina. She said she would have him back by December 23, but she was a no-show. She didn't even bother to call on Christmas just so Michael's big sister could talk to him or so that I could hear his voice. A lot of people gathered for Christmas at my sister's house, but I felt alone because half of me—my son—was in South Carolina with people who gave less than a damn about how I felt about not seeing him on Christmas. They kept my baby well until the New Year, and by this time I had grown fed up with how they were treating me and my family. Tasha said she tried to call. I saw that she called my cell phone once, but she didn't call my sister's house—that I know for sure.

It was now January and time for Michael's father and I to go to mediation. We all gathered in Williamsburg, Virginia, after getting lost trying to find the place, and tried to talk out what it was we all wanted. Darryl wanted things to stay the way they were. To me that meant he wanted someone else to keep taking care of his child. He even had the nerve to tell the mediator, "Really, I felt like Tasha was my baby mama, since she took care of him." He did not even speak to me, though it was my biological child we were discussing. When asked, he responded, "Why should I?" The bad words didn't even hurt anymore. Furthermore, Tasha and Darryl both claimed that we were all in agreement about Michael's name change, but in fact we weren't. They were in cahoots about that, not I. During the mediation meeting, we all said that we didn't have attorneys—I soon found out how that too was a lie. We got things said at the meeting, but still I was unclear on what I wanted, and we didn't come to an agreement that night.

Tasha, it turned out, did have an attorney. She claimed that Darryl and Joann had hired one for her, but that wasn't the case. There were lies and more lies, and then Tasha tried to get me to sign an agreement that her attorney had drawn up. One of the major truths that were unveiled was that Darryl and Tasha were not even blood relatives—she was his godsister. When the paralegal went over the agreement with me, I learned that it stipulated that Darryl and I would each have fifteen days of visitation during a thirty-day period, and Tasha would have Michael two consecutive weeks in the summer. Now what decent mother or father would agree to such an arrangement? More important than that, nothing about custody was mentioned, which meant that Tasha would keep legal custody of Michael. We kept calling each other back and forth and the paralegal went over the agreement with Darryl; he didn't have a problem with it. You are asking what I saw in him, right? That's what happens when you're in the sheets: not only do you become all hot, but you also become blind.

In the next few weeks, we made and cancelled appointments to get this agreement revised to something we all could live with. Everyone except Darryl met to look at the "new" agreement; I brought along my stepfather. I kept shaking my head as Tasha gave her rehearsed evaluation of the new agreement. My stepdad hung his head and shook it, saying that "not one of them was thinking about this child in the long run." Tasha's attorney tried to say that the agreement allowed that Darryl and I would have joint custody, or "shared" as they'd like to call it, but I did not read that on the page. I am a stickler for detail, and that's what I wanted to see written.

On March 28, the judge granted me a continuance pending the outcome of the mediation. Since I would not sign the agreement, we went to court on May 9. My family and I were looking sharp and all feeling confident. Tasha came with Darryl, her mom, and her cousin. I had my cousin Dee Dee and my dad's girlfriend, Ms. Shirley. I didn't know that I could bring witnesses to testify, otherwise I would have also brought my sister, mom, dad, and stepdad. Anyway, I had God with me all the way through and I knew that! Tasha's group came in and they sat right behind us in the courtroom. The whole time we waited it was a lot of nervous chatter. They kept talking about what Michael liked, and things they had gotten for him, and what he says and what he knows and all of these other things. My supporters were quiet, and I was in prayer. I had butterflies in my stomach and I prayed for peace to be still in me. My cousin wrote me an inspiring note, and it made me smile.

Believe it or not, Tasha's attorney called Tasha and me into the hallway and tried to get me to sign the agreement. You see, God had already told me this battle was won, so I wasn't about to sign that agreement. I told her that I would like to continue with the case and walked back into the courtroom. Before I made my way in, Tasha gave me pictures of Michael that had been taken the month before—he was as beautiful as always. These pictures were more appropriate than the picture she emailed me of herself and Michael with the subject line "me and Mommy." I went back into the courtroom and just sat there dignified and waited for my case to be called. I did not have an attorney with me because my legal-aid attorney said that he couldn't represent me without knowing who Tasha's attorney was. Remember, early on it wasn't clear whether or not Tasha had an attorney. I carried on with my silent prayer. I just knew God had this for me, and He has never forsaken His children.

At 10:15 AM we were called into the main courtroom and sworn in, and my witnesses spoke first. They told the judge what they could about my character, the circumstances of why I gave up my son, and what I have done since then. It was then time for my testimony. I talked to the judge from my heart, and told him that I did what was best for my child; I couldn't provide for him the way I wanted to, needed to. I told him that I gave temporary custody to someone who I thought I could trust—someone I thought God had sent to help me until I got back right again. I told him that I kept my older child, Tracy, because at the time her father was incarcerated, and she didn't have another family like Michael had. I made him aware of my accomplishments and my intentions for the future.

Tasha's attorney then asked me some questions, and here is where the agreement came up again. I told her that if the agreement meant that I have shared custody with Darryl, then it should say that! She responded, that is how the agreement is worded; I said, I don't like to assume, I like things spelled out. She even tried to suggest that I was seeking custody to lessen the cost of child support. As the noncustodial parent, I was still ordered to pay Tasha child support. The agreement that Tasha and Darryl wanted me to sign also stated that I wouldn't apply for any public assistance. The wording basically said that if I couldn't afford my child, then I didn't deserve him back.

After I got off the stand, Tasha's witnesses came up and basically lied. Darryl's mother actually said that I had people smoking around Michael even though he has chronic asthma, because he came home smelling like smoke. She said he came home in dirty clothes and in dirty diapers even though he had been provided with a change of clothes. Now what she failed to mention was that when Michael came back from South Carolina with Darryl and Joann, on different occasions, he had contracted ringworm, gotten sores on the back of his heels because his shoes had gotten too small, and had developed rashes on his body. Her cousin didn't say too much and admitted that she had only seen me maybe once with Michael, but to support her cousin she tried to make me look bad too. Darryl went to the stand last and he couldn't say too much—at least he didn't say anything disgraceful about me.

The judge was ready to render his verdict. While the attorney was giving her closing argument, he interrupted her. He said he hoped what she was about to say had some substance because he hadn't heard anything yet that made me a bad parent—someone undeserving of her biological child. The attorney said she understood and that the main worry was that I would do the same thing again—give up my child or become unable to care for him. She continued to defend her client, but the judge said he was sorry, but that he had no choice but to give custody back to me. He said that I have a right to my child and that we are not all perfect, and he said he was not going to issue any visitation at all to Tasha because there needed to be a breakage period. He stated that Michael could become confused because although he knows that I am his mommy and that Tracy is his sister, he'd been living with someone who was acting like his mother. The judge also said that I should be thankful to Tasha for stepping in to help raise him.

I had tears of joy in my eyes, and Tasha was on the other side of the courtroom crying. God made his presence known in that place. Praise Him! The judge wrote the order up and said that I was dismissed. I walked out of that courtroom with no expression at all on my face. I saw that my stepdad, my sister, and my uncle Michael had joined Ms. Shirley and Dee Dee in the courtroom, and I asked if they were ready. I kindly touched Darryl on the shoulder and said,

"See you later." When I got out of the courtroom and into the hallway, I looked at Dee Dee and said, "I got full custody." I broke down and cried in her arms, and Michael sang the praises and wonderful works of the Lord. We got in the elevator and more congratulations were given as I leaned against my stepfather with tears still streaming. My cousin and sister said something that I found very funny but true at times, "Only crooks needs lawyers."

In conclusion, I have to say God is true, He is here, and He is able. These people appeared at first to be helpful and kind and turned into something that even I couldn't fathom. I wanted to know what kind of God Tasha served that would make her think that keeping my child from me was right. To demean me the way that she did and to deny me my right to a second chance to be with my son and to have my family—my daughter and son—together with me.

This experience has made me so much stronger and wiser and that is why I wanted to share my story. It pained me to write this because it made me go over a time in my life when people hurt me over and over. I did nothing but try to seek out a better life for my child and I almost lost him. Instead of making my child suffer, I let someone I thought was decent help me with my child. During that time I improved my life so that he could have a better one, and I will continue to do that. I'm not going to apologize for the degree and the great grades I got while Tasha took care of my son, or for my job and the experiences—at least I didn't sit on my behind. I kept my house up and got a car for my children and me. You have to pray and intercede for those who come against you, and you have to behave in a manner that is reminiscent of Christ. The fact of the matter is, my beloved baby boy is coming home where he belongs. I love him so very much, his family loves him very much, and we cannot wait to bring him home on June 1st, according to the order. We all are going to Chuck E. Cheese to *party*!

Names have been changed to protect the individuals' privacy.

★ **TANIKA L. FEASTER** is a twenty-nine-year-old single mother of two beautiful children. A longtime resident of Newport News, Virginia, Tanika is an accounting specialist for a multinational company. She graduated with honors in 2004 from Strayer University with an associate's degree in acquisition and contract management, and received her bachelor's degree in business administration in 2006. Her future goals are to complete her MBA in Public Administration and Master of Arts in Divinity, continue to establish herself as a writer, raise her kids properly and help them all that she can to achieve their dreams, and get closer to God.

Movement Mamis
A Day in the Life of a Hip-Hop Activist Mami

C‡ɔ

JLOVE CALDERÓN

The young woman paused for a moment before she spoke. "Um, sure you can bring your baby! We wanna support you, sis." Not that she had much choice; I was presenting that night for the upcoming police brutality rally, so what could she really say?

An hour later I arrive at the small, overcrowded office in downtown Brooklyn. My son Gabriel, was crying, nose running, wanting his juice. But of course I don't have his juice, because I am not supposed to be on "Mom duty" tonight. It is my night off. My movement night, when I can reclaim my post-parent inner activist.

"*Mami! Jugo! Jugo?*" Gabriel cries in my ear as I struggle up the stairs, off-balance from my bag, papers for the rally, and his backpack from daycare. Damn, I shouldn't have worn these heels.

"Okay, baby, hold on, 'kay? We gotta get to the meeting on time. Mami just has to talk for twenty minutes, baby, and then Mami will get you your *jugo*. Can you be a good boy for Mami? Okay?"

But it isn't okay. I am late for the meeting; I have a hungry, tired, and cranky child. I have neither food nor juice nor alternatives. No toys to distract him. My mother would be so disappointed in my lack of preparedness. I am exhausted from working all day. Could I make this happen?

Pushing the buzzer, I pray for some strength. While I wait in the hallway, I take a deep breath, trying to stop my son's cries from gnawing at my nerves. Though I want nothing more than to just turn around and say, "fuck it," I think about the unarmed young Black man who had been shot in the back and killed by a cop in Bed-Stuy, Brooklyn. He was just walking to a friend's house. I *have* to make it to this meeting.

When my husband, a high school prinicipal, called me earlier, I could tell by his voice that things were bad. There was a fight among some students, and a rumor spread about some gangbangers coming to jump one of his students. He had to get the cops involved, which he detested, but there was nothing he could do; he had to protect his students.

As I listened and tried to be supportive of him, my mind began thinking if there was anyone who could pick up Gabriel. Although he hadn't said it yet, I knew that was the reason for the call. "So, honey, I know it's my turn, but you have to pick up the baby. I'm sorry."

I wasn't upset at my husband. If there's a crisis, he's gotta stay. No one's fault. It's just . . . it's just . . . *hard*: hard for me to keep it all together; hard for me to keep working for the cause, when the cause ain't working for me.

The door swings open and a new young volunteer whom I've seen around greets me, and my cranky, now snot-nosed toddler.

"Hey JLove, we're all waiting for you," she says sweetly, but she might as well have said, "*You're late!*" because that's all I can hear.

As I rush awkwardly through the crowded room, everyone turns my way, and my son begins wiggling, pushing his hands against my chest, trying to get down. With the two bags and the papers I can barely hold him.

Anya, a hardcore New York organizer, jumps up from her chair. "Do you need help?" I want to say yes, but what can I give her? What I need is for someone to take the baby, but in the state he's in

. . . well, with no other parents in the room I'm not sure it would do any good.

"No, no, girl, it's okay, just give me a minute." I'm sweating now, with my bulky jacket, the heat, the kid, my face flushed from all the attention.

"Mami! Let me down! I wanna get down!" he yells in my face, his hands still pushing against me, twisting his body.

"*Wait!*" I snap at him.

"Let me take him," says Suzanne, our coalition's legal-aid lawyer. I give in, just wanting to try and put my bags down, go over these security notes, and get the hell out of there.

"Thank you so much! Here, sweetie, go with Suzanne, okay?" Gabriel, who just a second ago wanted nothing more than to be out of my arms, now clings to me for dear life, pulling away from Suzanne's outstretched arms.

"Nooooooo," he wails. I can tell it is useless.

Ugh! "It's okay, Suzanne, thanks though, really!" She walks back and sits down.

"We need to get started," says one of the facilitators, glancing at the clock. I'm acutely aware of the fifteen or so other folks shifting in their seats, yawning, tapping a pencil on the table. Waiting. Just waiting for me to get it together. Shit! I remember when one of my girlfriends told me that it was impossible to be a good mom and a good activist, especially as a working mom. No way, I had told her, I would never give up my activism! I could do both! Now I was really beginning to wonder.

Like that time we organized a civil disobedience rally and the group was planning on getting arrested. That was nothing new; I had been arrested and jailed for protesting before, but at that time I was breastfeeding. There was no way I could get locked up. How would I breastfeed my baby? Of course everyone said they understood, but I felt like I was letting everyone down.

"JLove, are you ready?" Willie asks. He was the one who had brought the coalition against police brutality together. He once told me he never thought of himself as "political," but that was before the incident. A year ago, his Dominican cousin was maliciously attacked by cops in a bodega while buying a *café con leche*. Another case of mistaken identity. He was buying the coffee for Willie. After that incident Willie paid attention to the news, and when he heard about the sixteen-year-old who was killed, "I knew I had to do something," he had explained to me.

"Yes, yes, lemme pull out my notes," I put Gabriel down, drop my bags, and, holding on to him with one hand so he wouldn't crawl away, dig through my bag with the other, pulling out the security protocols.

"Okay, everyone, sorry for being late . . . last minute childcare issue," I look up to see tired, anxious faces. Luckily, Gabriel has quieted down, so I can focus a bit more. "Anyway, let's start with the color of the day." As I start going through my notes from the hours of preparation late last night, Gabriel starts picking things off the floor, and they head straight for his mouth.

"No, Gabriel, no! Don't eat that! It's *sucio*!" I grab it from his hand. "I'm gonna give you a *pao-pao* if you don't *stop*!" I am sure the Latinas in the room are cringing at my Spanglish.

My son looks up at me, mouth pouting, eyes tearing, and I know it is over for me. Why did I snap at him? Jesus! His fresh cries bring out a searing anger inside of me. I cannot do this. Not tonight.

"Willie, you're gonna have to take my notes and work this out. I gotta get my son outta here." He sighs and takes my papers. I know I am letting people down.

"But the security is the most important part of the meeting tonight, J. You know that." He looks at me with cross eyes. Gabriel sits down on the dirty floor, asking for *jugo* again. I swear, he is never this needy in my apartment!

The fatigue creeping into my body isn't just from the long day. It began when my maternity leave ended. I went back to my full-time job and my activist work when my baby was just three months old. We couldn't afford for me to take a longer leave. Every morning, dropping my little baby off for eight hours at a daycare, working to pay someone *else* to raise my baby? So yeah, it was hard to get back into the swing of things. I didn't have a lot of support; my family doesn't live in New York, and my husband's parents both have full-time jobs, and none of my activist peers had children. I was left trying to figure it out on my own.

The coalition folks tried to be supportive. Soon I realized they had no idea how, and we had no time to figure out what "being supportive" looked like. Time was a commodity we just didn't have. And I, feeling at times like the outsider, being a new mom, and still trying to figure it out myself, well, I didn't push. It felt egocentric to take attention away from our work to focus on *my* needs. That isn't activism . . . is it? Taking care of myself (ourselves)?

Nobody would say it outright, but "martyrs" were praised as the true activists. How so? The nuances of judgment, disapproval, or questioning whether someone is really "down for the cause" if they couldn't make it to the protest; if meetings ran late, and they actually had the nerve to leave before it was over; celebrating and honoring people who consistently took on too much to the detriment of their own health and well being.

When did this begin? Why did we activists choose to take it on? I don't know that I can answer that. What I can say is that in my community, the prevailing wisdom of the day was that the "the struggle" was exactly that: hard! It wasn't okay to have fun, to take breaks, to not be on *every* committee, to get exercise, to be healthy emotionally and physically, to be happy. It was as if we all had a censor in our head that said, *How dare you be happy when others are suffering? When there is so much work to do?*

Shoving the notes into Willie's hands, I pluck my child off the filthy floor, gather my bags, and practically run out the door, not even stopping to put on our jackets. As we leave the building and hustle to the car, Gabriel whispers, "Cold, Mami!" The tears start flowing down my face. What am I doing? Why am I out here in the cold with my baby without his coat on? What is my problem? I don't know if I can do this anymore!

That evening when we're back at the apartment, I put Gabriel in a bubble bath. I grab a beer, sit on top of the toilet seat to keep an eye on him, and call Willie's cell. It has been about an hour, and I know the meeting will be ending soon. Willie picks up on the second ring.

"Hey, JLove, did everything go okay with your son?"

"Yeah, he's fine. I was calling to see if you guys had any questions about the information," I say, smiling at my son playing with the bubbles.

"I am so glad you called; yeah, we just had questions on number six, the formation with the young people in the middle . . . do we have enough adults to keep them safe?"

Willie and I talk through the plan while Gabriel splashes water all over my papers. "Word, JLove, this is good; we'll be ready for them cops at this rally, for sure. Thanks for taking the lead on this." Willie and I hang up. I stay for a while, watching Gabriel go crazy with the bubbles, his happy sounds echoing off the bathroom walls. A heavy feeling emerges from my body. I was filled with despair and elation, dark fatigue and yet a hopeful spark of possibility.

It seems the rites of passage into motherhood come with complexities that many people do not speak of or share. And for my childless activist community, despite their good intentions, most of them simply do not understand my new life. It caused a schism between us that presented different challenges: How do you serve the movement and raise a healthy child? What does "balance" look like, feel like, taste like?

How do I measure the success of balance? Is it missing a critical meeting and dropping the ball so that I can be a better mother to my son? So that he gets fed on time, gets his bath, and is happy? Do I sacrifice his needs for the people's needs? Is it a trade-off? *Okay, Gabriel, tonight is gonna be hard on you because instead of coming home after daycare like we usually do, we're gonna pull an extra shift and handle some business . . . come on, Gabriel, it's called struggle for a reason!*

My friend told me she read about famous activist parents whose children felt abandoned by them because they were never there for them, only for the struggle. As she spoke I felt a pang in my heart.

Would my son say the same thing about me? Am I putting politics before my baby?

Years have passed since these questions first came to light, and I had another baby boy. It was life altering for my husband and I; Camilo almost died during the birth. He became our miracle baby.

Now that I have two children, my activism looks a bit different. Experience has taught me the difference between contribution and sacrifice. Part of the difference is in the intention. Part is the lived experience. Contribution feels good and whole. Sacrifice hurts, emotionally, and sometimes takes a physical toll as well. Years of not taking care of myself and having other priorities cost me my gallbladder and resulted in a lifetime of medication.

Wisdom provided by my mentors has taught me that "t*he* struggle" doesn't have to be "*a* struggle." Purpose has integrated my life, helping me prioritize and providing clarity. Leadership development and motherhood brought more capacity—the ability to hold more—gracefully.

Some of my single friends ask me how I do it, this *mami* activist thing. Although there are still many questions swimming in my mind and heart and I am learning as I go, there are some fundamentals that I have chosen to live by in my life: I am dedicated to truth, love, and freedom. I am committed to creating community, building a healthy tribe, and loving completely.

As a hip-hop activist movement *mami*, I promise to love my children *and* to love the movement; to understand that I cannot do it all, but to devote myself 100 percent to what I choose to take on; to stretch my capacity as a leader and a mother; to work within a framework of vision-versus-victim; to apply the wisdom of deep listening to the essential needs of my children, and to answer them. Sometimes that looks like a hug or an acknowledgment that I've "been on the computer too much" or taking time to talk to a teacher about something that is going on in the classroom. I promise to recognize when they do something well, as opposed to always harping when they don't.

Another huge shift for me is the understanding that it is not what comes first: movement or *mami*. This paradigm suggests that they are not interconnected. But they so are connected. I am a woman raising two boys. I am White, my husband is Latino, and our boys are of mixed heritage. An aspect of my movement *mami* work is bringing them up as feminist revolutionaries fighting for social justice worldwide. As a movement *mami*, my work is to show them, lovingly and patiently, the injustices of the world; to teach them their power in shifting male privilege; to explore the inherent harmony that physically created them; to love them. Love them. Love them.

As a hip-hop activist movement *mami* I pledge to serve the movement by being a good mother and being a good activist.

★ **JLOVE CALDERÓN** is a New York–based hip-hop activist movement *mami* with three beautiful guys in her life who inspire her daily. She coedited *We Got Issues! A Young Woman's Guide to a Bold, Courageous, and Empowered Life* (New World Library, 2006), which includes work by Marla Teyolia and was coedited by Rha Goddess, both of whom are also included in this anthology. JLove is also the author of *That White Girl* (Atria, 2007) and cocreator of *Conscious Women Rock the Page: Using Hip-Hop Fiction to Incite Social Change* (Sister Outsider Entertainment, 2008), a hip-hop social justice curriculum guide cocreated and edited by Marcella Runell Hall, who is also featured in this anthology. Her forthcoming book, *Till the White Day Is Done*, is an anthology about power, privilege, and hip-hop. For more information, please visit her at www.jlovecalderon.com.

Childcare Is Caring for Children

ASATA REID

When my midwife, Marsha, plopped my newborn's surprisingly warm, sweet-smelling and solid eight-pound, one-ounce body on my stomach, my days of punching someone else's clock were over. After all, I'd waited thirty years to have this child; I wasn't going to have someone else raise him, make him a cog in a wheel, a product of "the system." That was my philosophy, fueled by the ideal of being the most important influence on my son's life and the righteousness of new motherhood.

I'd heard stories of other women struggling at the dreaded end of a scant six weeks' maternity leave (twelve if they were lucky and used up vacation and sick days) and my eyes would well with tears. I'd think, how horrid to be pried away from this singular wonderful person/event/passion to go earn a slave wage or a mighty fine income at an anonymous job or stellar career. You can't put a price on the time spent with your baby, I'd think to myself, and snuggle my baby closer as if to shield him from a world hell-bent on separating us. What can I say? The weeks following birth are emotionally charged.

Still I was moved by trials of new mothers who had just gotten into the rhythm and flow of breastfeeding and establishing a good milk supply and then would suddenly find themselves struggling to produce or pump enough milk because of the stress of finding childcare for a precious newborn, learning the ropes of pumping milk (which is never as easy as the concept projects—finding a sanitary and relatively calm place to pump uninterrupted and a stable, sanitary place to store the milk), and many other untold stressors of simply returning to work. "How's the baby?" well-meaning co-workers ask the new mom, only to have her burst into tears. Or try explaining the pins-and-needles of "letdown" every time you proudly show off pictures of your new bundle of joy (while praying you don't leak through your nursing bra). So many women abandon breastfeeding because they go back to work. In a traditional work environment, breastfeeding is impractical, inconvenient, and usually not supported by co-workers and supervisors.

In online chat rooms I read web postings of mothers desperate to find affordable childcare, because the younger your baby, the higher the cost. The struggle of "having it all"—juggling work, home, and now parenthood—takes its toll on many women, who struggle to function normally while steeping in emotions like frustration at the lack of support at work and at home, anger at a system that forces them to choose between their livelihood and their family, and sadness and guilt for spending less time with their babies.

Between work and transportation I realized some mothers were spending nearly twelve hours a day apart from a child as young as six weeks old. I'd shake my head at a society that perpetuates this as normal. I imagined what this nation of tiny babies was missing in hours of being held, rocked, sung to, touched, stroked, and nursed—all of the things that research says make human babies grow to civilized, compassionate members of society, the little things that come naturally to parents. In childcare centers where five or more babies are relegated to two caregivers, babies spend more time "contained" in cribs, bouncers, high chairs, and rockers simply because there aren't enough hands, arms, shoulders, and bosoms to cradle them all simultaneously.

In a world where dysfunction has been accepted as the norm, where televisions are babysitters, how do you raise a thinking, feeling human being, not an automaton or a Worker Bee or a serial killer? Studies show that lack of human touch and skin-to-skin contact causes underdevelopment of parts of the brain linked to our socialization and abilities to feel empathy and compassion. Other studies have shown that boys and girls who don't have involved parents are more likely to commit violent crimes. As a mother—as a member of society—what responsibility do I have to raise a child who will be a contribution to our kind, and not a detriment? Can I do this, particularly when he is a young and impressionable infant, if I don't play the lead in his life?

But those were anecdotes, observations, and imaginings of a mother at home with her baby. In my mind, my sole purpose was to satisfy my son's every want and need until he became capable of expressing them and differentiating them for himself. My partner agreed: There was no excessive crying, forced independence, acceleration of the idea of self. One day when I was feeling overwhelmed by being a cow-on-call, being constantly harangued by this whiny little baby, my partner pointed out to me, "You're all he wants because you're all he's ever known." That struck me as profound. I was all my baby had known, my womb had been his universe and now I was the anchor, the touchstone in his world. It was humbling and empowering to realize I'd become the center of someone's universe, someone who had yet learned to differentiate himself from me. As far as he was concerned, my baby thought he and I were part of the same being—him.

The idea of being more than two hours away from my baby made my body ache.

Motherhood was my new addiction, backed by the biological realities of breastfeeding. Baby needs momma every two to three hours, and for momma's sanity, she needs baby just about as often. With breastfeeding, momma gets a delicious hormonal cocktail spiked with oxytocin, which to a sleep-deprived, achy, and anxious new mother is like Valium, or better. Breastfeeding, especially in the beginning, is a full-time job. Either you're nursing, preparing to nurse, putting baby to sleep after nursing, or pumping. Or you're fretting about your milk supply, crying over your sore nipples, delirious from that crazy newborn three-hour feeding schedule, or attempting to research solutions to any of the aforementioned through an addled brain fog. At least that was my experience, and somewhere in there the regular life stuff like bathing, cooking dinner, cleaning the bathroom, checking the mail, and—oh yeah!—paying *bills* has to take place.

Still, the decision to be with baby 24–7 was made and, by God, I was sticking to the plan. I was going to be a SAHM—a stay-at-home mom. I have to say that kind of commitment is probably crazy. New parents need breaks because parenting is a sudden, twenty-four-hour-on-call job that without previous experience is endlessly draining, filled with self-doubt, and despite the well-wishes of family and friends, rather isolating. Believe me, staying at home was no cakewalk. The issues of choosing to be home versus returning to the work world don't seem to get as much coverage as the dysfunctional state of working mothers and fathers. Everyone admits working parents get shafted, even if they're not willing to come up with creative solutions that are more family-centric. But most people look at "staying at home" with the baby as an option taken by leftist hippies or the wealthy who can afford not to work. Deemed as an "option," few people pause to give much thought to the struggles that arise from staying home with baby, much less the challenges stay-at-home parents face financially, emotionally, and socially. Most people are working and dealing with that set of stressors, so therefore the grass looks mighty green from that cubicle or cash register or assembly line.

Reality set in in the form of an overdue electric bill, and we set about trying to figure out how to have our cake and eat it too: Ill equipped, without a working set of realities as to the challenges we faced by not subscribing to out-of-the-home childcare, we determined to stay at home with our son while still earning a living. I became a WFHM, a work-from-home mom, pursuing assignments and clients, while my partner threw himself into the world of free-lance entrepreneurship chasing the elusive "gig." In a romantic-his-torical sense, I became the cultivator of our staples and he went out hunting the big game—very "Me Tarzan, you Jane." And with my baby safely tucked under a boob, it all felt right.

My plan was to really put that freelance notion into high gear and crank out witty and well-paying assignments left and right. The reality was, three days after I gave birth I was knocked off my birth-induced hormonal high and battled rounds of postpartum depres-sion that were at times so insidious and subtle that I didn't even see them coming. I mean of course I was tired; I was a new mother, right? Of course I was lethargic; I hadn't had more than two consec-utive hours of sleep in months. Of course I was emotional; I was a hormonal, sleep-deprived train wreck stressing over a thin trickle of income that wouldn't sustain a college freshman much less a grow-ing family. But the feeling that I was "sinking" wouldn't go away, no matter how I tried to rationalize it with logical stressors.

Finally I admitted to my midwife at a postpartum checkup that I really wasn't doing so well. At least not "in my head." Couldn't get organized, it all just seemed like a lot. Fuzzy. She recommended a low dose of Zoloft. I felt defeated because I'd foolishly viewed a phar-maceutical solution as a weak way out, but I also felt relief because I believed, or rather my midwife assured me, that it would help. And she should know, she's been bringing babies into this world and dealing with new mothers for over a decade.

Another reality: I couldn't afford to just "stay at home." I'd heard so many women say, "I wish I could afford to stay at home." We couldn't afford it either, but we did it. How? It was a matter of prior-ity, really. Food stamps or full-time employment? WIC or a forty-hour workweek? After being a tax-paying member of the gainfully employed workforce for fourteen years, I relied on public assistance to make up the difference. One cold December morning while my partner was working out of town, I bundled up my eight-month-old baby, packed some snacks, and went to the Division of Family and Children Services to get food stamps. Two friends of mine, also new mothers, had insisted that I go. One mother had experienced financial difficulties and got mental relief knowing that she could at least get groceries. The other worked as a counselor to women with children and she'd seen time and time again how beneficial food stamps can be when every penny counts. Armed with every possible official document of my existence as a U.S. citizen and mother of this baby, I stepped outside to load us into the car only to find that the repo man had visited in the night and that Chrysler had finally made good on their threats to repossess my car. Still I was a mother on a mission, and by God I was getting food stamps today if I had to crawl to DFCS. Instead, I took a slightly less dramatic route and drove my partner's car, though it hadn't moved in months, the tag was expired, and it wasn't guaranteed to make the trip there and back. At the DFCS office I endured the stereotypical and demoralizing long waits, regardless of preset appointment times. If I'd had a traditional job and was trying to handle this during a lunch hour I would've certainly gotten fired. There was endless paperwork required—forms, forms, forms—to get just over $100 worth of monthly food stipend.

We still struggled. Rent was late, the electricity and telephone were cut off. Arguments ensued. But we'd committed to staying with our baby and we did it. We could work from home as long as our baby was asleep (something newborns do a lot until they are four to six months old) or contained in a swing or bouncy seat. My partner and I were now eking a stable if paltry income by working from home, freelancing, and gigging, and things seemed to be going okay. Daddy and I would take turns entertaining the baby and getting work done, but that was all temporary because when "lap babies" get mobile, all productivity stops.

Besides the postpartum depression, I still struggled with my milk supply, adjusting to the amount of forethought it took to do anything or go anywhere with a child, and the crazy night-and-day change in the amount of perceived freedom I had: freedom to talk uninterrupted on the phone; freedom to schedule things on my time; freedom to take a leisurely, relaxing bath without listening to the baby monitor and jumping up at the first whimper. My normally laid-back personality, my long-cultivated water-off-a-duck's-back unshakable cool was certainly shaken. I was as tightly wound as a bedspring. Three months into taking Zoloft, I "leveled off," and the sinking feeling stopped. Had I gotten the hang of motherhood? I doubt it.

Mobile babies—crawlers, scooters, toddlers, walkers—have to be supervised. Constantly. As The Mother I either naturally stepped up to or was subconsciously pushed into becoming the vigilant watcher, constant entertainer, and regular food provider to a little being that always wanted more, more, more. More truthfully though, I was still wound so tight that as long as the baby was awake I was in monitor mode. I'd "take the baby" so that my partner really could get work done, especially since his work paid more, then I'd find my work getting pushed to the thin margins when our son was asleep, those times when I needed to be asleep myself.

When our son was eighteen months, a happy, healthy, successfully walking, spoiled little boy who was still nursing, a growing suspicion of mine took root. There *is* a time for childcare. There comes a point when a child has developed to the point of benefiting from socialization with other little peers and, more importantly, from developmental guidance by a professional who knows how kids grow and think and learn. And unless I was willing to learn a new set of skills to become a childcare pro, we'd reached that unmarked developmental milestone where as a mother I could honestly say my child was ready for childcare in the form of supervised tutelage, stimulation, and socialization. Not to mention I was ready to get back to work, work that couldn't be done in twenty-minute stints while *Barney & Friends* was on TV.

Fortunately for us, a friend of a friend's mother had been running a daycare for thirty years—a small, home-based daycare on the other side of town filled with love, attention, and home-cooked meals. It was a stretch for our dilapidated Honda and our thin wallets. No, it wasn't one of these newfangled "baby academies" with their programs and curriculums, but the children did have lots of learning opportunities and they all seemed genuinely happy and well cared for, if snot-nosed in the winter months (something, along with coughing, I've come to learn is typical for young children in daycare).

The first day was painful. And so was every day afterward for months. My son cried every single morning, but Ms. Jenel and Ms. Vita were always loving and swore as the weeks wore on that he stopped crying before I pulled out of the driveway. Because I was still working from home, I could drop in and peek through the window at any given time, and I loved what I saw: my boy playing, dancing, interacting, and having a genuinely good time. He ate well, he slept well, and he was often good and dirty at the end of the afternoon from playing outside in the fresh air and sunshine.

I stayed in the traditional work force for about seven months, working part-time from ten in the morning to four in the afternoon, four days a week. To say I barely managed it is no exaggeration. While initially I loved being back at work, working in my field, feeling productive, and getting a regular paycheck, I found that my priorities rarely lined up with those of my employer.

A job, in its traditional sense in this culture, is an endlessly "taking" partner in a give-and-take relationship. Jobs want more hours, more thought, more consideration. Jobs are the clingy, needy, smothering, codependent, time-consuming, high-maintenance partner that after you finally get rid of them you marvel over how expansive the world is and how much air there is to breathe out here. Jobs want you to think about them when you're not with them, on weekends and holidays and evenings when your mind should be your own.

Jobs work their way into conversations with your friends, families, and even strangers as you're standing in line at the post office. Jobs cause you to complain when you should be enjoying dinner, mope when you're getting the kids in bed on a Sunday night, and purchase clothes you just wouldn't wear in your "real" life if you didn't have a job. Jobs want to know what time you got in, when you plan on leaving, and what you're doing for lunch, and jobs have the audacity to weigh in on all three topics. It's hard to feel free when you're serving a job.

Interestingly, that's not so different from a baby. With a baby, however, my baby, I have a vested biological interest at least; he is carrying my genes forward another generation, so the game changes. And even though babies are definitely "takers," they are also gracious receivers, unconditional givers, and marvelous, crafty cajolers of good vibes. Babies can make you love them even when your mind is set against it. Babies can coax out stifled laughter, chisel a smile on the stoic, and bring on a case of the sillies in public places before you can check your adult decorum. And with their dazzling, drooly smiles; soft, dimpled hands; and warm, snuggly, sweet-smelling heads that fit right under your chin, babies are addictive. That's why people who have them (or puppies) have their pictures taped up all over their dreary cubicles, staunch offices, and even in magnetized picture holders on the wall appliances in commercial kitchens. People respond to babies, any baby, not just their own, because beyond those poopy diapers, there's magic to behold. The fountain of youth, the magic of childhood, is as close as the nearest child.

So as I sat typing away at my job, with pictures of my son taped to my cubby before a sunny window, I was relatively happy for a couple of weeks. I walked in frazzled every morning from the Daycare Drop-Off Drama, and the sweet receptionists (we went through three in the six months I worked there), who all had children, would smile with sympathy and drop an anecdote of when their children, now grown, were babies and how hard it always was to leave them. Always. Every day. "But it gets better," Liz promised. "When?" I asked. "When they have grandchildren."

I would jump into the tasks of the day with enthusiasm, empowered by my job, but then the job would keep making demands that seemed trivial, even childlike, and I would wonder what my son was doing, what he had for lunch, if he went down easily for naptime, what songs he was singing, what crafts he was doing, if he was playing nice with his little friends, did he miss me? The job would want me to work a Saturday (*with no childcare?!*) or worse, to stay late to finish a meeting. I would feel the sweat break out in my armpits and my breasts swell with milk (the surest sign of mommy anxiety). Being late to pick up my child was the worst thing I could think of. He'd already spent six hours without me, how could I ask him to wait any longer? What if he was the last kid there? Would he worry? Would he think I didn't love him?

Honestly, I don't think any of that registered with him the times I was late, or even when he *was* the last child. He was so well loved, but as a mom, being "kept" from her child by a job, these thoughts loomed huge in my mind, brought guilt into my conscience, and weighed heavy on my heart, not to mention my boobs. The more often it happened, the more the job came up in my time away from work, the more frequently the job forced me to choose it as a priority ("Love me or leave me"), the more I resented it.

I hated that on my one day off I was in a frenzy to get things done that I couldn't get done at The Job: phone calls, laundry, shopping, trips to the bank, post office, doctor. I hated that I couldn't make breakfast and dinner the way I used to before I had The Job, and that we rarely ate together as a family. I hated that the mornings were now in a time crunch because I had to get to The Job: no more story time, morning playground, pre-breakfast cuddle on the couch, pancakes with sausage and eggs. I hated that when I finally did pick up my son after a long day at The Job, I was tired from serving The Job and had that distinct feeling of "changing gears" to take on another "day part," or the "mom role." I hated that even when I wasn't at The Job I was worrying about The Job, and would sit at the playground at the end of the day and wish my son would "hurry up and finish" so we could go home and "get dinner over with" because we had to "get ready for tomorrow." What did tomorrow hold? The Job.

This was me as a mom working in a traditional job. Not a happy mother. Notice I didn't say "not a happy woman." I might have been okay if I was just a woman, but I'm not. I'm also a mother, and a mother is a different woman. Being a mother means that the *quality* of woman that I am now affects my child. Just like being a wife, the quality of the woman that you are will affect your husband, hence the old adages "Happy wife means a happy life" and "If Momma ain't happy, ain't nobody happy." Momma wasn't happy. Momma was snappy, irritable, and not much fun to play with. Momma wasn't painting, drawing pictures, and singing songs. Momma was making an awful lot of Tyson chicken nuggets and frozen green peas for dinner. Even though Momma had a child, Momma had lost touch with her child because Momma was trying to keep The Job happy. Well, you know how the Bible says you can't serve two masters? There's some truth there.

Things were complicated or maybe intensified because during this time my partner was on the road a lot, at least two weeks out of the month. So I was doing the "having it all" juggle single-handedly for stretches and it was stressful. Even when there were two of us, it was stressful. My hat goes off to single mothers. When the summer rolled around and our family grew in size again, as it does each summer when my partner's two children join us, I left The Job. I'd been toying with the idea for a while, but had fallen into the mindset of The Worker Bee: can't leave a job until you find another one . . . blah, blah, blah. Screw that. Life is short, and summer is shorter. If we were going to be a family of five we'd sink or swim . . . together! And swim we did, often. I reapplied the garment of self-righteous motherhood I'd worn when my son was a babe. There is no dollar amount you can place on the quality of mother that I am for my son, for *my family*. The Job was fired, and I would find a way to make a living without sacrificing the quality of myself. I have all three of our children to thank for giving me the impetus to make that move.

We took our son out of daycare for a couple of months so that he could get the most of this family time together, and interestingly during that time, we decided in the fall he should go someplace else. Not for any reason present, but for reasons pending.

My now two-year-old son was funny, smart, and a handful. We had been driving across town twice a day in a very unreliable car to take him to a daycare where I know he was loved and cared for, and that we could barely afford. I was happy to pay whatever we could to have him at that daycare, but sometime during the summer the realization that I was raising a Future Black Man kicked in. It struck me as a huge responsibility, not something to be left to chance.

The world, our society, has so many unwritten and written rules that Black men either learn to navigate or suffer, that I realized raising a Future Black Man has to be an active and constant process. He needs more than love, more than stimulation, more than education. He needs to see others like himself as role models (male teachers and administrators), he needs peers that are inspiring and reflections of his own greatness (other luminous young Black men in training), he needs his home culture and many others present in his daily environment (ethnocentricity and diversity). He needs to learn civility, compassion, and strength of character. He needs the benefit of structure and habit, and the growth that comes from expression of creativity, mirth, and spontaneity. He needs to "just be a kid" and he needs to learn how to be a person and one day a man.

Is it up to a daycare to teach all of this? Absolutely not. It's up to us, his parents, and his community. But aren't daycares, where we send our children every day, inside of the community? Shouldn't our nurseries and care centers reflect our community's interests, cultures, and needs? A daycare not connected to the community can't really serve the needs of the children it is caring for. Conversely, a community that isn't vested in its daycares isn't caring for its very children.

I came to the conclusion that as parents and members of this community, we needed to support local daycares that are supporting the children in our community. After weeks and months of searching, asking for references, reading local newspaper articles, and searching the Internet for various certifications both state and national, I found a wonderful daycare. We were able to afford the center because of a scholarship available thanks to community partnerships with businesses, charities, and donations. As part of the deal we would also volunteer at the center. Overall, the price of the new daycare ended up about the same as that of the old nursery. Those scholarships and bartering opportunities are a way that the center supports our family, part of its community, in return for the support we give. It's a mutually beneficial give-and-take relationship.

And here's where we are: Our son is nearly three. He's thriving at his new daycare-preschool, where, God willing, he will stay until the first grade. I'm working from home, my partner is gigging, the rent is still late, and the phone is off again. But we're off public assistance and we're doing this thing, living in balance for the most part. We're parenting, on our terms and in our own way. As a family we're growing stronger as we clear each hurdle. We're involved in a daycare that is invested in its children and supported by the community that in turn supports us. We're raising a Future Black Man *and* enjoying him in the process. It's a struggle sometimes, but it certainly pays more than a job.

★ **ASATA REID** is a writer and chef living in Atlanta with her son and partner in life. Her passions are food and family, including the liberation of motherhood. After receiving her bachelor's degree in Journalism in 1996 from Florida A&M University, Asata completed her degree in Culinary Arts from the Art Institute of Atlanta in 2000, and has been a professional chef for nearly a decade in some of Atlanta's top-rated restaurants and in luxurious private homes. Her publishing credits include *Essence, Upscale, Atlanta CityMag, AOL Living* and other publications. She is the founder of Life Chef, a culinary-education service that teaches her "food for life" philosophy using great-tasting and nutritious ingredients as the fun, delicious, and easy medium to enhance wellness.

Where We're From, Where We're Going

LISA CHIU

The first time I heard that taunt was in grade school. The last time I heard it was a year ago. From my own son. Nico was four years old at the time, gleefully mimicking something he had heard somewhere.

"I'm speaking Chinese," he explained.

"That's not Chinese," I said.

"Ching chong chongy chong!" he laughed.

My first-born child was breaking my heart. He had no idea those sounds stung me, but I couldn't help but feel betrayed. He may as well have called me a chink.

Many Asian Americans are familiar with the Ching Chong song. It often goes with "Chinese, Japanese, dirty knees, look at these!" and is sometimes accompanied by fingers pulling eyelids upward or downward until the eyes are stretched, slanted slits. I seem to associate the Ching Chong song with school recess, summer days at the community pool, trips to new places.

As a child, I got pretty good at predicting when a hearty rendition of the Ching Chong song would erupt. Growing up as an Asian girl in Cleveland, I was accustomed to looking different from everyone around me. It seemed like I lived in a black and white world, when I was neither.

When I was pregnant with Nico, I worried a lot about how he would fare as a Neither. Would he face an identity crisis? Would he acknowledge his Taiwanese, Italian, English, and American Indian blood? Would he be embarrassed by his Asian grandparents? Would he resent me for being responsible for his almond-shaped eyes?

Picking a name for Nico was challenging at first. We wanted to select a name for our baby that would honor his roots, a moniker that was accessible yet distinctive. It had to be a name I could envision on a college diploma. It also had to be a name my Taiwanese mom could easily pronounce. Eventually, we settled on two names: a Chinese name and an English one.

My dad chose the Chinese name, using my family surname, Chiu, and a specially selected given name. To choose the given name, my dad consulted his family tree manual that assigns designated names for each generation. For Nico's generation, each male child should have the character "ji" (meaning "continued") in his name. So my father named my first-born son Chiu Ji-an ("continued peace").

For Nico's English name, my husband and I settled on a long, somewhat cumbersome full name that included my husband's grandfather's first name and my maiden name as a middle name: Nicholas Alexander Chiu Thomas. To keep things simple, we decided to call him Nico for short.

Naming Nico turned out to be relatively easy, in the end. The real challenges came after he was born, when we had to help him define his cultural heritage. Coming to terms with my own cultural identity had been a struggle. It had always confused me, when I was growing up, when people asked me where I was from. I was never sure if people wanted to know where I lived or what my ethnicity is. It is a rather intrusive question for a stranger to ask, but I prefer someone asking than just guessing. I don't know how many times people have come up to me shouting, "Konichiwa!" This past Halloween, my husband asked me why I didn't correct the trick-or-treaters and tell them I'm not Japanese. It's better than Ching Chong, I said.

I don't know where Nico learned the Ching Chong song. For a while, my husband and I thought Nico was doing all right with his cultural education. We read him books. He liked that. We took him to cultural events. He loved that. We fed him foods from various cultures. He ate everything we ate—Chinese, Ethiopian, Indian, Italian, Japanese, Thai, you name it. He devoured my mom's pot stickers and fried rice until one day, inexplicably, he stopped eating Ah-ma's meals.

"I don't like Chinese food anymore," he said.

At first, we were alarmed. But then we saw that it was just a phase. Soon, he was back to eating Asian foods again, chowing down on sushi and dim sum with the rest of the family.

Then he started referring to my dad as "the Chinese guy."

When I explained to him that he, too, was a Chinese—or more specifically, Taiwanese—guy, he protested. "No! No, I'm not! I'm an American flag guy."

We tried to explain to him that he was Asian *and* American, but he didn't want to listen. Maybe he didn't want to be different from his friends. Maybe he just wanted to be a hot dog-eating, baseball-playing, American flag-waving regular guy. I understood his need to fit in. It hurt, though, to accept the possibility that my son was rejecting the part of his cultural heritage that I gave him.

Being multicultural, Nico has the opportunity to choose which parts of himself he wants to emphasize and which parts he wants to downplay. Although he has the choice of denying or embracing his cultural background, I'd be lying if I said it didn't matter to me how he chooses to identify himself. I want him to be proud of his Asian heritage.

To a certain extent, Nico will be able to influence the way that people view him. Sometimes, of course, people will make that choice for him. But as he grows up and is able to assert his opinions more readily, I want him to be able to tell people who he is and how they should address him.

Without a doubt, Nico's cultural journey will be long and bumpy. There will be bright moments too. Not long after his Ching Chong incident, our family took a trip to Taiwan. My parents, my husband, Nico, and I traveled there together and spent the entire time with my grandparents, aunts, uncles, and cousins. Immersed in Taiwanese culture, Nico soaked up his surroundings. In an elevator one afternoon, as we stood quietly waiting for the doors to open, he suddenly announced, "Hey! I'm a Chinese guy!"

Fleeting moments like that one aside, if he's anything like me, Nico will struggle through adolescence to understand his cultural identity. For me, as a child, I wished my eyes were rounder. I wished my mother wouldn't embarrass me by speaking Taiwanese in public places. I wished she would just bake a normal casserole for potlucks, like the other moms did.

Now that I'm a mom too, I look back at how I was ashamed of my mother when I was a child. I cringe when I think about the moments when I wanted her to be someone she wasn't. When I was born, she was a first-time parent navigating a foreign world. She had to learn English and raise a child in an unfamiliar country. When Nico was born, I was a first-time parent too, but I didn't have to face the same struggles my mother did in learning a new language and culture. I won't share the experience with my son of coming from a multicultural background, but with both of us speaking the same language at least, communication between us should be a little easier.

With a language barrier and cultural divide to contend with, communication between me and my parents had its rocky moments. At times, growing up, I sensed conflicting messages from them. Although I was raised to be pious and deferential to my elders, I was also encouraged to express my opinions. I was confused about this.

One day, at a parent-teacher conference, my second-grade teacher told my parents I rarely spoke up in class but when I did, I offered valuable contributions to the discussion. My parents talked about it with me later, and I agreed to raise my hand at least once a day. Naturally shy, it was hard for me to force myself out of silence and into speech, but gradually, I became more comfortable with it.

Beyond grade school, it took me a long time to figure out when to speak up and when to shut up—I'm still working on that, actually. I think the key lies in finding a good balance of instinct and experience. It is important to know when you're facing a receptive audience and, perhaps more critical, when you're not. As a parent, these are lessons I plan to pass down.

It's a tricky thing trying to raise a child to be assertive but respectful, persuasive without being pushy. As a mother and a writer, I want my child to go out into the world as an effective communicator—a diplomat, but not a doormat. As a parent, naturally, I want my child to be spared pain and suffering, as impossible as that is. Yet, there are certain life lessons I know Nico will have to experience. Most likely, he will be teased at some point. Maybe someday, someone will say Ching Chong to him. It is important to me that he knows what to do if that moment occurs.

So how do I prepare my child for the questions of race and culture that surely await him? To begin, following my parents' example, I am introducing Nico to various cultural traditions. My mother and father did all they could to teach me and my sister to take pride in our heritage. They spoke Taiwanese to us, they prepared Taiwanese meals, they enrolled us in Chinese school on Saturdays and they took us on family trips to visit relatives in Taiwan.

I felt very comfortable in my Taiwanese American household and among my Taiwanese American friends. Still, I was always conscious of looking, and being, different from my classmates at school. It's one thing to appreciate your own culture when you are immersed in it, but it's another to do so when you're all alone.

It wasn't until graduate school, really, that I fully embraced my Asian heritage. Ironically, that was when I was really on my own for the first time, hundreds of miles away from my protective parents. For the first time in my life, I met Asian American students from all over the country. It was not a conscious choice that I picked a school that enrolled many Asian American students, but it was a welcome surprise. I bonded with others who faced the same cultural challenges I did. I learned that other people had also developed their own repertoire of answers to the "Where are you from?" question.

It was a valuable experience for me to live and learn among fellow Asian Americans. I became more comfortable with my cultural identity as I built a supportive network of people who looked like me and understood me. As a mother, I want my children to experience this too. I want them to value diversity, but they need to feel comfortable in, and connected to, their own community too.

Since my own cultural confidence took years to develop, I have to accept the possibility that for Nico too, it may take a long time for him to acknowledge and appreciate all the components that shape him. Right now though, Nico is in kindergarten and still trying to nail down the basics. I can see that his world view is starting to develop, though. His drawings include images of dinosaurs and monster trucks mostly, but every once in a while, they feature people in his life. The other day, he brought home a crayon drawing of him and his friend—he was orange, she was brown.

I have started to initiate discussions with Nico about race and culture, but usually, he listens for only two or three minutes before he runs off to play. Our conversations on these topics typically begin with my responses to stories he writes and pictures he draws. Since I know he will only tolerate a few questions before he gets fidgety and impatient, I am careful not to cross-examine him. "I really like this drawing," I said in our last conversation. "Is this you? The orange one?" He nodded. "And who is the brown one?" After he answered, I told him, "I like this picture a lot. You both look very happy."

I hope that some day, when Nico has the attention span, vocabulary, and sophistication to understand it, I can have a long conversation with him about these issues. I hope to explain to Nico that his multicultural background is a valuable asset and that being different sometimes allows you to develop a set of social antenna you might not otherwise have. Perhaps when you're neither Black nor White, or when you're both, you can see the world around you in a different way.

Some day, I will tell him that I know what it is like to be different from the others around me. For me, I will tell him, I think that experience has helped me gain an ability to empathize with people who are marginalized, who often don't have a voice. For him, I will tell him, I hope that he will develop understanding, sensitivity, and compassion for people from all backgrounds.

Nico's classmates haven't yet asked him where he's from. But when they do ask—and they will—I hope he will answer the question with clarity and confidence. I hope he will respond in a way that educates people, informing them not just of his own cultural background but of a world that is multihued, complex, and complicated.

It took me years to come up with my own succinct answer to the question, replying that I'm a second-generation Taiwanese American woman who was born in Canada and raised in Cleveland. It took a long time for me to learn how to define myself. Now, it is time for me to guide my son along his cultural identity journey. I know where we're from. And I'm gaining clarity in knowing where we're going.

★ **LISA CHIU** is an Asian American writer who lives in Cleveland, Ohio, with her husband and two sons. Her work has appeared in *People Magazine*, the *San Jose Mercury News*, and other publications. Her Chinese name is Chiu Jia-ying ("beautiful light").

Four Pushes

MEILAN CARTER

The Fresh Prince *of Bel-Air* made me cry. I watched agonized as a teary-eyed Will Smith confronted his absentee father and later asked his uncle, "Why doesn't he want me?" "That's going to be Kamau!" I yelled at the television, and then erupted into tears. Malik laughed at me.

Yes, I was eight months pregnant and emotional, but it was true, my unborn son's father didn't want to be a father. I go alone on the bus to doctor's appointments and into baby stores that make me feel Black and poor. I am a cliché: a young Black girl on the verge of raising a Black boy alone; people in the street sing 2Pac's "Keep Ya Head Up" to me, not knowing it is adding insult to injury. Although it took the Fresh Prince to make me cry, I have been contemplating raising my son without a father for months. Malik dismisses my anxiety-filled projections; is that because he's considering taking the job?

Now I am here. Pushing out a new son and a new mother. One of the nurses says I'm the only woman she's ever seen smile in labor. Woman? Me? Me? Just two months past my twentieth birthday? Who just made a wordless plea to her mother to stop the pain? My mother looks helpless; her baby is becoming a mother. The second push knocks everything coherent out of me. I cannot respond but I hear everyone, especially him. No second thoughts, no time to think. *A Love Supreme* is my theme music, although in this moment I have no idea of how appropriate it is. I can see smiles with concern just under the skin from my sister and a smile of disbelief from my brother, who just flew into town that morning.

The room is on mute, except for Malik's stream of encouragement: "That's right baby, almost there." The voice sounds so naturally strange. I glance down at our fingers interlocked as I try to unearth what feels like a Buick from my uterus; his fingers look pale—too pale. This baby will not have those bony, pale fingers. They might be crooked and brown like mine. They might not. I truly don't know what this baby's fingers will be like, because I am starting to forget what his father looks like. Is nine months really that long? Nine months feels like two lifetimes plus one life sentence, equalling forgotten fingers that used to touch me.

I don't look at Malik, but his face still surprises me. It was only a few months ago, before learning that Lamaze was out, that I asked him to be my labor coach. He said he didn't know if he'd be around when the baby came. Is it possible to be left by two men when you are carrying one baby? But he is here, not being a father, but playing one on TV. Five months of chess games, riding shotgun in the Mustang, and sex that reeked of his guilt. Him. With one foot teasing the doorway, laughing at my hormonal bawls, but always saying the right words. Both of us playing a house destined to topple over.

I want someone to tell me what to do. All of the books I read about labor stories have faded. The IV is not pulsating any wise words, emergency exits, or fire escapes through my bloodstream. This is it. I feel it. I have to push in a way I only understand in this minute. But now I am pushing out my impatience to see this baby. My baby. This baby now belongs to me; he has been revoked from the wandering sperm donor. I smell adrenaline, blood, and fluids I don't want to know. The tingling flutters around my head and through my chest and the epidural does not soften elbows and shoulders, or the heavy burning of my body opening up. "All right, one more and we're home free." It is the doctor's words that make me realize that there will be another life in the room with us that was not here two hours ago. There is a half second when I feel like I have crossed the state line/gates of St. Peter/have been accepted into the secret society of women. Of mothers. In four pushes I am one of them.

I talk silently to my mother, sister, and all the women in the room with my new language, because there are no words for this. We are now sisters with beautiful scars; my mother praying her child back to life, my best friend who gave birth alone at fifteen, my sister pacing her son's colic away. Our blood runs differently. I want to parade my new battle wound.

"Well, reach down and pick him up." I reflexively follow the doctor's instructions. I don't remember moving, but there he was: slippery, gross, and beautiful. Kamau Malik Carter. (Yes, Carter, because he cannot carry the name of a ghost.) I hold him against my chest and cover him in hard tears, the ones reserved for heartbreak and death. My family is flooding us with smiles and Malik kisses my cheek before cutting the umbilical cord. The pride is leaking out of the corners of his mouth, and I know he will look for his eyes or mouth on Kamau's face. All of the staff assumes what I wish to be true: that Malik is Kamau's father, and no one is denying it. I can hear my mother telling me that the fact that I chose the name Kamau Malik before I met Malik was a sign. According to her, he is a godsend.

Even after the nurse hands him back to me, clean, weighed, and measured, I am in disbelief. This baby, this boy, this tiny human being, is a creation of me, and I am holding the proof in my arms. His face, squished and covered in dark hair, is almost eclipsed by his eyes. The huge black marbles seem to look through me and assess me. There is such confidence in his stare that it overshadows the ruptured blood vessel next to his right pupil. I study his dark earlobes and fingernails for some hint of the man with whom he shares genes. I don't want to call him the father, so much so that I leave his name off the birth certificate. The nurse glances over the clipboard with a look of both curiosity and boredom. "Do you want the father's name withheld?" I feel that sensation of climbing to the top of a rollercoaster—I feel the drop before I make it to the top. I answer loudly to quiet the cork-screws in my stomach. "Yes. I do, thank you."

I am waiting for someone to stop me, but everyone is off making phone calls. Am I doing the right thing? Will my child be on *Oprah*, hating me for leaving his father's name off the birth certificate? I want my mother to tell me I'm right and Malik to say, "Don't worry about it, I'll be his father." I know he won't. Instead I sing "Summertime" to Kamau and daydream about my perfect family. I think about Kamau and a baby sister with overcast-colored eyes like Malik. I know he is the kind of man I want to help me raise Kamau. He will teach him about our culture, family—he will teach him how to be a man.

I don't want to spend the rest of my life watching music videos for Kamau to see his father. My son's legacy is a smoky concert T-shirt and a CD jacket where his father is barely recognizable. He stares at me from the page like a stranger; is this the man I almost left school for? Him. The bad-boy poet; no, he is not family material. I do wish I could take his beautiful promises and spool them from Malik's lips like a ventriloquist. I try to drown out Malik's disclaim-ers with the look on his face as he cut the cord. It is so close, isn't he here now? How long is now? Malik's two-week departure time bled into five months, his feet always poised for the exit. My mother looks at him with experienced eyes and tells me to be patient. She also tells me she can see Malik in Kamau's brand-new face. I just smile at her.

Even in my fantasy I cannot forget it. I am thankful Kamau is sleeping through my lonely tears. My life-changing moment was shared by four of the closest people to me, who have all returned to their regularly scheduled lives. My friends who waited impatiently to be "aunties" have chosen to sleep in. I am alone with a little stranger. I am trying to hide from wistfulness and weakness. This is supposed to be a family moment: two people counting toes and claiming features. The quiet is suffocating; it makes the recollections reverberate. *I'll stop going on tour . . . I won't be like my father . . . my son will always know he's loved . . . you are my reason to live right.* I just pushed out a seven-pound, fourteen-ounce, nineteen-inch person; how could I still be vulnerable to a memory? I want to curse at him, hit him, and make him hurt. I make haphazard U-turns for anyone on the street that reminds me of Kamau's father. I want to slap his face every time someone tells me, "You better go find his father," as if he was waiting to be found. I want to despise him for making me scared and alone. I want to, but I can't.

Malik stops by briefly on his break from work to sneak in some pizza. He is still wearing his hospital bracelet that says FATHER. In three days I will smile because he will still be wearing it.

After he leaves all I can do is watch Kamau sleep. I try to mimic how fast his chest rises and falls, but I can't without feeling dizzy. Now that I am completely alone with my son, I realize what has happened. This is my child. I am responsible for this person, this open mind that knows nothing. I will have to introduce him to the moon and blood and butterflies. Help him walk, say prayers, ride his bike. I have to teach him about art, fear, and sex. I'm the one who will have to nurse him, bail him out, and teach him to fight. What if it's not enough? What if I make a mistake? What if I don't have all the answers?

Before I am entirely overwhelmed, Kamau opens his eyes and looks at me in the simplest, most pure way, and I know that he was given to me because I do have the answers. Even if we learn them together—and we will. At this moment I do not know that neither Malik nor his father, Dana, will help me raise him. I do know that from the moment my son stared at me, just a few hours old, that he and I were already the perfect family.

★ **MEILAN CARTER** is interested in crossing literary genres, documenting family history, and challenging language. The beauty in death, magic, and the complexities of relationships, are some of the themes that appear in her work. A writer of both fiction and creative non-fiction, Meilan recently completed her MFA in Fiction at Mills College. She is currently working on a creative non-fiction novel about the loss of her father titled *The Etiquette of Death*.

The Baby Bank

KATHY BRICCETTI

"This has got to be the strangest thing—" I whispered as Pam and I eased onto a Naugahyde loveseat the hue and texture of a lemon rind. The sofa in our private room whooshed under our weight as if farting, and, like kids, we laughed at the sound. In one corner, a low bookcase held a pile of worn *National Geographic*s, a pink plastic tub holding children's ABC blocks, and a Raggedy Ann doll flopped on her side, legs crossed at the socks.

The windowless room was deep in a labyrinth of hallways in the Sperm Bank of California, an office building in the heart of Pill Hill, Oakland's medical quarter. For us, the building was an oasis, a safe island in the center of a world that in 1992 did not yet fathom, much less accept, what we were doing. Although cryobanks had been selling the goods to infertile heterosexual couples since the 1940s, the Oakland sperm bank had been founded only ten years earlier and was one of the few clinics in the country providing semen to single women. Nowhere in the brochure, though, did it mention that the clinic catered to straight *and* lesbian single women, as well as to lesbian couples. We'd heard about that through the local lesbian grapevine.

Outside the clinic, a winter wind whipped down the street, but once past the heavy, opaque glass door, the only sound came from a fax machine whirring down a hall. I felt insulated there, both from the January chill and the attitudes of the outside world. For a time, we were safe from judgment, safe from fear.

When I look back on this scene, the trepidation I felt then surfaces briefly. My gut tenses, and I have to remind myself to take a couple of deep breaths. Although same-sex marriage is in the news regularly now, and gay couples are having babies via all sorts of methods, it was a different era at the end of the twentieth century.

In the fall of 1992, when we arrived at the sperm bank, the "Gayby Boom" was about to explode in the Bay Area and around the country. We were trailblazers, not at the front of the pack but near it. We'd met a few lesbian couples at the sperm bank's monthly support group, but had no role models and few books telling us how to do what we were doing. Because Berkeley was one of the most liberal and tolerant cities in the country with its antidiscrimination laws and protections for the disabled, and since San Francisco, the gay mecca, was just across the bay, I held out hope that the area would feel like home for our family. Still, though, I feared what it would be like each time we told the truth to someone outside our safe nest. I struggled with whether we should try to pass as heterosexual women and if we would be tempted to lie to outsiders in order to protect our child. *Pam and I are roommates*, I imagined saying, years before Don't Ask, Don't Tell.

When my friends announced their engagements, people threw them parties; when they married, they threw them even bigger parties. But when I announced that I had found my life's love, reactions were muted. I felt like Cinderella, never expected to fit my foot into the slipper. We had told very few people about what we were planning

Pam and I had come to the sperm bank because we wanted a donor who had relinquished his paternal rights, who could never take our child away from us. We had briefly considered asking Pam's brother to be our sperm donor, but it would have been too strange for our children to be the cousins *and* half-siblings of his three children. And we'd been tempted to ask our unmarried, straight friend Jack for a huge favor but came to realize we didn't want to co-parent with a third adult. We didn't want to share our child, or worse, lose our child to a man when he married and convinced a judge he was the better parent. We wanted an anonymous donor who would release his identity when our child reached eighteen. And we were not alone. While 80 percent of the sperm bank's clients requested identity release donors, only 60 percent of donors were willing to be identified.

"No way will I keep my child's beginnings from him or her," I'd told Pam earlier. "Not with all the divorce and adoption in my family." I didn't want my children to be frustrated someday by secrets, closed records, and dead ends.

Now, after almost a year of charting my daily basal temperature and examining the fluctuating viscosity of my cervical mucus, I knew when my body was ripe, receptive. When I menstruated next, we would call in our order, and two weeks later would carry home a vial of frozen semen in our six-pack cooler full of dry ice. But first, we had to choose the father of our child.

"Are you sure you want to do this?" Pam asked, eyeing the tower of folders on the low table in front of us. The creases in her forehead deepened, and she gave a tiny shrug of her shoulders. When she caught me looking at her, she found my hand and squeezed it.

Privately I was questioning my judgment, and I longed for reassurance that we were not making a huge mistake. I was thirty-four and, with characteristic impatience, believed that time was running out. I was writing a doctoral dissertation while working as a psychology intern at a San Francisco hospital's psychiatry clinic, pushing myself to finish the degree on time so we could start inseminating as soon as I was free of school obligations. "You have your life mapped out on the head of a pin," a friend said when I told him my plan to give birth during my summer break the following year.

"If we have a boy," I had asked Pam before our trip to the sperm bank, "how do we teach him to pee standing up, to shave?"

She laughed. "We'll figure it out."

"What about wet dreams?" I asked. "How do we explain that?"

She shrugged and said nothing.

What concerned me more than guiding a boy through puberty, though, was the possibility that someday our child would hold me responsible for the way we made him or her. "Are we being selfish?" I'd asked Pam. "Making kids this way, without a father?"

"Two mothers can do just as good a job as a mother and father," she said.

"And if we have a girl?" I asked. "What would it be like for her to grow up without a father?" I hadn't let myself think about my own absent father. I needed to believe that since I had turned out just fine thank you, my daughter would end up even healthier, since I'd be an educated mother and I'd know what she needed to compensate for the lack of a father. Part of me felt wise, but I also knew that I was too close to it, and that this made me biased, defensive.

Even if they didn't suffer from being fatherless—after all, many children are raised by single mothers, widows, and grandmothers and not only survive it but flourish as well—I wondered whether my children would be subjected to people's harsh judgments, whether insensitive people would tell them they were created unnaturally and since they were not a "love child" produced by a man and a woman, they were unworthy.

But, I argued with myself, *is a three-minute fuck in the backseat of a car a better way to make a baby? What about a man who forces his wife to have sex? Is that "normal"?*

Pam handed me half the stack of file folders and flipped open one from her pile. "Come on, Ms. Virgo," she said. "We're paying by the hour."

"Excuse me?" I asked. "Look who's talking, Ms. Virgo."

Our similarities—efficiency, goal-directedness, and sense of fairness—were partly what had attracted me to her. We still negotiated tasks like who would wash the dishes. "I'll do them tonight, love," I'd say. "No, you did them last night," she'd say. "Let me."

I opened to the first page of a donor's chart. I was our self-appointed secretary, jotting notes about each sperm donor—his education, resume, medical history, how much alcohol and which drugs he'd used, or at least those to which he had admitted using. The records would also give us his hobbies, eyesight, exposure to toxic chemicals, and the causes of his grandparents' deaths. Then we'd go home and from these notes choose the father of our child. We needed to list donors in order of preference, because the demand was higher than the supply. We had been warned that if our number-one guy's deposits hadn't cleared quarantine yet, we'd have to settle for our second or third or maybe even fourth choice.

"Good God," I said, reading from the chart. "This guy weighs 220 pounds and he's five-nine."

Pam glanced over her reading glasses and scrunched up her nose.

"I guess he could be a body builder." I lowered my voice. "Or do you think they use fat guys?" I did a quick check of the room, searching for a video camera in a corner near the ceiling or a little sliding window with tiny double doors, the kind you slip your urine sample into. I imagined the staff listening in and laughing at us, or worse, finding us unworthy recipients of the precious goods and sending us away.

"Mother had breast cancer," I said. "Reject pile." My mother had a mastectomy when she was fifty-two, and I did the recommended monthly breast exams every Monday morning in the shower. I didn't want to stack the deck against my daughter by giving her two grandmothers who'd had breast cancer. As if I possessed that Godlike power, or control over any of this. This genetic prioritizing we were doing seemed wrong, but I was afraid of scary diseases, Coke-bottle eyeglasses on toddlers, imperfection.

The ancestry list of each donor was interesting, and it didn't matter if our donor's family immigrated from Ireland, Greece, or Russia. But we had decided not to cross races. Our children would be challenged enough having two mothers. Why add the struggles of a cross-racial family? I had a secret bias for tall, fit men and wanted to make babies who looked like me. However, I kept this from Pam, my physical opposite. She was almost a half foot shorter than me. Her jeans were size 6 and so were her feet.

Pam didn't share my desire for pregnancy and childbirth, but did want to share mothering with me. She'd also agreed to my request about what our children would call us. "I've always wanted to be called Mommy," I'd said. This may have been the final vestige of the heterosexual parenting fantasy I was unwilling to relinquish. I would give up the wedding, but not the kids, nor being called what I'd called my mother when I was a child. "Is it all right if they call you Mama?"

I reached for the next folder in the pile. "This is ridiculous; I *slept* with guys I haven't known this much about," I said. "If I were doing this the regular way, I doubt I would interview the man, subject him to blood tests, semen analyses, and a study of two generations of his family's medical history." I slapped the folder down on Pam's pile. "I don't think we want this guy. His vision's 20/200."

At home, we'd found humor in the pamphlet that had come in the mail from the sperm bank, *What Is Semen?*, but, sitting there making the choice, the situation seemed more serious. We were paying $30 an hour to read the donors' files. The vials went for $75 and $108 a pop, and most inseminees took home a couple of vials at a time in order to better their chances. We could recite the three most important factors in semen analysis: sperm motility, count, and shape. We knew that donors had undergone an eight-month medical screening and testing for sexually transmitted diseases. We knew that they were checked again six months before their semen left the building. We also knew that, despite all the tests and waiting periods, the sperm bank could not guarantee the semen to be free of disease-causing organisms.

We lapsed into silent reading again, tuning out murmurs in the hall. I wanted to know whether sperm donors and prospective parents ever met here, eyes lingering over each other, wondering, are you the one?

"Only a high school education," I said, flipping a folder closed. "I'd rather go with the PhD in physics; he's also got a master's in nuclear engineering."

"Lemme see that." Pam snatched the file from me. "High school education. Kath, he's only eighteen years old! How could he have any more education?"

"An eighteen-year-old?" I took back the folder. "I could be his mother."

We both snickered. It was anxious, *what-the-hell-are-we-doing-here* snickering.

Thousands of babies had been conceived so far with what has been called *artificial insemination*, but I hated this term. Artificial implied the negative, something not genuine, something false and unnatural. It implied that what we were doing was creepy, like a basement laboratory experiment. I appreciated the recent, less judgmental term, *alternative insemination*, and, finally, I found in the sperm bank's brochure the term I liked best: *donor insemination*.

Three hundred thousand children had been conceived this way since World War II, so could it be that bad? Yes, it could, according to a group of donor offspring, who in the 1980s organized a self-help group and developed a doomsayer's pamphlet. In *101 Things to Consider before Choosing Artificial Insemination*, an adult looked back on his life: "Never did I worry about being a bastard. No, what upset my whole sense of being was that nobody knew my 'real' father. It was as though half of me did not exist. My mother clearly felt a sense of shame for I was sworn to secrecy. It has haunted me every day of my life."

Even if we did everything right—told the truth to our children and the world, didn't get uptight and pass our anxieties to our kids—I still worried that conceiving them this way and raising them without a father would screw them up. I didn't know if Pam would be an equal partner in our parenting or whether she'd lack the quality that would allow her to truly attach to our child. Maybe, like some heterosexual mothers, I'd be possessive of our baby and insist on doing things my way, take over the parenting. And she'd let me.

Each morning, when my eyes were still fighting the light, I groped for the thermometer on my nightstand and slipped it under my tongue. I was afraid of falling back to sleep and biting off the end, spilling slivers of glass and silver teardrops in my mouth. Every evening before bed, I plotted my daily basal temperature to a tenth of a degree on a graph, zealous about the orderliness and predictability of the charts I'd been keeping for nearly a year. If I had placed my monthly graphs together side by side in a line, they would have resembled the leitmotif from a symphony score: *da da da dee da dum. Da da da dee da dum.* I ovulated to a precise clock, on the fourteenth day. If those sperm were healthy, and we could awaken them from their deep freeze nap and prod them back into service, we might get lucky on the first try.

At home in Berkeley a month after our sperm bank visit, her hands in grass-stained garden gloves to protect her from the dry ice, Pam rummaged through our six-pack cooler. Its lid, once red but now sun-faded to salmon, lay overturned on our bedroom rug. Her movements were slow, as if she was in awe of the ghostly vapor and potent cold.

"It's not here," Pam said, placing the largest chunks of dry ice on the cooler lid and digging a little deeper. The disappointment in her voice mirrored my fragile feelings. Although it was a balmy evening, I felt a chill sitting in my nightshirt at the end of our bed, my feet swinging over the edge like a child's. It looked like we'd miss our chance to make a baby that month. By the time we got to the sperm bank the next day and then returned home, it would be too late. The egg would have popped out and made its journey alone.

All the anticipation, the surreal experience of ordering semen, of bringing our cooler home, of waiting for the right day had tenderized my emotions, pounded them pulpy. I wanted a baby so badly I'd ignored the eeriness of our method and plowed ahead. Perhaps the missing sperm was a sign that we should abandon the crazy plan. Instead, I could find a man in a bar for a one-night stand. Or we could adopt one of the many children awaiting a home. Or we could forget about kids altogether and enjoy summers of traveling. I longed to stop riding these frenzied waves of feelings—cresting anxiety, roiling anticipation, deep hope.

"Here it is," Pam said, and I flinched as if startled by a jack-in-the-box. She pulled a ziplock sandwich bag to the surface of the milky icebergs. Inside lay a tiny plastic vial, the size of department store perfume samples that I collected in junior high school. She held up the frost-coated tube filled halfway with a dropperful of frozen white liquid. On its side, written across the length, ran a code in fine tip permanent marker: #042–75; 5 c.c.; 8/4/91. She removed the garden gloves and tucked the vial under her arm like a duck in its nest settling over her egg.

"That ought to do the trick." I laughed, and motioned for her to join me on the bed. "That should bring them back to life."

I didn't tell her I feared the stuff might hurt me somehow, that I imagined a tiny alien coming out of me in forty weeks. I fluttered the insemination instructions against my bouncing legs, which refused to keep still.

"Are we doing the right thing?" I asked, my voice wobbling. "We don't know this guy."

We did know that he was just over six feet with sandy brown hair, green eyes, and good vision. But we'd never seen a photograph, never heard his voice. He was not three-dimensional to us but a faceless cardboard cutout. "Talk about a leap of faith," I'd told Pam when we'd gone through the charts at the sperm bank. Was he gorgeous like a model, striking in some way, or plain looking, homely even? Did the sperm bank staff ever reject a guy, telling him, *sorry, you're too ugly to be a donor*? I'm embarrassed to admit my superficiality, but at the time, I speculated on what features this stranger would bestow on our child, whether our child would look like him or me. I guess it wasn't much different, though, than my checking out the faces and physiques of men I had dated for their potential genetic contribution to our future children.

"I wish I knew what kind of person he is," I said. "Would we like him? He could have lied on his questionnaire; he could be a drug addict—"

"That would have shown up on the blood and urine tests."

"—or a serial killer." I took a breath. "Or a closet Republican."

"Ha ha," she said, not laughing.

"Why do you think he donated his sperm? I mean the real reason, more than the money. They have to go through all those medical tests, then fill the cup at the sperm bank a bunch of times." My legs no longer belonged to me; they were swinging on their own.

Pam inspected the vial, tipping it. "How do we tell if it's thawed out? I think it's still frozen in the middle." She stuck it under her other arm and took the instruction sheet from me.

"Do you think we'll ever meet him?" I asked.

"Depends on our kid," she said, reading the insemination steps to herself for the fourth time. "Anyway, don't you think you're jumping the gun? We need to get this to work first."

When Pam tipped the vial again, the semen rolled gently back and forth, coating the sides. Our precious sample was ready. She twisted off the miniature cap and gently placed the slim syringe, blunt without a needle, inside the vial, then pulled back the plunger in slow motion. She looked as if she was working with a volatile substance, and I snickered.

"I don't want to kill any of them," she said. "Do you want to do it?"

"I'm sorry," I said, shaking my head. "You're doing fine."

When all of the liquid was withdrawn, the rubber tip of the syringe briefly stuck to the bottom, making a soft sucking sound.

"Okay," she whispered. "I got it. Are you ready?"

I lay back on the bed, propped my hips on several pillows, and lifted my nightshirt to my waist. With warm fingers, Pam gingerly inserted the cool, plastic tube, narrower than a tampon, and slowly engaged the plunger, releasing the newly roused swimmers on their upstream journey to the entrance of my womb—the land of Os. The irony was not lost on me at the time, that after years of paying for birth control to keep that opening impenetrable, I was now paying big bucks to sow seed in my fertile tunnel; that I had become the Vaginal Welcome Wagon.

I wondered how many trips to the sperm bank, how many months or years, it would take to get me pregnant, and whether the gods would mess with me. *So now you want to get pregnant. At thirty-five? You had your chance before, so you'll just have to wait until your turn comes around again.*

Pam placed the spent syringe on the table and eased herself onto the bed. She lay next to me nuzzling her head until it rested on my shoulder. "We did it," she said.

"Yeah, we did." Unexpectedly, I began to cry—a jumble of emotions finally releasing. "This isn't how I thought I would make my babies, though." I hadn't needed scented candles or sitar music, but maybe we should have put massage oil on the list, or exchanged our not-exactly-sexy nightshirts for something slinky from Victoria's Secret. "It's so clinical," I said.

"I know, sweet love," Pam said, tracing the path of my tears with her thumbs.

Following the directions from the sperm bank, I swiveled my hips and swung my legs onto the wall, letting gravity help in the Miracle of Conception. There was some debate at the time about whether or not an orgasm following insemination would increase our odds, so we'd come to bed early in order to check that off the list too.

I finished my half-hour spider pose and settled into bed. Pam's soft fingers searched for my belly under my nightshirt, and finding it, she stroked in a light circle between my jutting hipbones. Her touch descended, I reciprocated, and, afterwards, we fell asleep nestled in the middle of our bed, my legs cradled in the soft, warm curves of hers.

★ **KATHY BRICCETTI'S** work has appeared most recently in *Under the Sun*; *Dos Passos Review*; *The Writer*; *So to Speak*; *upstreet*, *Brain Child*; and the *San Francisco Chronicle Magazine*. Her essays have been published in anthologies, including *The Maternal is Political*; *Herstory*; and *The Essential Hip Mama* as well as on public radio. An essay taken from her memoir manuscript was nominated for a Pushcart Prize. Some of her work-in-progress can be found on her website: www.kathybriccetti.com.

Colorblind

The Very True Story of a Woman Who Didn't Notice Her Sons Were Different Colors

LORI L. THARPS

First you need to know the backstory.

I met my husband during my junior year of college. I spent that year in Spain chasing my Josephine Baker/James Baldwin fantasies of an expat's bohemian existence. I didn't find the race-free utopia I'd been looking for, but I did meet the man of my dreams. I admit I am a sucker for a guy with an accent.

El hombre and I followed each other back and forth across the pond for almost a decade, until we finally decided to settle down and make it official. We chose the gloriously diverse, tragically hip borough of Brooklyn to plant our roots. Once we found a mouse-and-cockroach-free apartment to call our own (after approximately two years and a lot of tears), it only took us a short little while to produce our first child, a healthy baby boy. Three years after that, another boy-child joined the family. Once I got over the fact that I would never be the mother of girls, that my children would never attend my alma mater (single-sex Smith College), and that the levels of testosterone in my home might one day overwhelm me, I realized that being the mother to boys brings its own bag of joy and bliss.

Here's where I get to brag a bit.

Both of my boys are beautiful to look at in their own unique way. They both have sweet dispositions and neither one of them can think of a better way to begin the day than by crawling into bed with mommy and papa for one big snuggle fest. They are curious and funny and mercifully, they have both inherited my great love of books and reading. Even as babies they loved to sit in my lap and be read to at any time of the day. Yes, they have an almost inhuman fascination with cars and trucks, and yes, their manic energy levels sometimes make me want to run away and hide until they're twenty-five, and yes, their idea of a joke must always end with the words *booty* or *poopy* in the punch line, but as God is my witness, I couldn't love either one of them any more. To quote the great Mary Poppins, I think they are "practically perfect in every way."

Which is why I found it perplexing, bordering on offensive, when over the years, people kept pointing out to me that my sons are two different colors. "One is brown like his mama and the other one seems to be White like his Spanish papa," they said. I never saw it. I looked at my children every day, and never saw their color. I literally couldn't see a difference. I looked into their beautiful faces and saw only love reflected back.

Even when pressed by well-meaning friends, I honestly didn't believe their skin color was really that different . . . until this past summer. We were on the beach in the middle of paradise (actually we were really on the southwest coast of Spain, where Europe almost kisses Africa) and my sons were splashing in the waves. And suddenly I saw it. My older son is the color of warm caramel, while my younger son is all vanilla, with maybe a dash of cinnamon for flavor. I don't know why I never noticed it before, why the veil was lifted then, but it was. Watching them from behind, the sunshine casting them in her vivid light, it was obvious even to me: My sons are two different colors.

So what does it mean? Why should I care?

Again, we need to go into the backstory. And this story goes way, way, back.

In America, back when White people owned Black people, the

color of your skin along with the texture of your hair laid bare all of your family's history and, by extension, the potential for your future. The black skin of Africa meant you were destined to work under the yoke of slavery until you mercifully died. A lighter hue meant the blood of the master flowed through your veins, which meant maybe, just maybe, that very same master might set you free at some point in your life, or at the very least, take even the smallest bit of interest in your well-being. And that little bit of interest could mean more food for you and your family, a chance at getting a formal education, and sometimes just a shred of kindness instead of the constant threat of an overseer's painful whip. And finally, if you were Black, but your skin was light enough to be mistaken for White, you could pass. You could pass right into freedom and leave human bondage behind.

By the time the emancipation proclamation was issued and Black people could no longer be legally held as slaves, the psychological damage had been done. The significance of having lighter skin was hardwired into our brains. "If you're light you're all right, if you're Black get back." We even developed a name for our collective disorder; we call it the color complex. From Booker T. Washington to W. E. B. DuBois, from Marcus Garvey to Elijah Muhammad, Black history has been underscored by our obsession with the shades of our skin. We didn't create the problem but we can't seem to let it go.

In the twenty-first century there are still Black organizations, social clubs, sororities, neighborhoods, and churches that still operate with unofficial, color-coded membership rules. There used to be names for these rules, like the paper bag test (if you were darker than a brown paper bag, then admission was denied). Now such vulgarities are never expressed aloud, but the rules are still in effect. Mothers of dark children whisper in their kids' ears at night that they better find a lighter mate so that their children won't hate them. Generations of light-skinned Black people partner only with others of the same hue to maintain the same tawny complexion for years to come. And just to show that the complex goes both ways, there are plenty of light-skinned men and women who yearn to be accepted as authentically Black, so they partner only with the darkest berry that will have them. And as a result of these color wars amongst colored folks, dark is pitted against light. Tensions and distrust grow and an "us-against-them" mentality emerges. Will this be the future, I worry, for my dark and light sons?

My older son started noticing color when he was three years old. He came home from his Brooklyn preschool and listed off for me all of the children in his class who had the same brown skin as him. This was neither a good thing nor a bad thing, he just noticed. But now at age six, he has realized that in our family of four, he and I have brown skin while his brother and his papa have white skin. It seems to concern him, although he cannot or will not verbalize why. Nor does he claim to think one is better than the other, but we are different, and to a child of six, different is not a good thing. For a while there he wanted to say that even his father was in fact brown, just a very, very light brown. He really just wanted to be the same as both his father and his mother.

Is that even possible?

Now it is just wishful thinking, but I reason that if we were going to try to get this family all the same color, we're going to have to get the pale faces to darken up. I know my husband can get a really nice tan (thanks to his Moorish ancestors), and then I find myself wondering if it's still possible that my younger son may ripen up a bit naturally. It happened to my cousin, the one with the Black father and the White mother. He was as pale as my son until he hit puberty, and then like overnight his skin darkened to a ginger brown and his hair went from curly to kinky. (Those raging hormones are mighty powerful!) Why do I go there, though? Why is it important for me to make my son more colored? He's healthy, funny, smart, and sweet. Why do I need him to be a different color?

I could say it's just a safety issue. There have been times, and I mean more than one, when people have mistaken me for the nanny. What happens if one day he gets lost and I come to reclaim him and the authorities won't hand him over because they doubt our blood relations? Okay, that's a little far-fetched, but it is really annoying and hurts my feelings when people point out that my son looks nothing like me. (True story, at a mommy-and-me music class once, this woman suggested I get a DNA test done because sometimes they mixed babies up in the hospital.)

But it's not really about safety. It is just that common desire to have our family be the type that doesn't make people stop and stare in restaurants and ask us dumb questions like, "No, really, who does he look like?" that makes me fantasize about having a cookie-cutter, monochrome clan. And it's not just my feelings I'm worried about. Honestly, I worry that one day my older son is going to start placing a value judgment on the hue of his skin and compare it to his brother's. He's going to notice, like my husband and I already do, that certain people pay more attention to his brother than to him. I'd like to think that's because the little one is still graced with baby fat and is quite the charmer, but my husband isn't so optimistic. He thinks (and worries) it's because the little one looks White. Whether that's true or not, if my older son believes it to be so, then trouble begins. And that's the kind of trouble that only years of therapy, an emotional trip to the Motherland, and multiple choruses of "Kumbaya" can heal.

In this instance I do thank the gender gods that I have boys instead of girls because I believe this issue would be more heart-wrenching if I had daughters instead of sons. I hope and pray that it is true that boys don't place too much of their self-worth on their physical appearance, or at least not in the same ways that girls do. If that is the case, then I think we can prevent this color complex from destroying our multihued family. More than ever, I compliment my older son on the color of his skin and his overall physical appearance. I encourage him to be proud of all of his features because they are uniquely his. I, of course, have to be careful not to make it sound like brown skin is prettier than white skin because then I'd be rejecting my younger son in the process. He needs reassurance too. The message I try to impart to both of my children is that we are all flowers from one garden. Each flower is a different color and that's what makes the garden so very beautiful.

In our family garden we are four unique colors, no two of us are the same. People may stare at us or ask silly questions, but at the end of the day, I remind myself that we are healthy, happy, and supremely blessed in so many ways. Would being the same color change any of that? I don't think so. We are our own minirainbow coalition and I think we are all practically perfect in every way.

★ **LORI L. THARPS** is freelance journalist, editor, author, and teacher. Originally from Milwaukee, Wisconsin, she attended Smith College and received a master's degree from Columbia University Graduate School of Journalism. After graduation from Columbia, Lori was a staff reporter at *Vibe* magazine and then a correspondent for *Entertainment Weekly*. She has written for *Ms.*, *Glamour*, *Suede*, *Odyssey Couleur*, *Bitch*, and *Essence* magazines. She is the co-author of the award-winning book *Hair Story: Untangling the Roots of Black Hair in America* (St. Martin's Press, 2002). Her work can also be read in the anthologies *Young Wives' Tales: Stories of Love and Partnership* (Seal Press, 2001), *Naked: Black Women Bare All About their Skin, Hair, Hips, Lips, and Other Parts* (Perigee, 2005), and *Women: Images & Realities; A Multicultural Anthology* (McGraw-Hill, 2006). Lori is the creator and writer of the blog My American Meltingpot. Her memoir, *Kinky Gazpacho: Life, Love & Spain* was released by Atria/Simon&Schuster in March 2008, Lori lives in Philadelphia where she teaches magazine writing at Temple University.

Is Life without Kids Worth Living?

LIZ PRATO

Quick, what do these circumstances have in common: severe depression, alcoholism, a shortened lifespan, divorce, and having no children? They're all conditions that participants in a Yale University study said they would choose over obesity. The study concluded that obesity is perceived as a truly horrible fate if it ranks as more dire than severe depression and alcoholism, both of which can result in the loss of job, relationships, and life. Divorce's devastation of love, family, and dreams is also preferable to obesity, as is living ten fewer years. And not having children, well that's a fate worse than . . .

Here's where I got lost. Would I give up having kids in order to avoid obesity? Hell, I'd give up having kids in order to avoid taking out the trash. This study failed to recognize that many adults don't see forgoing childbearing as a devastating loss. In fact, so many people have happily made this choice that they've rallied against the term *childless* (which implies they're missing something), and instead opt to be called *childfree*. But the Yale study's inclusion of childlessness as a fate as dire as death just goes to show that the choice not to reproduce is hardly embraced, or understood, by our society.

My husband and I decided not to have children for a variety of reasons, which range from the mess and noise commonly described as "kid chaos" to feeling that raising children would prevent us from achieving our artistic dreams. Neither of us ever wanted our ten-year-old to discover the collection of dusty musical instruments or stack of never-finished novels in the garage and ask, "Dad, how come you never play music anymore?" or "Mom, how come you stopped writing?" The honest answer to that question would be, "To raise you, my darling lamb." Would it be worth giving up our dreams in order to raise a child who we'd love more than our own lives? Maybe. But the thing is, I've wanted to be a writer since I was five. The same can't be said for wanting to be a parent.

When push comes to shove, the reason my husband and I are childfree is probably less about kid chaos and putting aside our own dreams than it is about lacking some fundamental drive to reproduce. After all, there's not a parent alive who hasn't, at the very least, been inconvenienced by, and most likely made sacrifices for, their children. What constantly amazes me is how many of our friends were surprised when those situations arose. "We had no idea it would be so loud and messy all the time," they've said. "I didn't know we'd have to stop traveling internationally so much," said one couple. "I didn't realize I wouldn't have time for myself anymore," said another. Here's the thing: My husband and I have always known these are conditions of parenthood. We've known them without having children—by only watching people with children and extrapolating what it would be like for us—so why were these otherwise intelligent, thoughtful friends of ours incapable of reaching the same conclusion? Biological drive, I think. It's like they have some chip in their brain that sends out a reproductive signal so strong that it makes them oblivious to how difficult parenthood can be. For whatever reason, the chips in my brain and my husband's brain are malfunctioning or absent.

Maybe it's biological, maybe it's environmental. My husband was an only child raised by a hippie mother with a laissez-faire parenting style. He was free to run barefoot among the orange groves in rural California, and earned his allowance harvesting the pot plants in the garden. Unfortunately, being raised by a hippie wasn't all daisy chains and "Kumbaya." It was also illicit drugs and Mom's addicted boyfriend and a lack of structure and discipline. It was fear and a kind of emotional repression that I'm sure his mother never considered. In order to counteract all the instability in his childhood, my husband chose to be good. He didn't fuss, he didn't raise his voice, and he rarely got in trouble. And while that all may sound like the model child, it meant that as an adult he had no idea how to voice his opinions, to stand up for his own feelings, or to identify his own needs.

My childhood, on the other hand, was enacted in the middle-class suburbs amid well-manicured Kentucky bluegrass lawns. All the houses on our block were occupied by married couples with children. There wasn't a divorce for miles around—until my parents'. It happened when I was thirteen, and even then I was well aware that divorce was a kinder option than fighting and lovelessness. Mom and I were pretty happy, setting up house the way we wanted. There was a lot of laughing and dancing in the kitchen, and long, soulful talks that lasted late into the night. There was also her alcoholic boyfriend and money struggles and, years later, I discovered she was frequently visited by severe bouts of depression.

My mom died when I was twenty-six. She was fifty-eight, making her the longest living survivor in her generation of women in our family. My two aunts both died in their mid-forties. That means that my cousins and I all became motherless—most of us before we'd had children of our own. At least half of us still don't have children and, it looks like, never will. It seems that knowing the parent-child relationship can come to such an abrupt end has shut down our desire to have kids.

I'm also adopted. This mom who I loved so much was my adopted mother, and the woman who gave birth to me is a stranger. I apparently have brothers and sisters (from both my biological mother and father), but I will never know them. Maybe the reason I never inherited that drive to reproduce is because my bloodline is totally mysterious to me, and continuing it is therefore irrelevant.

In the long run, though, whether our reasons are born out of nature or nurture shouldn't matter. The only reason they do matter is because we must justify our choice time and time again to people who are trying to decide what's wrong with us. It's not uncommon for us to be told, "You can still change your mind."

"That seems unlikely," I say. "I'm forty."

"These days women can have healthy pregnancies in their forties."

This is when I hold out my index and middle fingers and make the *snip-snip* motion. "Really," I say. "It's too late."

One couple never called us again after this conversation. Maybe it's because they're Catholic, and having children is a condition of marriage for them. Maybe it's because they assume that because we don't want children, then we would not value theirs. Listen, I'm not one of those childfree people who proclaims, "I love other people's kids, I just don't want my own," because that's simply untrue. I don't love kids, and by that I mean I don't love *all* kids unconditionally. I love *some* kids, the children of my friends, whom I have played with and had conversations with and have been able to watch grow into pretty spectacular personalities. I love them because of who they are as people, not simply because they're kids. And when I see some random two-year-old jumping in a puddle like it's the coolest thing ever (even though he can barely walk, much less jump), I get a big kick out of it. And, really, kids do say the darndest things. But, honestly, most times when I encounter kids in a restaurant or the mall or the grocery store, I think only one thing: *Shut up!*

Wait, that's not true. That's not all I think. What I mostly think is, *Thank God we didn't have them.* This parenting is hard work. It's loud and messy and time-consuming, and the results are critical, so I can't imagine why anyone would encourage people who don't want it to jump into the fire. My decision was not arrived at lightly or quickly. It was well thought-out. I'd like to think that people who have chosen to raise children put as much thought into their reasons for doing so.

Many of our friends with kids tell us they envy our lifestyle.

On Sunday morning we get to wake up slowly and read the *New York Times* and drink coffee in silence. We can go out to movies and dinner and concerts pretty much anytime we feel like it, and our futures belong to us, and no one else. But that moment when their children snuggle up to them and say, "I love you," makes being a parent all worthwhile. Seeing them master the alphabet or graduate from high school or welcome their own children into the world makes all the kid chaos fade into the background. The best part is, I feel no envy for them. It's true, the *New York Times* can't snuggle up with me and say "I love you." But, when I'm tired or bored, I can put it away—by choice.

★ **LIZ PRATO'S** fiction and essays have appeared, or are forthcoming, in several magazines and literary reviews, including *ZYZZYVA*, *Iron Horse Literary Review*, *Massage & Bodywork* magazine, *Cream City Review*, and *Subtropics*. Awards include a Pushcart nomination, first place in *Berkeley Fiction Review's* 2005 Sudden Fiction Contest, and runner-up for the 2007 *Juked* Fiction Prize. Excerpts from her recently completed novel appear in *Gertrude*. Liz teaches creative writing in Portland, Oregon.

Perpetual Choices

PAT D. JEAN

My personal definition of feminism includes all rights for women, but more importantly, it encompasses the love of women. Not romantic love, since I am heterosexual, but love on a more spiritual level. I love being female. I love that every twenty-eight to thirty days, my body reminds me that I am meant to and will one day give birth. I am fascinated by the fact that women are God's special creation in that we can simultaneously carry another human being in our bodies, think, and speak, and men don't and cannot. Don't misunderstand me, I love men; I just believe that women are sacred.

I got my first period when I was eleven years old. I was in complete denial and proceeded to change, wash, and hang my panties to dry three times before my grandmother went into the bathroom and asked me what I was doing. Each time that I checked to see if the bleeding had stopped, a bright red bloodstain surprisingly greeted me. I was then handed a box of gigantic (or so they seemed to an eleven-year-old child) box of Kotex and a sanitary belt (which I swore everyone could see the outline of through my clothes), forced to endure the long and painfully uncomfortable speech about staying away from boys, given a full permanent relaxer, and then we all went to Chinatown for dinner. I was finally a woman.

I embraced puberty during the early eighties and always had an advanced knowledge about sexuality. I had my first kiss at nine years old, and at twelve years of age, the same boyfriend tried to initiate sex with me. I adamantly told him that I was too young and not ready to become a mother. A classmate of mine, with whom I share my birthday, turned up pregnant earlier that year. Everyone was shocked. I wasn't. I clearly understood that the young lady in question was absentminded and didn't know anything about birth control. I think it was then that I subconsciously vowed to never, ever let that happen to me. I was going to find out everything I could about sex and contraception and wait until I was much older and truly ready to have sex.

In hindsight, the early eighties were for me a time of evolution. I was just a kid from Brooklyn, but at the same time, I was the embodiment of my mother's, grandmothers,' and aunts' values and beliefs. While mainstream women were having their sexual revolution, I was absorbing information, which would be regurgitated later in my life, about "broken homes," women leaving husbands and choosing new ones, single motherhood, and more importantly, women taking their sexuality into their own hands.

Growing up in a Haitian household of first-generation immigrants, I often found myself caught in the chasm of my grandmother's old-school theories about men and family, and my mother's newfound independence and courage in pursuing and obtaining the things she wanted. In my opinion, many women from my grandmother's generation were economically dependent on their men more so than were women who were raised in or migrated to the United States. This dependence caused women to marry young in order to leave their parents' homes. The marriages often became self-inflicted traps from which they couldn't escape, mostly because their culture demanded that they stay with their husbands, whether they were happy or not. Without many options for generating income, the women choose to accept their plight.

Migrating to the United States gave immigrant women more opportunities to work and to contribute to household expenses than they had in their home countries, and allowed them to take active roles in making decisions concerning their families. My mother, who has still had some "old school" in her, left and divorced my father in 1978 with only $80 in her pocket. The marriage was abusive and life threatening, but I strongly believe that the economic opportunities afforded to her empowered her to leave. There was never a moment that my mother didn't have a steady income, and yet she still managed to raise us up right. She worked hard, not out of some need to be equal to men, but out of the sheer necessity to survive. I inherently learned that women couldn't rest on their laurels, waiting for a knight in shining armor to rescue them; black women just did not have that luxury. Again, I took an unspoken vow concerning my future: Never depend on a man for anything.

My grandmother, mother, and I agreed on the need for women to work; we often bumped heads, however, when it came to men. Although the tone was set for women's independence, the undertone of "needing" a man was ever-present. As a teenager I believed that women could do anything and everything that men did. The generation gap between us widened as I began dating.

I didn't want to find myself pregnant at sixteen like another classmate, so I went to Planned Parenthood, got a six-month supply of birth control pills, and stocked up on condoms and spermicide. I was still a virgin. The clinic was very welcoming and brightly decorated in pink and white, I think. The staff was keen to making sure that I had an ample supply of prophylactics and foam (do people even use that stuff anymore?). In addition I was sent home with pamphlets about other various methods of birth control and information on STDs. I proudly felt like I was part of a grown-up collective.

My pride shriveled when I got home; I hid my goods in the back of the bathroom cabinet under the sink, behind the bottles of shampoo and cleanser. For some reason, still unbeknownst to me, my mother decided one Saturday morning to clean the bathroom. That task was one of my chores. My heart began to pound in my ears when she snapped on the rubber gloves and knelt before the sink. My mother nearly had a heart attack when she found my stash. I still remember how time moved in slow motion as she reached into the cabinet and asked herself out loud, "What the hell is this?!" I instantly regressed into a five-year-old who had been caught doing something very bad. My throat dried up and my tongue felt heavy. I was admonished about promiscuity and the dangers of letting boys take advantage of me. I was warned with the Haitian euphemism about unwanted pregnancy: If a person burns wood, they will eventually make charcoal. She poked my breasts with her angry finger and asked numerous times if I was pregnant, and mind you, I had not yet had sex. I tried explaining this to an irate and disappointed mother, but to no avail. I told her that she should be glad that I was smart enough to prepare myself for what was coming. She was not amused.

My burgeoning sexuality was my weapon of choice when it came down to me differentiating myself from the women in my household. The thought of premarital sex never entered my grandmother's mind, or so I would still like to believe. My mother married young, but remarried a man out of desire and not necessity. I however took the damned thing to another level. I was determined to get my swerve on, college education and career, before even thinking about marriage.

I was careful and religiously used birth control, but sadly joined the population of the 5 percent of women who may become pregnant while on the pill. Again I was in denial. The first home pregnancy test was positive, but I took two more before I accepted my reality and scheduled an appointment with a doctor. That visit to the clinic was the antithesis of my visit to Planned Parenthood.

Having absolutely no money for treatment, I went to a clinic in a county hospital, where I was relegated to a testing center. I was greeted by other seemingly stunned teenagers. My best friend for life accompanied me in order to offer moral support. As I suspected, the official test came back positive: I was six weeks pregnant. I cried as I walked out of the room. An ignorant and equally pregnant teenager said to me, as we passed each other in the corridor, "Did they say you was?" I cried even harder. My best friend cried with me too. I cried for months after the father-to-be told me that I had a problem and needed to take care of it. The decision to terminate the pregnancy came after much lamentation. People often think that pro-choice women go skipping off to the clinic to kill their babies. They could not be more wrong. Ask any woman who has made the choice to have an abortion, and she will likely tell you that her first period signified childbirth, motherhood, and all the glories therein. When the craft is terminated, for whatever reason, the woman is scarred for life. On the day of the procedure, the doctor asked if I was sure that it was my first pregnancy. I prayed for forgiveness. And I added to my checklist of vows to choose very carefully the man to whom I will give my ovum. Six months later, I went off to university in Philadelphia and tried to make better choices. The education factor was strictly ingrained in me from my first day of kindergarten. Many children in Haiti don't have the opportunity to go to school, I was told. I was raised to take full advantage of this country's education system, and having done just that, more doors opened up to me than my predecessors could ever have imagined. I wrestled through personal struggles during my college years, but the day I graduated with a bachelor's degree in economics, I realized that I had taken the course of my life in a direction where I would be able to support myself. I didn't have to settle for marrying early in order to escape poverty.

I'm not so naive as to believe that all people who marry young do it in order to escape poverty. My theory is simply based on what I've witnessed happening to the women in my immediate circle. I met Mr. Right, right at that time, when I was twenty-one years old, and one week before graduation, he asked me to marry him. I declined the proposal with great anxiety, and opted to move back to New York in order to pursue a career in corporate America. I consciously decided to delay marriage and motherhood. I loved him, but I felt like I had not yet lived and I wanted so much to really experience life as fully as possible. And anyway I was just developing sexually and could not see myself at twenty-three being tied down to just one man. My return to New York was the best decision that I could have made. I have never regretted it. I came back in the early nineties and started working eight months later. Having a salary, though paltry as it was, allowed me to provide decently enough for myself. I looked forward to my weekly paychecks and dreamed about the things I would buy. I spent them just as quickly as they came in. I hung out with my girlfriends a lot and dated men, who like me, were single and free. My circle of girlfriends began to shrink in my late twenties, though. There seemed to be an epidemic. Everyone was getting married. I attended weddings back to back and always seemed to be at Babies "R" Us or Toys "R" Us buying baby-shower gifts. "What was the rush?" I asked. The most common answer: "I'm turning thirty soon, and I can't be single at thirty!" "What's wrong with being thirty and single?" I asked. It was as if I had blasphemed in the house of the Lord. I watched many women marry Mr. Wrong. I asked my grandmother to slap me if ever I ran down the aisle to marry out of fear of being thirty and single. The economic trappings of my grandmother's generation had morphed into the old-maid syndrome of my generation. The old maid had always existed, but with our educations and paychecks in hand, I was foolish enough to believe that we could transcend the need to have a man just to satisfy society. Some marriages lasted and grew into loving, supportive families. Some did not. During this time I added another unspoken truth to my list: Never marry out of fear, and never try to catch a man in a baby trap. That's right, I said it, "the baby trap." This is the snare that is laid out, deliberately by some women, with lingerie, slamming sex, booty calls, and the famous phrase, "It's okay, I'm on the pill." I knew one woman who poked holes in her diaphragm. I have seen many guys shake their heads and wonder, "How did this happen to me?" My thought on their situation: In the infamous words of my mother, "When a person burns wood, they are bound to make charcoal." Again, please don't get me wrong; I hardly believe that all accidental pregnancies are not actual accidents. These things happen. I know this from personal experience. I simply made an active choice not to purposely bring a child into this world in order to coax a man down the aisle. If he is not willing, then neither am I. No one plans for divorce, but seeing so many young couples end up in divorce court led me to examine my choices more carefully.

I did meet Mr. Right, but he turned out to be someone else's Mr. Right, and my Mr. Wrong. That relationship ended very painfully, but I learned something very valuable: that I want to have children with someone I love and am married to. I have neither the support network, nor the courage really, to be a single parent. I am fiercely independent, but am scared to death of the prospect of having to raise a child alone. I honor women who develop the courage to be single moms. I have chosen the word *developed* because I imagine that much like myself, before they actually became single moms, they too were very afraid. If I should find myself pregnant and single, I know that I would develop the courage to do it, but for now, I am praying for marriage first and babies after. My decisions to wait for a loving marriage before having children and to delay marriage until later in life both stem from the childhood experience of my parents' divorce. I didn't wake up one day and decide that I would be thirty-eight, single, and unmarried. I decided over time that if a relationship didn't feel right, I would not "go along to get along"; I would end it and spare myself and my partner a lifetime of sorrow. Some of my relationships have lasted years, some only months. Only two felt like they would lead to marriage. When my gut tells me something, I listen to that inner voice. I worked hard at not fooling myself into believing that I could marry a man if my feelings were not genuine. I simply could not do it. During different intervals of my life, I compare the person I am with the person I was in the past. I gauge my personal growth and am so thankful that I chose this route. I have discovered some things about myself that I believe would otherwise have been buried underneath marriage and babies. I wanted to fully develop my individuality before becoming a wife and mother.

This choice is a very difficult one because many of my peers do not support this ideal. I have been the object of mean-spirited ridicule. "What the hell are you waiting for?" "You pick, pick, pick, until you'll pick shit." "You think you're too good for just any man." And my all-time favorite, "Thank God for auntie Pat, who doesn't have a life . . . priorities of her own. God knew what he was doing when he didn't give you kids of your own." This one is from someone who is happily married. I believe these women are trapped in unhappy lives. At first the allure of the big "poofy" dress, diamond ring, and babies is irresistible, but after the honeymoon ends, and reality sets in, things can get ugly. I have always believed that houses built on sand eventually wash away when the tide comes in. I am still chiseling the layers of bedrock that my life is built upon, and most of the time, am very happy with my decision. I sometimes question my choices but eventually am given the exact answer that I need. I was down-and-out last year about getting older and still not having found my Mr. Right and not having any children. I sought and found solace in my mom when she simply said to me, "You are slow, but sure. It takes you a long time to get what you want, but when you achieve something, you are certain that it is right for you." If I am blessed with a child before I wed, I will lovingly welcome my little bundle of joy into the world. For now, I will continue to stick with my principles and anticipate marriage first, and babies second.

★ A thirty-eight year old Haitian-American Brooklynite, **PAT D. JEAN** began her career at Temple University where she studied economics. Shortly thereafter, she became a derivatives consultant on Wall Street, yet all the while aspiring to become a creative fiction writer. To date, Pat has taken continuing education classes both at New York University, where she studied Writing Basics I and II, and the New School, where she studied Beginning and Intermediate Fiction. She anticipates applying to an MFA program in the near future.

Which One's the Mother?

MARY WARREN FOULK

After many years and countless conversations with law-yers, doctors, financial planners, family members, and friends (as well as anyone else who would listen), our son Grady was born. His eyes were wide open and we took each other in. I've never held anything so beautiful.

I had always wanted children and a family of my own. I just wasn't sure how I wanted them. I never saw myself pregnant, couldn't imagine the "feeling" in my belly, couldn't imagine myself in maternity clothes. My domestic partner/spouse/wife/best friend/ lover (not roommate) was the exact opposite. Alyson would frolic around our apartment in her worn baggy overalls, stick out her stomach, and say, "Look at these hips. Meant for babies."

I met Alyson in January of 2000. I was dating John at the time. Not just dating, we were contemplating engagement, even looking at rings. We had been together for nearly two years. Let's just say it had been a tough two years. I lost thirty pounds, dropped from a size 8 to a size 0. I took Zoloft and Wellbutrin. Two therapists analyzed my ambivalence. I met John after several years of dat-ing disasters, including a lesbian heartbreak. (My second? Third?)

Mutual friends had set us up, friends I hadn't known very well. (Red flag, red flag!) Our differences were apparent from the start, but we both felt the need for "security," for answers and guarantees. I knew my answers, but had long denied them, giving into "should/would" and years of internalized homophobia, years of wanting acceptance. Our ending was not my proudest moment. ("Dear John . . .") I regret my lack of maturity and awareness, my fears about being gay, about being me.

My first coming out was at the Holly Ball, Christmas 1987. I was eighteen and a debutante making her debut. My father and I danced awkwardly to "Thank Heaven for Little Girls." My mother glowed. This was her dream and I was her reflection. Eight of us wore white and were presented to the "bachelors" for picking. I had grown up with these girls but never quite related to them, never quite felt a part. The ninth deb had dropped out months prior (scandal!). I admired her courage. I learned years later that she was living with her long-time girlfriend in New Hampshire; that her parents refused to visit. Looking at the photographs from that night, scenes of me in taffeta, pearls, long white leather gloves, I wonder, painfully, "Who was that?"

My second coming out was ten years later in Santa Fe. A recipient of an academic grant, I spent June and July studying the cultural landscapes of the Southwest—and Roxanna. My mother came for a visit and found me a mess. I was "totally" in love (lust?). We talked around the obvious until I couldn't help but be honest. The confession didn't stick, for either one of us. Nor did the relationship.

The third was in 2002 after my eldest brother's sudden death. Cleaning out Stephen's apartment, wading through his things, my parents found the years of hiding. Although I had the opportunity, I didn't conceal the evidence as I had during his lifetime. I wanted his truth at last, for his sake, for my own. The pain was too great for me to reveal my own closet, except in writing. After the funeral, I wrote my other brother David and my parents a letter, thinking that would be easiest for us all to digest. My mother was "shocked" (denial runs deep in our DNA). My father, ever noncommittal, said, "Whatever you want, babe." David flew to New York where Stephen and I both lived. He took me out for our favorite Mexican, bought margarita after margarita, and at the end of a tender but laden evening, told me with welling eyes, "I love you. Please be happy. Life is much too short." Stephen had been forty.

Alyson and I took our time in dating, resisted the pressure of some lesbian stereotypes (U-Hauling?), and gave into others (sex on the first date? hours of processing?). Having both been mired in relationship messes, we decided to go slowly, to be present, not to predict or fantasize what the future might hold. Nearly eight years later, we still follow those mantras. When I tell people why I love her so much, I often mention the first time I saw her apartment, the moment I noticed her bookshelves and saw all of my favorite books as well as all the ones I had ever longed to read. Meeting her felt like coming home. I had never felt so known nor had such desire to know.

I was honest with her from the start about wanting to have a baby and my uncertainty as to how. At the two-year mark, I very subtly asked, "What in the hell are we doing? Are we committed? Do you want this (read: me) or not? And what about kids? I'm not getting any younger." Note that this conversation happened in the early morning before Alyson could process a thought. She sighed deeply and grunted, "I love you. I'm in. Give me two years before deciding on kids." Then, she went back to snoring.

In many ways, the path was easier with John. I could fall back on a common, known script. Date, get engaged, marry, buy a house, have kids, and then divorce when they go to college. At least that was what my parents did. Literally, the papers were filed the day after I graduated. Upon seeing me receive my diploma, my mother nearly fainted with relief and then declared, "That's it. I'm done. Gerry, move out." Thirty years she (they both) had endured, sacrificing herself for the sake of her children, what she had been taught, what had been modeled. I vowed I wouldn't do the same.

Alyson and I never really talked about marriage. As of 2003, it didn't seem like an option. We didn't know anyone who had gone to

Canada. None of our gay friends had had "commitment ceremonies." In fact, many despised the notion—why be a part of a tradition and institution that actively and historically excludes you? We had been fixtures at myriad weddings. Often we were the only lesbians, symbols of liberalism and progression, always seated off to the side or at the back, next to the crazy neighbor, colorful colleague, or thrice-divorced uncle who incessantly asked us to dance and couldn't quite comprehend that we were a couple. "Are you sisters?" *Um, no.* One summer, invites reached the teens and we thought we should rent ourselves out: "Rent-a-Lesbian: Prove you're progressive. Put the *blue* in blue state!"

We had to draft our own "script." After the aforementioned what-the-hell-are-we-doing conversation, Alyson and I moved in together. Slowly, repeatedly, repeatedly, we came out to all of our family members, friends, and colleagues—to varying degrees of acceptance and "success." Also, to varying degrees of openness. Every conversation is an outing, and depending on the context, level of safety and trust, more of our selves are revealed or hidden. And there's the fatigue factor. It's exhausting to explain who you are all the time. For example, I have yet to tell my 105-year-old aunt Myrtle. Where do I start? And to have to scream, "I'M GAY" at such a volume the entire nursing home would hear? Such fun.

In 2003 we moved to Portland, Oregon, for a job opportunity. We opened a joint checking account, despite my panic attack in the parking lot of Washington Mutual, and eventually bought our first home.

On March 3, 2004, our friend Kathy woke us up with an early morning phone call. "Get down here now! The county is issuing marriage licenses to same-sex couples!" Kathy and her wife, Tay, had gotten married in San Francisco. None of us thought the revolution would happen in the City of Roses. Alyson had to go to work, but I took the day off to celebrate the happiness and history that was finally being afforded, that was long overdue. I couldn't wait to share with Alyson what I had witnessed, and when I did, our conversation turned to our own future.

We stayed up all night debating "should we/shouldn't we." Were we ready? Should we wait and see what happens? Should we plan a ceremony for a later date, one that would include all of our community, our family, and friends? Could we afford to wait? What if the opportunity didn't come again? It was this question and the thought of participating in such a wonderful, profound act of civil justice, a political demonstration for true equality, that inspired us to get out of bed, put on whatever clothes lay around us, and get to the county office by five in the morning to wait in line with hundreds of others, who had traveled many miles and years and imaginings and fears to get to this place. March 4, 2004, was one of the greatest days of my life, the day I said, "I do." We partied for days, months, reveling in our newfound freedoms, until a judge, whom I do not know, deemed our marriage invalid and denied us the one-thousand-plus privileges/protections/securities enjoyed by heterosexual couples everywhere (including serial killers in Sing Sing). Our check for $60 was marked VOID, returned in the mail. We put it in our wedding album, amid the smiling photographs. Despite the disappointment and anger, we continue to see ourselves as married. How many weddings, ballot measures, court cases will it take before I can enjoy fully what my neighbors have, what my brother has?

Sometimes I fantasize I'm a guest on *Oprah*. (Who doesn't?) She's interviewing me about my lesbianism and marriage. I wax on about what it means to me to be gay. I assert, "There have been gay people since the dawn of man. They are your mothers, fathers, aunts, brothers, and cousins. They are your doctors, lawyers, teachers, talk-show hosts, ministers, and politicians. They are the EMTs who will save your life, the person sitting next to you on the bus or on the pew. Always have been, always will be." And then I turn to Oprah and ask, "What were you doing on March 4, 2004? Anything special that you remember?" She ponders the question and replies no. "I got married on that day, Oprah, and you weren't invited nor was anyone in this studio audience. My marriage had nothing to do with you and no impact on you whatsoever. You and Stedman didn't split, divorces didn't skyrocket, and the world didn't collapse."

That's gay marriage—an intimate moment and promise between two people who love one another.

House, marriage, fantasies about Oprah, we endeavored the next step—kids. I wish I could write that we planned romantic evenings of wine, candles, bubble bath, and sex, but breeding for lesbians is a challenging, deliberate, multifaceted process. Forget foreplay, we called a lawyer. Having been denied marriage, we had to ensure as many legal protections and securities as were allowed by Oregon law. We met Marlene through mutual friends. She was known throughout Oregon for her expertise on same-sex legal matters and on second-parent adoption. A married, lesbian mother, she had navigated this journey herself and had been instrumental in influencing Oregon lawmakers to recognize same-sex families. For an absurd amount of money, we purchased the "adoption" package, which included wills, health directives, legal guardian documentation, and, when ready, all the paperwork necessary to establish that both Alyson and I would be recognized as the parents of any children we might have.

Like any good lesbians, we made our next call to a therapist. We interviewed several. One was a little bit too titillated by the thought of working with lesbians, clearly not his usual clientele. Another never called us back. We later heard from the acquaintance who had recommended her that she had had a crisis of conscious and left the country. Probably a blessing. Another had a very specific method, which he would not name, that essentially would improve our communication skills. We kept reiterating that we thought our communication was rather effective; we didn't have a problem processing or talking with one another. He just didn't seem to listen or couldn't quite go off method. And frankly he just kept repeating what we said. ("So I hear that you want to start a family. So I hear that you are lesbians who want to start a family. So I hear that you are lesbians.") Alyson and I knew the art of therapy. We loved our individual therapists and were deeply moved by the teachings provided as well as by the level of awareness and changes achieved. We also believed we were pretty good at it. We often role-played analyst at home. ("Okay, now you lie on the couch.")

At long last, we met Susan. Earth mother extraordinaire, she nurtured us to a better understanding of why we wanted to be parents and how we could achieve our family.

Under a patchouli haze, we came up with three plans: Plan A, I would get pregnant; Plan B, Alyson would get pregnant; Plan C, we would adopt. It then became a matter of which plan to execute and what that execution might mean.

Since I had initiated the conversation about children, our first focus was Plan A. We analyzed my fears about pregnancy, my ambivalence (a pattern?), the rationale and reasons for my feelings, as well as the parenting models I had inherited (too involved versus not involved). Months passed and a decision could not be reached. We felt stuck.

I then contacted several of the larger adoption agencies. In my mid-twenties, I had a recurring dream in which I adopted a child from Thailand. In the dream, I was walking through JFK holding a little girl. We were walking towards baggage claim where my parents and eldest brother were waiting. I was nervous to greet them. The dream wasn't far from reality in that at the age of twenty-five I did spend a year in Chiang Mai. During my time there, I volunteered at an orphanage and met children living with or orphaned by HIV/AIDS. The orphanage had asked simply for arms to hold and rock the babies. How quickly they had learned absence. My therapist suggested the little girl was me.

None of the agencies I spoke with were willing to work with lesbian parents. I would have to act as a single mother, complete the adoption process, and then later we would file for Alyson's legal status as parent. The costs were extraordinary on many levels. There also was the possibility of home visits in which we would be scrutinized, judged fit or unfit to be mothers. There were no guarantees and years could pass before we might embrace a child as our own. We ruled out Plan C, for now.

Driving home one night from therapy, we got caught in a lengthy traffic jam. Alyson turned to me and said, "Do you feel it in your bones?" "Do I feel what in my bones?" I replied. "Do you feel

pregnancy in your bones?" "No, I don't," I sighed. "I really don't."
I realized that I had been the one holding up the process. I was the
obstacle, which was such a painful observation given how much I
had pushed her on the topic, how much I had projected onto her.
Our friend Claire always jokes about how great it would be to have
a two-womb family, but two wombs can be more complex than one.
Plan A was out. As we neared home, she turned to me again and
said, "Well, I'm ready. I want to get pregnant, and I want to get
started." Plan B was in.

One Sunday, shortly after we had made our decision, Alyson
glanced through the opinion section of the *New York Times*. Every
Sunday, we relax by reading the *Times*. At least we attempt to
relax. The Op-Ed pieces tend to enrage us. We noticed an article on
same-sex parenting and sibling donor registries. The article argued
that children of same-sex couples feel a void in not knowing their
"father," in not knowing their "siblings"; that their lives would
be quests for blood connections. We felt nauseous. We decided to
write a letter to the editor. In it, we questioned the author; her
intent, which leaned conservative and heterosexist; her research,
which was narrow and bordered on ignorant; and her use of language, including the equivalence of "donor" and "father." The letter was published, one of three, all denouncing what had been
written. We were particularly moved by the response below ours,
written by the executive director of a sperm bank on the West
Coast. She defended sperm banks, donor insemination, the often
arduous routes that individuals and couples must take to have a
family. Her response was intelligent and humane and represented
values in which we also believe. It became clear that she would
be someone to whom we could turn for help, that her organization would be the place to begin. We spent the rest of the day
online, reviewing the sperm bank's website. We were more and
more impressed by the work they did, what they had achieved. We
liked that the bank was small, that they took time to get to know
their donors, were highly selective, and wanted to ensure that all
parties felt deeply cared for. We signed up for their newsletter and

commenced our search for the "perfect donor." How would we make this choice?

We used our therapy sessions to talk about the fact that there is no perfect donor. We analyzed what mattered to us. Should the donor look like me? Or Alyson? Should the donor be Irish/Jewish/Catholic, representative of Alyson's lineage? Or Swedish/English/Southern Baptist/Presbyterian like mine? How healthy need he be? How many joints would be okay? What if he didn't eat leafy greens? What if he was eighteen, in his early twenties, mid-fifties? What if he failed math, didn't have a college degree, wasn't a cardiologist? What if, what if? The questions were dizzying. We were thinking too much. We stepped back, reflected on faith, reaffirmed the leap.

We reviewed the donor profiles again online. We chose three. We ordered their medical histories, interview results, staff impressions, and personal statements as to why they chose to be donors. When the packages arrived in the mail, Alyson and I agreed that each of us alone should take time with them, read through them carefully, garner some impressions, and then rank them in order of preference. Our rankings were the same.

Donor #2279 made us laugh. He felt familiar, familial. He seemed earnest in his answering, even asked to update his profile over time. Dated notes dotted the margins. He was healthy, yet admitted he didn't eat enough broccoli. He had smoked a few cigarettes but didn't really like the aftertaste. Raised in the South, he admired manners and grace. He was a film student, creative and bold in his imaginings. He wanted all families, including gay families, to have the same kind of happiness and closeness and love that he had known. We ordered six vials.

Friends and family questioned us about our choice. What do you really know about this guy? How can you trust him? How do you know he isn't lying? They shared horror stories about eighteen-year-olds wanting cash, about kids showing up unannounced on their donors' doorsteps, about every cynical and destructive stereotype and every misinformed *New York Times* article. We thought about his words. As a writer, I well understand that you make choices in how you express yourself on the page. We honored his choices as well as our own. Alyson and I held fast to our belief in one another, in the child we would create, in the family we would be.

I have always respected the saying, "Timing is everything." I gained newfound respect for the phrase when attempting insemination. After months of charting temperatures, peeing on sticks, testing the viscosity of mucous, we contacted our nurse practitioner and told her, "This month's a go." It was June of 2006. When we hit the seventy-two-hour window, we called the sperm bank and told them to overnight the goods. A tank the size of a small car arrived on our doorstep. Out of the corner of my eye, I had watched a poor FedEx employee struggle to bear the weight. I ran to find Alyson. "What did we order? And how big are the vials?" It felt like we had ordered a small country of sperm. We called Kaiser, our HMO, and said, "The tank's here," at which point they asked us to come in. We arrived, sweating and anxious.

"That's the biggest tank I've ever seen!" the technician remarked. The other lesbian couple in the waiting room looked at us with disdain. Their tank was so hip and sleek and cool. I felt like I had the word LOSER etched on my forehead. I had failed the tank test. LuAnne called our names and brought us back to a dimly lit room. Pictures of vaginas colored every wall. She calmly and carefully explained what our appointment would entail. She reviewed the technician's lab results in which he had examined the motility of the sperm as well as sperm count, then prepared us for the IUI and potential outcomes, forewarning that it was very unlikely that we would get pregnant on the first try. I held Alyson's hand as LuAnne inserted the long syringe, we breathed together, and tried to imagine sperm meeting egg. Weeks later, Alyson got her period. We shared a bottle of red wine and told ourselves that the baby would come when he or she was ready.

On the next attempt, we miscalculated our ovulation window, thinking we had more time than we did. We ordered the tank to arrive as the window was closing. I canceled all work meetings to wait for FedEx. Alyson took a half day. When we saw the truck pull up, we rushed to greet the messenger, grabbed the tank, heaved it and ourselves into the car and sped to the hospital, where LuAnne greeted us warmly. There was an excitement and optimism in the air, a levity we hadn't felt for days. Analyzing the technician's results, LuAnne remarked, "Wow! Great counts! Where did you get these guys? I haven't seen such a specimen." Perhaps she says this to all the ladies, but it didn't matter. It put smiles on our faces. We assumed our positions: Alyson with legs in the air; me by her side; LuAnne, donning miner's light and magic wand. Before inserting the syringe, she called to me, "Mary, get down here. You have to see this." I inched my way towards her, looked at Alyson to see if it was okay, and took a slight, nervous peek. Of course, I had perused the area many a time, but not in public or under such circumstances. I blushed a bit. "Look how open and primed she is. Just beautiful." Clearly LuAnne loved her job, and I loved her for loving her job. As she inserted the syringe, LuAnne chanted, "Swim, swim, swim." Then she urged us to do the same. The three of us sang and laughed in chorus. LuAnne reminded us to think good thoughts. She turned on a CD player, which whispered wave music and ocean sounds, then left the room to attend to another patient. When she came to check on us and say good-bye, she hugged us tightly and said, "I'm so happy and excited for you both and for your family." We all had tears in our eyes.

Is it weird that we still have our positive pregnancy test? It sits on our bathroom shelf, by the toothpaste, dental floss, and facial creams that have not halted my aging process. Alyson woke me with her screaming. "OMG, a plus sign! I knew it! Babe!" When I didn't respond immediately, she came bounding into the bedroom and laid the stick next to my pillow. "Look!" I couldn't believe what I was seeing. So many feelings, from disbelief to not knowing what or how to feel, to thinking, "So soon? Second try? Who does that?!" My fertile wonder.

Reality didn't quite hit until the ten-week sonogram. To be honest, we weren't even sure of the purpose of the appointment. To be more honest, I had missed most of Alyson's first trimester due to the fact that my mother was nearing the end of a too long, valiant struggle with leukemia. It was miraculous for me to have made the appointment at all. When our nurse practitioner brought in the machine, we thought, what exactly are we going to see? Then, the tiniest head, a beating heart, racing arms and legs appeared on the screen. "Our baby," we whispered, "our baby."

As Alyson grew, so did my concerns and fears. I worried more deeply about being the "other" mother, about the lack of blood history or genetic connection. What if the child was a mirror image of Alyson or a member of her family? How would I feel? I had thought about and examined these issues before, in therapy, over coffee with friends. I had researched the Internet as well as the library and local bookstores, looking for perspectives from "other" mothers. Another couple we knew suggested we attend a PLOP meeting, Parenting/Pregnant Lesbians of Portland. (I kid you not.) The hosts' house was a sea of kids and lesbians. I had never seen such a gathering. I became enamored of a little girl, approximately four years of age. She was blonde, blue-eyed, a boisterous mini-me of her mother. I said to Alyson, "See, genetics do matter." I learned later that her birth mother had been the older woman sitting shyly at the dining room table, the one with brown hair, brown eyes.

Three baby showers were thrown in our honor. Much was made of the belly. It wasn't that I felt envy, rather, apart. Alyson and I had traveled so many roads together, but this was different. This required dissimilar roles, conjured disparate emotions. I wasn't sure of my role. I feared a playing out of stereotypes, ones we had inherited. I wasn't the "father." I hadn't gotten my wife pregnant. (Our contractor Kate, when she heard the news, looked at me and said, "You old dog.") I got very offended when two good friends said, "Way to go, Dad." There are lesbians who do call themselves Dad, but that wasn't for me, that wasn't what I needed or wanted. Also, I didn't want to feel like the nanny. I was very afraid of rejection. Alyson knows me well (at times, much better than I know myself) and could sense my apprehensions. She made a point of using inclusive language—our baby, our pregnancy, our labor, our parenting—and of complimenting me anytime she received a flat-tering remark. She truly is my partner, in every sense of the word. We agreed that we would be open to what comes, to let language, roles, parenting styles develop organically, on our terms. We would continue to draft our script.

On the hospital tour, we were the only lesbian couple. The tour guide insisted on repeating, "The father will sleep here on a cot next to the mother's bed. The father cannot store his beer in the room fridge. The father will not be served food. The father will . . ." Hello! We're standing right in front of you! Know your audience. I had even asked a question in which I referenced our partnership. It was as disrespectful for us as it was for the lone single woman in the group. We felt very uncomfortable and understood better why most lesbians try to give birth at home. We actually ended up hir-ing a doula to help facilitate interactions with hospital staff, frankly to guard against any inappropriateness or tension that might occur based upon the fact that we were two moms. Nothing like hear-ing a fag joke while you're pushing. We also were the only lesbian couple in the birthing class, which didn't bother me until a father-to-be made a point of talking about the "husband stitch" (ha ha ha). Alyson didn't get the joke. I had to explain that the husband stitch would help to shrink the vagina post-labor and post-pregnancy, to ensure maximum penis pleasure. Ewww. The instructor looked at us and laughed nervously.

Fear and anxiety were not my sole emotions. I was filled with tremendous love and respect for Alyson, for the choices we were making and had made, for the life we had built and were building, together. I was filled with raw hope and wonder. Having just lost a mother and now about to become one, I marveled at the life cycle, at mortality, at the blessings I had been given and those to come.

The contractions started at eleven at night. Hours earlier we had gotten home from our second-to-last birthing class. Alyson had felt uncomfortable all day and jokingly asked our instructor, "What are some things that induce labor?" She listed a few including pine-apple and cohosh tea. We knew we had pineapple in the fridge, so when we got home we had a few bites. We settled into bed to read the three thousand books we had been given on pregnancy (*The Penultimate Guide to Lesbian Pregnancy*, *The Ultimate Guide to Lesbian Pregnancy*, *The Irreverent Guide to Lesbian Pregnancy*, oh, and *What to Expect When You're Expecting: The "Lesbians Not Included" Guide to Heterosexual Pregnancy*). After an hour, Alyson turned to me and said, "We need to go to sleep *now*, it may be a long night," and clicked off the light. At three in the morning, we called our doula to prepare her. At five, we called the hospital to let them know we would be coming in. At seven, we got in the car and Alyson was in the zone, nearly beyond my reach. On the way, Rachmaninoff played on the radio. I tried to focus her attention. The contractions were coming every two minutes. When we arrived at Kaiser, she was five centimeters dilated.

Hospitals scared me. I associated them with loss. My friend Habiba had counseled me to remember that there was reason and purpose to pain, what she had learned intimately during her own labor. I held on to that thought as we entered the ward and were greeted by Beth, our midwife. She smiled gently, said "you're doing great," and led us to our room. I knew everything would be okay.

Our first phone call was to Marlene, our attorney. "Congratulations! I've been waiting!" She needed to initiate the documentation that would ensure my name was on the birth certificate, ensure that I would be recognized as Grady's parent. It would take at least six months. And once completed I could opt to go to the judge's chambers to have him bang the gavel and officially declare me sane and sound and Grady's mom. At first, we thought about making the trip downtown, perhaps having a ceremony on site, but then we thought harder. How demeaning to have someone you don't know tell you that you are a parent. I had had enough degradation and dehumanization after our marriage was deemed void. Our second call was to our therapists, who all cried on the phone, reiterated how proud they were of us, how they thought we were pioneers. (Therapist as parent?) We then contacted our family and friends, who sent flowers and enough food for the first year and came to visit.

Visitors continue to arrive nearly nine months later and we are so thankful for their presence in our lives. My brother has sent box after box of toys, hand-me-downs, black-and-white photographs of us as children. He listens eagerly and empathetically to my stories about sleepless nights, diaper rash, gas grins. My father stayed for nearly a week, his first trip to Portland, and couldn't stop holding his grandson and telling his daughter-in-law how much he loved and missed her. He likes to remind us that the baby is his spitting image (bald, blue-eyed).

There are days I look down and swear I see my mother's hands, changing Grady's diaper, caressing his face. Days, I hear Stephen's laughter as if he's in the nursery with us playing. I feel them with me, my angel guides, and am grateful for their eternal lessons, undying memory, Grady's legacy.

As he drinks from his bottle, Grady reaches for my fingers. I see his smile behind the plastic nipple. I can't help but smile in return. I love his weight in my arms, the weight of all these moments.

★ **MARY WARREN FOULK** is a writer and educator who lives in Portland, Oregon, with her amazing wife, Alyson, and their beautiful son, Grady. She loves being a parent and never realized how deeply challenging, moving, fun it could be. When not doing laundry or attempting to put a onesie on a fidgety baby, she enjoys exploring the incredible views of the Pacific Northwest, critiquing lesbian movies, and attempting to read something other than an anxiety-provoking parenting guide.

Mommy Maybe . . .

CHRIS MURPHY

On the Saturday before Christmas, I had a lazy day. I watched sappy holiday movies, read a quirky chick-lit novel, snacked on ice cream and microwave popcorn, and reveled in the fact that at three in the afternoon I'd neither showered nor changed out of my pajamas. A week prior I had completed a two-year writing program that culminated in a master's degree, and this reprieve was my reward. My husband was away while I'd frantically prepared for the holiday, and I'd grown weary of shoving through panicked shoppers and potentially unwanted gifts amid department store aisles. But my shopping was finally done, the cards sent, the bird purchased and ready for roasting. I'd done it all with the intention that on December 23 I was not going to leave my apartment or fight one more painfully long line. I basked in my space and the background noise I chose to surround myself with that day. Part of me felt guilty for indulging, for not tending to anyone or anything. But that didn't stop me from luxuriously wrapping myself in a blanket and snuggling up in the freedom of it all.

As I lay there, all comfy in my self-made nest for one, my eyes strayed above the entertainment center to the Christmas card photos lined up on top. The cards were from my old girlfriends, the ones I rarely talk to, the ones whose faces are notably absent from the photos they now send. I see only their children's faces, two by two, smiling back at me. It's not that I don't enjoy their adorable little mugs, but where have my friends gone?

Since my friends had their babies, our paths are continually diverging and picking up speed. I imagine these women, now primarily known as "Mommy," running around their single-family homes, chasing after bobbing heads and stubby legs, playing with building blocks, making meal after meal, and pushing for naptime. These friends live in suburban sprawl on the East Coast, I in a garden apartment in the West. They each have two kids. I have two cats. They plan details for their kids—Gymboree, playdates, nutritionally balanced meals, and cleanup time. I plan for Italian classes I'll take, self-imposed writing deadlines, details of upcoming travel, and takeout.

Recently, I heard a phrase recounted, from a friend, that is simple but true: "There is a difference between those who have children and those who do not." At this point, I am definitely of the *do not* variety.

Christmas day and my thirty-seventh birthday arrived. My husband and I normally spend the holidays in Florida with relatives, but this year we were strapped for cash and couldn't make the trip. Some parts of not being there are a blessing. Last year my mother gave me a giant box of lingerie, complete with hot pink thong underwear and see-through frilly teddies. I pulled out each lacy garment as though I were a magician pulling scarves out of a hat, astonished at the faux silk slipping through my fingertips. "To give you a little shove in the right direction," my mother giggled while the rest of my family looked on with cheeks as blushed as my own. With my absence this Christmas my mother couldn't embarrass me publicly. But I should have known she'd find a way. This year I was passed around via telephone receiver, speaking to each family member gathered around the holiday table until my messages of merriment were halted by my brother Mike.

"So you're how old now?" Mike asked me. "Thirty-seven? Let's see, that gives you three more years. Better get on it."

"Get on it" referred to the baby train I've considered riding, but for which I have never actually purchased a seat. Mike told me he was speaking for my mother, who has been waiting patiently for years and now resorted to sending the message by proxy.

Honestly, I hadn't had much pressure lately, from my friends or my family. I'd assumed they'd all but given up, so this upfront confrontation was refreshing coming from my brother, who normally didn't care at all. It's funny how no one ever pressures *him*. He's forty-six, childless, and unmarried. I'm sure he's taken his fair share of pressure to get down the aisle, but he'll never be pressed for time in the baby department. The running-out-of-time phenomenon is reserved for women. Our eggs simply have a limited shelf life. Men on the other hand can plant their seeds and procreate until they die. Look at Michael Douglas. Wasn't he a new papa when he was pushing sixty?

After I laughed to myself at Mike's comment and messenger status, I couldn't help thinking about the enjoyment of my lazy day. If I had a baby, there would be no days like that, no more time that would truly be my own. Writing would be difficult, especially in those early, mind-numbing, no-sleep kind of years. I've heard stories from my friends about them losing their thoughts, identity, and sanity in those early years with baby. And yet, they endured. I suppose I could too. Since I'm at that age of give-birth-or-shrivel-up, which is extreme but the message I'm getting, I feel the pressure of planning for an event that may or may not happen. Planning requires a list of questions and contingencies on my part, especially for my potential maternity. The questions I've devised are not about if I simply *want* a baby. I'm pretty sure I do. They are about my qualifications as a mother, whether or not I could handle motherhood. This I don't know at all.

In our earlier post-college years, my three closest friends and I never talked about kids. It seemed that our immediate goals did not invite babies or the dream of domesticity. We wanted to get out into the world, working women with strong supportive men at our sides, men who would share the housework, cook the occasional meal, and celebrate our achievements the same way we celebrated theirs. We wanted to work for a life of freedom and travel, not settle down into the depths of predictable suburbia. We couldn't foresee the chores of motherhood or the lackluster of parenting. None of the baby commercials on primetime TV or the church arguments for procreation or the gaggles of articles on the joys of motherhood could convince us that being a mom was inevitably a rite of passage. We thought that motherhood may one day be our destiny, but we first wanted the knowledge gained through life experience that we felt was a prerequisite to teach another human being to be curious about the world and to be as fiercely independent as we were. At least this is how I thought we all felt.

In our twenties, my friends and I were becoming women in Washington DC, pursuing careers, promising mates, and, well, fun. We were women who sought out the best in ourselves and the best in one another. We labored long hours at the office and reveled in new positions and increased pay. We worked out, kept up with politics, called Mom on Sundays, and depended on each other to support the ground we stood on. We got riled up discussing our neurotic bosses, our incessantly nagging mothers, impending wars, and the state of the world. We read the *Washington Post*, indulged in glossy magazines, and swapped around the latest John Grisham books. We were women who were curious about the way other people lived and were accepting of all walks, to each his or her own.

We were primed for marriage, the shared-support-and-friendship kind, and the idea of "forever after" dominated our thoughts. By the age of twenty-seven, all three of my friends got married but continued pursuing their careers. Katie would marry first, and go on to own her own pet-sitting business and triple her clientele in a year. Laura's nuptials soon followed, after which she went on to pursue a master's degree and land a job as a research analyst at a software company. Julie would marry next and thrive in a new position as a traffic manager at an ad agency. I was a bridesmaid in all of their weddings, but left after the receptions, disillusioned in my job working for trade associations, and without even a boyfriend in the mix.

I decided to move home to Florida to be closer to my parents and to start a new job as a corporate meeting planner and a life independent of my friends. It was as though I had married off my own children, for they were like the air I breathed, absolutely necessary to my existence. But I had to revel in their happiness from far away while trying to create a path for myself. Within a month of arriving in Florida, I met my love. Three years later I married him, my new best friend, and allowed my parents to breathe a sigh of relief.

After the honeymoon, we moved to California. My new husband was just like my friends—adventurous, spontaneous, fearless. He was looking for an agent to boost his comedy career. I was looking to recreate myself. He encouraged me to pursue long-buried dreams—"You want to work for yourself? Then do it"—and I started my own meeting-planning business. It took a while for either of us to make even the smallest income. We commiserated our losses and celebrated our gains, worked from a makeshift home office in our living room, and dreamed of the day we'd have a second bedroom. While we were scraping by and charting a course, my friends were onto their next step.

They were all around thirty when they got the itch. Julie was the first, and I remember she cried when she got the news that she was pregnant. She and her husband had started trying that month and she never thought it, the big "it," would happen so soon. She'd confided in me that her freedom was taken away much sooner than she'd planned. A couple months before baby was born, her husband accepted a job in Florida. She left her pending promotion, and they bought their first house in a country club subdivision in Orlando.

Katie was next and didn't get so lucky with the first-try thing. After two years of no luck, they gave up, stopped the hormonal supplements, the doctor visits, and the worry. She kept repeating her mantra to me over the phone: "I don't want to be an old mom." But when she decided to stop trying, she became pregnant with a baby girl, who became my goddaughter.

Laura would struggle the most. She had laboriously planned the arrival of her child, taking all the proper steps—be off the pill for at least a year, quit smoking, lower her stress level. But when she decided that all was in place, no baby came. She was devastated. She prayed a lot. She tried fertility pills and something called sperm spinning. She checked into adoption and artificial insemination. All options proved unfruitful or prohibitively expensive. After two years they took a break, but within a year began the process all over again with new doctors and a new set of disappointments. I remember her muffled cry over the telephone, like a wounded animal, each time her period would arrive. She couldn't bear the pain, nor the words of her mother vibrating in her head: *You're not getting any younger you know.*

Laura was given hope. She was notified of a previously misdiagnosed condition called endometriosis, that if removed, could make it easier for her to conceive. She had the surgery and received shots as part of her recovery, which temporarily put her thirty-year-old body into menopause. Hot flashes, sleepless nights, and mood swings; no baby to hold, just the mock end of menstruation, as though her young body were on the fast track to senior citizenship. She bore the six-month process, and when it was over she was told not to expect anything right away. But within a couple of months, first time out after her normal cycle returned, Laura became pregnant and achieved the long-awaited glow of motherhood. After all the due diligence, the hand-wringing, the hard life questions, Laura was finally promoted to Mommy.

I listened to my friends' baby struggles, but I never quite understood their angst. This is where the divergence began, the difference between those who *know* they want to be mothers, and those who don't. I've always arrived late, from the time that I was born it seems. I was my mother's fifth child, surprising her pregnant at the age of thirty-nine. I arrived nine days late, induced just *after* Christmas dinner. Of the four of us friends, I was the last to fall in love, the last to marry, the last to finish school, and of course, the last to have a child, and when and if that will happen is still a debatable point.

Kids? Sure I want them someday, but I'm not sure when that day will arrive. In my seven years of marriage, I've only seriously considered the job of Mommy once and the moment was brief. I was thirty-three at the time. My father had just passed away, and I was confused. On a long walk a couple days after the funeral, I turned to my husband and said, "I want to move back home to Florida and have a baby." I remember feeling immediately proud of such an absolute statement. But it was a farce, a trickery of grief and denial. I wanted to fill the emptiness of death with the fullness of life. And even as my husband, trying to be supportive, readily agreed, I quickly changed my mind. The resolution of the statement dissolved as soon as it came on. I didn't want a new life. I wanted the old one that was just lost.

With my hasty baby plot vaporized, I began a search for a new kind of baby that year and its name was New York City. I proposed the venture to my husband while on vacation, where among the madness of midtown Manhattan, I simply said, "We should live here." And he replied instantly "Yes!" He could pursue stage time in the city and work the road; I could follow a new voice that told me to write while still keeping my previously secured freelance job. Just what we needed, just what I needed—a place to immerse myself and seek out what's next. Six months later we traded in our meager savings to pay four month's rent in a five-hundred-square-foot sub-let in the East Village, and made the cross-country move. While my friends were birthing their babies, I was emerging from the Lincoln Tunnel on my way to another adventure, and I felt proud of that fact, freer than I've ever felt.

My friends couldn't imagine my life, one with so little security and so little an apartment. I couldn't imagine theirs, with mort-gages and the knowledge of how it feels to create life inside them. I couldn't imagine responsibility for a tiny hand. They couldn't imag-ine what I did all day. My friends seemed to grow up while I glori-ously remained a kid, taking in the world one crowded street at a time. The ring on my finger extended my hand to seek out whom-ever I wanted to be. I took writing classes and attempted to teach myself how to play guitar. Every few days my husband and I would discover a new museum or a hidden secret garden. Everything was perfect, and when I got that crazy feeling, the little fluttering in my belly where a baby could possibly be, I buried it. *This is my time*, I kept telling myself. At the age of thirty-five I created another step. I would go to graduate school, a decision that allowed me to keep warding off the mommy question while I finished off my degree.

When my friends became mothers for the second time, we began to talk less frequently. When we do, we usually end up reminiscing about old times, since that is where our commonality lies. They no longer ask when I'm taking the plunge. They probably figured that since I've passed thirty-five, my options are limited anyway. Just thinking about conceiving now has me envisioning myself as "the old mom," what Katie so feared being. And when Julie told me about a childless friend of hers who she said was too selfish to be a mother, I couldn't help but wonder if I was selfish too.

Questions of myself keep arising. No absolutes, just questions. What could I possibly teach a child? Am I smart enough? How will a child affect my marriage? My career? Me, me, me? Maybe I am that selfish girl. But, I'm not taking away from a child who doesn't even exist, am I? I'm simply questioning my own intentions.

When the time came, my three fabulous friends seemed prepared to commit to motherhood. They all had a row of ducks that quacked in unison—ducks in the form of money-market accounts, husbands with jobs and benefits, thirty-year mortgages, good school districts, and homes with playrooms and backyards.

My husband and I have never had any of these things. We are self-employed with income that arrives in large doses or small trickles. We have mounting debt, loads of frequent-flyer miles, journals full of thoughts, a crowded rented apartment, and each other's hand to hold. We live month to month, day to day, moment to moment. We don't have backup plans or "what if" scenarios. We confront life as it arrives and plan for the next big trip.

It's only recently, since I've finished my final degree, made the right steps to begin a new career, and find myself inching closer to forty, that I'm starting to hear the incessant call that my friends answered long ago. "Someday" is now followed up with a question of "when." But it's not like a job offer is on the table and I need only make a call to accept, it's more like the independent business that I began years ago; you have to make a plan and go after it. But timelines and to do lists seem wholly inadequate to prepare for the unknown.

My whole adult life has been about justifying my capabilities in résumé form to get a job, in essay form to get into graduate school, in compatibility testing to get married in the Catholic church. I need to consider why I would make a good mother, be able to justify it, to my husband, to my family, to my creator, to myself. What makes me think I could handle the job and all its duties, me, a person who enjoys spur-of-the-moment travel, long nights drinking wine, reading leisurely for hours, making love to my husband in the afternoon? Will my marriage be able to take constant pressure from another? Will I fade away, cease to exist, as my child takes center stage? Will the answers present themselves in time?

Some people seem to think that parenthood can be sold as the dream job and that they are just the headhunters to do so. For example, a couple of months ago we met up with some of my husband's high school buddies while on a trip to his hometown, all of them blessed with children. I made the error of telling one of the wives that we're considering having a baby. Word spread through the bar that night like a tornado through a tunnel. We weren't prepared for the bevy of arms ready to embrace us. We were soon caught up in a chorus line of "about time," accompanied by pats on the back. These mommies and daddies united at once, joined forces to yank us into baby oblivion. "Parenthood is so rewarding," they said with reminiscent eyes and cunning grins. "You've got to do it." I was flabbergasted by how all these seemingly normal humans instantly turned into opportunistic salespeople at the mere possibility of a full womb.

One by one, a woman would sit next to me and describe how motherhood changes your life, how once you get through the first year, "it's cake." I explained that we are trying to prepare, waiting for the time to be right. "The best-laid plans never work out with a kid," one of them said with her arm around my shoulder. "You never know what you're gonna get."

These couples told us it is our responsibility to bring a child into the world; that we're going to produce a well-behaved kid who will turn into a productive, well-behaved adult. How in the world can they know how our kid will turn out? Do they know what terrors my husband and I were to *our* parents? The thought of raising someone like me, a snotty little girl with a tendency to scream at her mother *"leave me alone!"* is terrifying. How would I deal with a mini-me? Will I be able to use my own experience to teach the kid some manners, teach her to respect her elders, her classmates, herself, me? Isn't there some test I can take, some kind of certification exam that rates my maternal skill? *You're running out of time.*

Time is coming at me like a fist banging on a window. At any moment the glass will break. There is never a good time to have a child, I tell myself. Jobs and plans, poor economic situations tend to get in the way. But I keep hearing voices telling me *just do it, jump in, take a chance.* How can our friends be so sure, when I'm not? I remember marriage as a huge step, a lifelong commitment that began after the wedding. I was prepared to spend my life with my husband; I know him. But in entering the realm of motherhood, I'd go in blindly—*you never know what you're gonna get.*

I remember saying aloud in my mid-twenties, a year or so before I met my husband, that I could die happy tomorrow—happy, except I'd never fallen in love. Time could have left me stranded. But love arrived when I least expected it and led me to the joy of sharing my life with another. I've since forgotten all the empty dating dilemmas, how painful it was each time another relationship ended, how when I finally met the man for me all that inner turmoil disappeared. Love came when the time was right, when I was ready to receive it. Could the same be true for a baby?

These voices and questions continue to collide, and I'm waiting for answers. Maybe they'll never come. But I'm in love, content, and fulfilled. I could die happy tomorrow—happy, except I've never had a child.

★ **CHRIS MURPHY** recently graduated with her MFA degree in Creative Writing from Antioch University. She is currently writing a book-length memoir involving social identity and the process of emerging from grief. She is a volunteer for WriteGirl, an organization that fosters young women writers, and plans meetings and events for nonprofit groups. She lives in Los Angeles with her husband and their two cats, George and Simone.

No Kitty Crack, Leather Diaper Bags, or Little Black (White) Babies

KERSHA SMITH

I am thirty-three, happily married, financially stable, and childless, and at this point in my life I am okay with that. I'm not completely opposed to children. On the contrary I think someday I would like to have a baby . . . one at the very least . . . someday. As my biological clock beckons, it presses me to imagine the experience of carrying a child and basking in the glow of pregnancy. Once I forget the pain of labor I am sure I will gain immense joy from taking our child to museums and sitting in the audience of our progeny's first dance recital or basketball game. But to be quite honest, I am not there yet. Even with the ticking clock and the mounting societal pressure, I have failed to become fully comfortable with the idea of bearing a child.

While my husband and I are in no hurry to have a child, it's almost as if there is a kid-free grace period for couples. It's very short, though. After the second or third year of marriage, people expect you take it to the next level and procreate. These looming expectations don't come from my husband, since he essentially shares my ambivalence. Even our families have been pretty cool about letting us live our lives without the pressure of little ones.

It's actually random people, people whose opinions in all actuality shouldn't matter, who pick, prod, question, and get me going.

At work everyone always asks me when I'm going to have a baby, as if it is the natural order of events. They inquire with a mixture of wonderment and judgment. I can almost hear them saying, *What's wrong with this girl? She has a husband who loves her. She has a secure job, a PhD for God's sake, why is she waiting?* In some ways I feel guilty, almost puerile, simply saying, "I am not ready." The times I do say this, my reply is typically met with the standard retort, "No one is ever ready." Thus I've moved on to more practical defenses like, "I just started my career," or "It's just my husband and me and we don't have family here." These seem to garner more sympathy and prevent me from looking "underdeveloped."

The fact that my husband and I don't have any family here in New York is not just an excuse I use to quell interrogation; it is a very real concern that has definitely influenced my feelings about parenthood. I was fortunate enough to be raised by a host of aunts, uncles, cousins, neighbors, and family friends. It makes me sad to think that if we were to have a child, he or she would not be cradled by a gaggle of extended family. Both my husband's and my own family are thousands of miles away, so the most we can ask for by way of closeness is extended summer stays, Christmas and Thanksgiving visits, and Sunday morning telephone conversations. This is unfortunate because I have such fond memories of waking up on Saturday mornings, running down the stairs, and seeing my mom and grandma sitting at the dining room table chatting over coffee. As a young girl, skinny legs and all, my aunts and uncles were forever picking me up to go to their basketball games and track meets. And I know for a fact that afternoon shopping and lunch dates with granny were the stuff of real girlfriends and have helped shape the woman I am today.

With our biological families far way, we've created a circle of friends who have become our surrogate family. Essentially they are our fictive kin, play brothers and sisters, whom we have come to love and respect. Many by and large are just like us, burgeoning adults and couples, who are in the throes of navigating and contemplating life's big decisions. Most of our close friends in New York remain childless. For better or worse, our lives are devoid of kids. My husband has a larger contingent of friends with children, but his circle is much smaller than that of most married men. For me I can count on one hand the number of friends who have children. What's more interesting is that I have noticed that being surrounded by friends who do not have children reduces my pressure to have one.

In some ways I think New York creates the illusion of youth, so no matter if you're twenty-five or forty-five you can still engage life fully sans the emblematic trajectory of school, marriage, house, and children. Here you can be educated, have a good job, yet forever be relegated to writing out that monthly rent check. The simple fact is that life, especially in a place like New York, may not progress in a stereotypically linear way.

For example, the possibility of owning a house can remain elusive. The volatile nature of New York's housing market has been difficult to get used to for this Chi Town native. After moving to the Big Apple I had friends in Chicago who were purchasing their second or third home by the time I had moved out of the seven-hundred-square-foot Park Slope fourth-floor walkup that I shared with a roommate. When my husband and I moved into a third-floor two-bedroom brownstone, my newly constructed (New York) schema had me thinking that I had moved into a mansion (a brownstone, what, and it was well over eleven hundred square feet!), but when my girlfriends came to visit me for our wedding they looked worried. I told them what we were paying in rent and they all but thought that I had lost my mind. They didn't understand and still don't. If you don't carry the love for New York in your heart, most of the grind that characterizes this city seems silly. For those of us in love with its allure, we're okay with forfeiting homeownership if that means that we can live in a place that nourishes our soul. Thus for many of us, rent is a reality and until we can get membership into the home proprietor's club, it is what it is. Therefore the cycle continues, and as our linear movement toward homeownership gets interrupted, so too does our movement toward parenthood.

For me however life in this crazy city is not the only culprit molding my ambivalence about motherhood. If I were being completely honest I would have to reveal that a lot of my maternal energy gets sublimated onto our cat, Malik. We have had him for close to thirteen years. He was a birthday present from my husband—at the time just a boyfriend—who realized his girl missed her family cat, Shorty. I suppose I do with Malik some of the things that mothers do with their own children. For instance, I take hundreds of pictures of him in "cute" (or at least "cute" to his mother) positions. Thankfully they remain the private stock of our family photos. I have never had the gumption to send them out as funny emails or donned him in a red and white Santa hat and christen him our official Christmas card. I have, nonetheless, done other things that one might qualify as maternal. Right now as I type he is happily playing with his catnip toy. He has a couple; one is shaped like a carrot, the other like a lemon. I only buy fruit- and vegetable-shaped catnip toys for Malik because I care about his nutrition. No table scraps or "kitty crack" for our little guy. At one point we bragged that Malik was a vegetarian. We touted to friends and family about how he only eats cat food that is free of meat and contains the right amounts of crude proteins, fats, and fiber. When we took him to the veterinarian, we explained our cruelty-free diet, and the cat doc all but laughed in our face. He reminded us that cats by nature are carnivores.

Now before a picture of a crazy cat lady is constructed, let me disrupt that idea. First and foremost I'm into Malik, but to a point. Unlike most mothers I have no compunctions about leaving him for extended periods of time. He's used to it. I think by now he knows that when the suitcases come out mommy and daddy are about to leave. At this point it is relatively easy for us to travel, and we have mastered the art of packing. Right now we can comfortably travel for at least two weeks with just two suitcases and a carry-on. There is no need for us to worry about diaper bags, limited amounts of breast milk that potentially get flagged at security checkpoints, or crying babies that are sensitive to changes in altitude. We get to travel a lot, and we can financially do a lot of things that I presume might be cut short if we had another mouth to feed, or a college fund to think about. Life without children, so I have been told, equates to freedom. Everyone says, "Just wait, when you have a child, your whole life will change!" This does not put me at ease.

On a more serious note, it's scary to think about the time and energy that goes into raising a socially conscious, emotionally stable child. Parenting is hard work, and although your parents may not dictate who you become, they definitely help shape it. I want to be a good parent. Every fiber of my being would want our child to be the best person he or she could be. Like all mothers, I would want his or her life to be full of opportunities and free of hardships. I would hope that our child's uniqueness would be characterized as an asset and that he or she would honor their person even when they question and struggle with it.

It is possible that because our child will be biracial he or she would struggle with his or her identity, but I hope that my husband and I will have the wherewithal to help him or her navigate, with integrity, this aspect of their self. If and when they struggle I hope we can effectively communicate how we have all struggled at one time or another with our identities. I think I'll be ready to speak from my heart and from my mind, retelling stories about my teen years interweaving William Cross's Nigrescence theory and Erik Erikson's eight stages of psychosocial development. I hope to teach them that identity is complex and that figuring out who we are is by and large how we come to know and appreciate ourselves.

The simple fact remains though, your caregivers affect how you see yourself and the world, and in that notion I find comfort. I feel blessed by the love and friendship I have built with my husband. I can proudly say that I feel no more or less Black in being with him. We both have very healthy relationships with our racial identities and have not felt the need to compromise this fabric of ourselves. Neither my husband nor I revel in a colorblind ideology. We have no illusions about the ways in which the world is constructed. We both believe that race is a lived experience and has a role in shaping one's identity. We have open and honest conversations about critiquing the privileges race affords certain individuals. We also try our best to fight against those social structures that create disenfranchisement. But outside the sanctuary of our minds' ideology and of our home (and sometimes within), remains a world full of racism and marginalization. We are nowhere near the pluralism that might assuage the concern I have about our potential child or all the children who might become victim to racism and race privilege. So even with all the gains our country has made in disrupting certain aspects of racism and marginalization, I still cannot be relaxed in my thinking about this matter.

Perhaps my concerns are typical, and all parents worry about paving a way for their child. I suppose we all hope the world accepts our children in all the fabulous glory we see them possessing. Maybe my contemplation gives me a sense of agency, and the true beauty of choice is one's ability to reflect on it. Perhaps my ambivalence is healthy and it gives me time and space to make one of the biggest decisions that I will make in my life. Whatever it is, I hope there comes a time when I can safely land and resolve the uncertainty, but until that day I will continue to vacillate . . . and I am okay with that.

★ **KERSHA SMITH, PhD,** is the chair of the Psychology Department at the College of New Rochelle, School of New Resources in Brooklyn, New York. Her current research interests involve the nature of transformative learning. In addition to teaching and writing, she likes to spend time traveling with her husband, James.

A Pellet of Poison
I Don't Want to Feed Racism to My Children the Way My Mother Fed It to Me

EILEEN FLANAGAN

One morning two years ago, I awoke suddenly angry at my dying mother.

To take my mind off caregiving, I had rented the film *Restaurant* about a White bartender who can't escape his dead father's racism. Although he dates Black women and defends a Black co-worker, the bartender faces his own prejudice when, in a moment of rage and grief, he punches a Black teenager and calls him a "nigger" in front of their shocked co-workers. The film triggered my own memory of shock the one time I heard my White mother use "the *n*-word." It was the first time I was asked out on a date by a Black man.

I never gave in to my mother's admonitions not to date men of color, though I never actually married any of the men she objected to, either. I was 99 percent sure her objections were not the reason those relationships didn't last, but the morning after seeing *Restaurant*, that 1 percent of doubt felt like a pellet of poison that rose up in my throat. I was happily married with two children and suddenly furious about a fight with my mother twenty-five years before. I knew morphine and an oxygen mask weren't likely to improve our communication about race, which had never been easy. I tried to forgive her and focus on the many positive legacies she left me.

A month after my mother's death I stumbled onto the book *Learning to Be White* by a Universalist minister named Thandeka. Quoting the childhood memories of White adults, Thandeka argues that White children learn to conform to the segregationist expectations of their families and communities in order to be accepted, a process that leads Whites to feel shame about their own White identity. The book gave me a little more compassion for my mother, who had grown up in a heavily Irish neighborhood where dating Italians was taboo. My schooling and friendships had been more diverse than hers, but I understood the threat of being disowned for crossing the race line. It made me grateful that my children's experience was different.

But when I mentioned this to a Black friend, he asked, "What makes you think it's different?"

"Because I'm different from my mother," I answered smugly.

He said, "Hmm," with just enough doubt in his face to shift my focus from what my mother had learned about race to what my children were learning.

A few nights later my children and I were spinning the globe, discussing whatever country our fingers landed on. When my six-year-old son hit Russia, he exclaimed, "That's where Julia is from! She was adopted." Then, remembering there were two Julias in first grade, he added, "The white Julia, not the brown Julia."

With *Learning to Be White* fresh in my mind I asked, "Do you think of people in those terms, "who has white skin and who has brown skin?"

"Kind of," he shrugged, as if it were just another category, like boys and girls, or first graders and third graders.

What struck me was the speed with which my nine-year-old daughter interjected, "Not me!" She had already asked me about *Learning to Be White*, and had been horrified to hear that some children grew up segregated from other races. "Ashley is my friend, and no one could tell me we couldn't be friends just because our skin color is different," she added emphatically. Ironically, she had vehemently denied that she thought of people in racial categories and a breath later had named a Black classmate to prove her point. A typical White liberal, I thought.

At least my children are not learning to be segregationists like the kids in *Learning to Be White*. They go to a diverse school, have diverse friends, and read diverse books. Still, my daughter's vehement denial made me realize that she's absorbed more than just tolerance. She's also learned that it is taboo for a liberal White girl to acknowledge the racial categories so clearly at work in the world.

I recalled a moment four years earlier when my daughter's kindergarten was reading the Addy series about a girl who escapes from slavery with her mother. One day my daughter begged me to read *Happy Birthday, Addy!* on the bus, which we were taking while our car was in the shop. We happened to be on the chapter where Addy gets kicked off a Philadelphia trolley for being "colored," a passage I read very quietly on a Philadelphia bus in which we were the only Whites, not to mention the only people making noise at 7:30 AM. I raised my voice a bit and added, "Isn't it great your school is teaching you about injustice in kindergarten!" I felt like an idiot. Rationally, I knew the people around us would figure out it was a children's story; still, I felt self-conscious.

In hindsight I wonder if my daughter noticed my discomfort on the bus. It's not that I consider racism a taboo topic, by any means. I teach a class on South African history and discuss race with Black friends. Still, like many Whites, I become cautious when race comes up with strangers of a different race. There's a lurking fear of being misunderstood, accused of being racist, maybe being unconsciously racist, like the *Restaurant* bartender. I remember my cringe when my daughter, at four, asked loudly in the vicinity of a Black woman on a cigarette break if people with brown skin smoked cigarettes more than people with white skin. Today I wonder what my daughter has picked up from such cringes over the years: a healthy sensitivity toward a legitimately sensitive topic, or the shame identified in *Learning to Be White*?

At first Thandeka's concept of White shame didn't quite ring true to me. After all, I didn't shun Black friends as a child or join a segregated fraternity in college, like many of those interviewed for the book. I dated Black men, despite the objections of my mother, which does help me understand the process the book describes. If I had left a man I loved because of my mother's objections I might be filled with shame too, but those relationships failed on their own merits. I didn't quite buy Thandeka's implication that all White Americans feel this shame.

Still, the longer I sat with her thesis, the more truth I saw in it. It's hard to imagine any of my White friends wanting to celebrate White History Night the way we celebrate Black History Night at school, and not just because White history is already in the curriculum. Much of the history that binds Americans of varied European backgrounds is shameful, which is part of Thandeka's point. In fact, she argues, Whites find it painful to even think of themselves as White (as opposed to Irish or Italian). As evidence, she cites the difficulty Whites have in playing the "Race Game," an exercise where for an entire week we're asked to use the adjective "White" whenever we refer to a person of European descent. Her point is that Whites often describe others in racial terms, but never themselves. To say "my White friend Julia" makes us uncomfortable, even though we might say, "my Black friend Julia" without thinking. My own glimpse of this came when a Black writer friend convinced me that "Black" and "White" should be capitalized, since they represent distinct cultural groups, and I found it easier to capitalize the *B* than the *W*.

My children never speak of themselves as White, though I'm beginning to realize how their racial identity affects their perception of the world. One night at dinner, after the globe incident, my daughter mentioned a classroom presentation on slavery, which led my two children to speculate on how nice they would have been to their slaves had they ever had any. When I explained that there was no such thing as owning someone nicely, they switched to the word "servant" and assured me that if they ever had servants they would pay them really well and let them have lots of time off. (My son added that he would like to have a butler, but when he gave the job description it sounded suspiciously like what I already do for free.)

What struck me, and what I pointed out to them, was that they were both assuming that they would be the owners/employers, not the slaves/servants. When I asked them to imagine *being* a slave and hearing someone say, "I'll be really nice to you and let you have some time off," they immediately understood my point. Still, the incident suggested to me that along with tolerance, and maybe even shame, they've also absorbed a sense of entitlement, an assumption that people will serve them, not the other way around.

I don't want my children to expect a privileged life, though that is what they'll probably have. Since reading *Learning to Be White*, I've been steeped in books and articles on racism. More than personal prejudice, I've realized, it is privilege that I've inherited and privilege I'll pass on to my children, whether I intend to or not. Even if they never even think "the *n*-word," my children will still benefit from the institutional racism that is endemic in our country. Like my immigrant grandparents—who worked hard for what they achieved, no doubt—my children will find it easier to find a job, a house, or a cab because of their skin color. Of course I want them to be able to find a job or a house. I want their way to be smooth, just not at anyone else's expense.

And so I'm left with the question of how to teach my children about race in ways that will make the world better, not worse. It would feel good to applaud my daughter when she says she doesn't notice skin color, but I know that's too easy. Numerous studies show that children absolutely do categorize by race, at least by kindergarten, usually earlier; it's just that White children learn to deny it as they progress through elementary school, as my third grader denied what my first grader acknowledged while spinning the globe. Studies show that, by adulthood, many Whites have convinced themselves that they really are colorblind, so they don't notice if they are subtly more friendly to the White job applicants they are interviewing or subtly more mistrustful of the Black boys they are teaching. Like the bartender in *Restaurant*, they don't realize they've swallowed some of their parents' poison.

Actually, I should say "their culture's poison," rather than laying it all on parents, who carry enough guilt. The truth is that even if parents never say anything negative or stereotypical about people of another race, children of all races will observe stereotypes, not only in the media, but in the world around them. They will notice, for example, if most of the doctors and teachers they meet are White, while most of the supermarket cashiers and garbage collectors they see are Black, and they will figure out which jobs carry more status. They might never mention their observations to their parents—especially if the adults around them cringe, the way I cringed when my daughter asked if people with brown skin smoked cigarettes more than people with white skin—but just as most boys learn not to wear dresses by watching the adults around them, most children figure out the racial hierarchy still at work in our country by observing the world we live in.

I'm trying to be more aware of what they notice and more open to processing it with them. When my daughter, at four, made the cigarette comment, I did cringe, but then I asked her about her observation and discussed the places where she had noticed people smoking cigarettes. I pointed out several adults with brown skin she knew who did not smoke, as well as some with white skin who did, feeling grateful that we live in a diverse enough community that I could offer her such personal examples. I concluded that it wasn't a good idea to generalize about people based on their skin color.

Now, a few years further along this journey, I realize how tricky it is to acknowledge the real cultural differences between groups, without falling back on stereotypes. I'm not always sure how to strike this balance with children, who like simple explanations, not college seminars, from their parents. Sometimes it's just easier to punt, like last spring when I took my son to hear the internationally known Morehouse College Glee Club, which was singing at a local Black church. As we were getting ready to go, I told him to put on a nice pair of pants and a shirt with a collar. He looked at me with surprise. "Why? Aren't we just going to a church?"

I thought of the casual attire in my mostly White Quaker meeting and the left-wing church my husband attends. I wanted to say, "Because Black people dress better for church than White people," but I could see this leading to a whole discussion that I just didn't feel like having on the way out the door. I decided it was enough I was bringing him to the Morehouse performance, where rows of sharply dressed Black men sang beautiful harmonies. I was fighting a stereotype, I figured—the image of Black men in handcuffs that so often appears on the Philadelphia evening news—by offering another image to counteract it. That was enough for one day.

I've come to think of racial prejudice as one of the toxins I have to try to protect my children against, like lead or formaldehyde. The problem is that our world is so full of toxic chemicals, a diligent parent could drive themselves crazy with worry. I just heard that there is lead below the surface of the orange glue caps that I've often opened with my teeth when the cap gets glued shut. I felt like throwing up my hands—who would have suspected the glue caps? I felt similarly when someone pointed out to me the racial stereotypes in *The Lion King* movie. Yes, the stupid hyenas in *The Lion King* have African-American voices, while the evil lion has dark skin, and bad me, I let my children watch it. It's exhausting, trying to be a diligent parent, always being on guard against something that could harm my children's bodies or psyches. I've had to accept that I won't be 100 percent successful all of the time. On the chemical front, scientists have gone to the Antarctic to see how far human pollution has traveled. It turns out even the penguins are poisoned.

Although racial stereotypes are widespread and insidious, like toxic chemicals, that doesn't mean we parents are powerless. Just as I try to choose healthy food for my children (without being a total fanatic), I try to feed their minds with the least toxic material I can find—the Morehouse College Glee Club instead of the evening news. Likewise, after reading how saunas help our bodies expel the toxins we are invariably exposed to, I've started sitting in the hot little room at the gym, sweating out the harmful stuff I've inhaled or eaten. Like the penguins, I will never be pure, but I can reduce my toxicity. In the realm of race, I can also face the heat of my family history, sweating out whatever I've absorbed and teaching my children to do the same.

Stories are like saunas that can help draw the poison out of us. In the two years since my mother's death, I've read slave narratives, abolitionist histories, Toni Morrison, and Addy. I've also listened to the struggles of other parents, like the Black friend who fears her son will be unfairly labeled by White teachers, and the White friend who fears her children will learn stereotypes just by driving through a poor Black neighborhood on their way to private school. I know that sharing such stories won't solve the unemployment in the poor neighborhood or make our education system fair. Stories are not enough. But as a writer, I believe honest stories have the power to open hearts, and that's a start.

Eventually I sweated out my own first story about race. As my mother told it, I was about three when a "colored" woman took my hand and stepped onto an elevator with me. Fearing I was being abducted, my mother leaped onto the elevator and took my hand back. The story, like my mother's prejudice, never made sense to me. My mother couldn't explain the woman's motives, or why my mother had stayed silent once on the elevator. But now as a mother myself, there's one piece of her story I understand: My mother was afraid she might lose me. That was always her fear.

I may blame my mother for the way she tried to protect me, or blame those who taught her to be afraid of people who looked different, but in the end, a mother's fear is something I can understand, if not forgive. Perhaps the one difference between us is that I fear, not just for my own children, but also for the Black boy who may be stereotyped in class and for the White girl who may swallow those stereotypes.

★ **EILEEN FLANAGAN'S** publications include *God Raising Us: Parenting as a Spiritual Practice* (Pendle Hill, 2008) and *The Wisdom to Know the Difference* (Tarcher, Fall 2009), a book which offers spiritual tools to discern when to let go and when to stand up for what matters. To learn more about her writing and the workshops she leads, please visit http://www.eileenflanagan.com.

Walking Your Talk

CHARISSE CARNEY-NUNES

Memories are like flash photography. They are disjointed records that play in our minds over and over, which we know (somehow) fit together into our stories. My memory is filled with pearls of wisdom, ironically from my father. "What's fair? Is life fair? Is anything fair?" It was one of his favorite maxims. "If you want an *A* and you're Black in America then you've got to earn an *A+*," was another one that he actually shared with my mother.

All of these flashes from my past have certainly contributed to who I am today. But since I joined the ranks of parenthood a few years ago, the adage that flashes most often in my mind was one of his favorites: "Do as I say, not as I do." Whenever my father threw those words at me, I promised myself I would never grow up to be so hypocritical. I swore I would set an example for my children, that I would always be able to tell them to "do as I *do*!"

Fast-forward from my childhood to the day that my six-year-old queried me as to why I was "allowed" to watch *The Today Show* while National Turn-Off-the-TV Week had her missing her favorite shows. With no other tools at my disposal, I resorted to my father's retort. I must admit that I quite pleased myself when it worked, since quieting a precocious first-grader is certainly no easy task. Yet my quick adoption of this language that I'd sworn would not become part of my parental lexicon caused an uneasy tugging at my nature. I wondered if this all-too-convenient answer was nothing more than a parent's attempt to opt out of that part of parenting that requires responding to difficult questions. Alas, I let the moment pass because, quite simply, I wanted to watch *The Today Show* before work, and I was convinced that if my husband and I could triumph over Disney Channel for one week then we'd somehow be validated as better parents.

Do as I do? Well, it would be okay to fall off course. *Just this one time*, I thought.

I once knew a woman who never fell off course. She always lived by her words. She was almost twenty years my senior, yet her soul was centuries older. When I imagine the wisdom of time, the birthing of nations, the nurturing of young, and the devotion to truth, Andrea's portrait is drawn in my mind. She was the quintessential example of a mothering spirit, yet she'd never birthed a child of her own. Maybe that's part of the reason she was able to stay so true!

Still, she not only walked the walk and talked the talk, but Andrea was committed to *walking her talk*.

Sadly, my model for obedience and faith passed on. She slipped away from this world into the next, arriving, I imagine, triumphant, triumphant over her disease, triumphant over her death. She arrived in that place, I am sure, still donning a crown for her dynamism and devotion to her words.

And as with many spirit queens who went before her, her transition caused the rest of us to reflect. Facing an unwelcome mortality can be a curious experience of "waking up" for the loved ones left behind. So too, for me, was Andrea's passing. As I listened with my left brain to our mutual friend deliver the news of her transition, my right brain selfishly reminded me of mine. *Andrea lived her words*, it admonished me; *she truly practiced what she preached. What about you*, it continued ominously, *are you* really *walking what you talk?*"

"Answering this question," I told my right brain, "is some formidable task." It cannot be mastered within the confines of the written or spoken word. Yet my right brain reminded me that words give such opportunity to express and extol the wonder of our minds that, for me, they were the only place to start.

As I think about Andrea's obedience to her words in the context of my father's adage and my acquiescence to *The Today Show* and conveniences of everyday modern life, I'm unsure. It must be sufficient, if only once in a while, to tell our children to do as we say and not as we do. To the contrary, perhaps our parenting paths must necessarily include a personal journey to do as Andrea did and "walk our talk."

Though I pondered the contradictions on the surface, not surprisingly, my type-A personality convinced me to explore the latter—my journey to "walk what I talk."

In order to figure all of this out, I first needed to get clear on "the talk." In other words, what is it that I actually purport to stand for? What is it that my life is trying to say?

Being a mom has made such an impact on my being, I tend to divide my life into two eras: "BC," meaning "before children" and "AC," meaning "after children." In my earliest BC years, I was incessantly shy. I can recall at least three "memory flashes" where as a grade-schooler I opted to pee on myself rather than to risk opening my mouth to ask an adult to use the restroom. After the third instance of the "golden shower" I'd thrust upon myself, I realized, in my child's mind, that "this shyness thing" was way too debilitating, and I made a clear decision to abandon (or at least suppress) it.

As I matured as a young Black woman growing up in America, I grew more convinced that God put me here to make an imprint on the world. Coming of age in a predominately White town, I could not help but to strongly identify with my race. Identification, in this sense, was quite frankly akin to survival, and even to this day, this is much of what my life stands for. I will never forget the uncanny mix of fear and defiance I felt when racist vandals scribed nigger on our house. I will also never forget my father's answer when I implored him to erase the slur after it had remained for two weeks: Quietly but defiantly he refused, telling me that if "they" wanted to mark our house, then let it stand so that the whole community would see. Ouch! Though I cannot remember when my father finally agreed to the erasure, his racial identification, composed disobedience, and sheer dignity entered my consciousness and took root.

My ensuing BC years brought much of the same cultural connectedness with my community—a connectedness that remains a large part of who I am today. I attended a historically Black university, pledged Delta Sigma Theta Sorority, ended up as president of the Black Law Students Association at Harvard, and championed endless Black causes. I studied environmental racism twenty years ago, and made it my business to put my academic well-being on the line to show Harvard the error of their ways with regard to their perpetuation of White-male dominance in their faculty hiring and their too-reluctant (and still exclusionary) acceptance of women professors of all races.

This fight with Harvard challenged my father's commitment to the "composed disobedience" I'd learned from him earlier. After all, it was a lot to ask of him to endorse helping me through professional school, only to risk an Ivy League expulsion.

The Harvard fight represented another milestone in my life. It was my first (but not my last) personal introduction to the intricacies of race and gender. My early professional years gave me countless additional examples of this challenge as I witnessed woman after woman (inevitably mothers of all races and ethnicities) fall victim to the recalcitrant old boy network.

The incident that drove this home was when an African American male attorney whom I deeply admired dismissed the ability of a colleague of color to give a legal analysis simply because she was at home "thinking about her new baby." I don't think the situation would have stirred me so much had it not occurred in front of my colleague's White male "competition" for partner, who sat smugly by, observing the entire exchange (his wife, of course, was home with his kids).

Though I was ardently BC at that time in my life with no desire to become a mom anytime soon, it was the first time that I knew for sure that my dichotomous existence as an African American woman (and eventually a mom) would profoundly shape my value system and outlook on the world.

It is no surprise to me that the most profound experience I have ever had was becoming a mom. It was profound to serve as a vessel for a growing soul within. It was profound to bring to life a tangible being that had begun as an intangible expression of love. It was profound to witness my body transform itself into a source of nourishment to offspring, reminding me that although humans like to think of ourselves as "higher beings," we exist quite simply in nature as one part of the cycle of life.

What did surprise me, however, was the cumulative effect of it all. Any of the impacts on my life in isolation would have been easier to comprehend. But essentially what I have found is that the *most* profound aspect of becoming a mom for me was the way in which it pervaded literally every other area of my life. It has impacted my political views, my social and cultural values, the company I keep, the music I like to hear, the food that I eat, drinks that I drink, and even the way in which I choose to wear my hair.

In my BC life, I never once thought maternity leave was a politically sexy topic. And one of my earliest lessons from my AC years was that my employer (Uncle Sam himself) apparently didn't think so either. Uncle Sam, I found, was actually part of a good old boy network masquerading as someone who "cares" about family values. My AC mind could not wrap its head around the fact that in the United States, where I hear endless rhetoric about family values, female federal government employees did not have a category of leave called "maternity." The only thing I had more difficulty understanding was why colleagues looked at me as "political" or "raising a ruckus" simply for pointing this out. Maybe I was too distracted with my BC attitude in the 1990s to have recognized that the debate about the Family and Medical Leave Act was all around *unpaid* leave. "What?!" I wouldn't call my shock and outrage "political." To the contrary, my views are quite "personal."

Another part of my life invaded by my AC status was my friend-ships. While I had plenty of BC friends that stuck with me once I became a mom, consistent with my new values and my spirit, one of my first acts as a new mom was to help create a network of moms on whom to rely. I banded together with like-minded women, and together we co-founded Sistermoms, Inc., a support network for African American moms and their families. Its mission was profoundly important to me in my new space in life, and this network of women quickly became a lifeline. Sistermoms marked a major milestone in my journey as an African American mother who understands and acts on the imperative to create the kinds of sup-portive networks—the village—that her children need to thrive.

Sistermoms also inspired me to a writing renaissance resulting in three books representative of my soul. My first book, *Songs of a Sistermom*, was my initial attempt to explore what I call the sym-phony of motherhood. I reflected on what I find to be four different phases, or movements, of motherhood and celebrated the diversity of feelings that mothers experience every day. Through poetry, I explored my feelings about romantic love, pregnancy, and child-birth, the crazy ups and downs of being a mom, and finally the larger life issues that motherhood affects. Though many of my feel-ings were inextricably intertwined with my (previously singular) identity as a Black person living in America, others were singularly maternal.

One day, after a three-hour session of doing my daughter's hair, I reached another milestone on my road to understanding who I am. African American hair is steeped in a tangled tradition. History tells us that our mothers and grandmothers and great-grandmothers sat us on their laps with love as they worked a comb, trying to tame those tresses at whatever cost. But on this *particular* day, my three-year-old's scalp was especially tender. We broke a comb. She ran out of her chair. And unable to bear the drama, I cried. I wondered if it was really worth it. Maybe her hair didn't need to be "tamed" like a tiger, maybe it was meant to be free. But then I thought about all of the women in history who came before us overcoming insurmountable challenges. Clearly, this "hair meltdown" we were experiencing on this particular day was barely a blip on the historical landscape of Black women. So I wrote a poem to my daughter, *Nappy* (which I later turned into my second book), teaching her to embrace her hair, her history, and her*self*. I told her, as part of that poetic message, that "God didn't give us nothin' that we couldn't handle." And while I could not answer my internal question of whether her hair should be "conquered" or "free," I knew for sure from that day forward that we would be one with each other until she could decide for herself. I left my own hair relaxer behind that day, seeking unity and peace between my natural locks and my daughter's. Notwithstanding my strong racial identification, I'd never been a natural hair zealot. I had no problem holding up my fist and shouting, "Power to the People," while simultaneously sporting chemically-produced slick and shiny hair with no resemblance to my God-given natural naps. But as a mom, I felt differently. And today, there is not a curling iron, bottle of neutralizing shampoo, or even a hair roller to be found among my things. And when my natural-hair-loving brothers and sisters talk to me about solidarity, I know that it really isn't about that for me. It's just "personal."

My third book helped me to reach my latest milestone—a redefining of my life's purpose: to explain big issues to children. After publishing my children's book, *Nappy*, I had the opportunity to work with an amazing organization known as the Jamestown Project. Essentially some friends of mine from school had joined together to form an organization committed to making democracy real. They wanted to show people that democracy is something that should be an action that is taken with careful and critical thinking. It was the first time in my life that I was ever so drawn to an organization that was not, by definition, identified by race. What I loved about the Jamestown Project was its bold pronouncement that race does matter today, as it has since the beginning of the American story with founding of the Jamestown settlement in 1607. But the Jamestown Project also recognized that race generally is not a stand-alone issue that needs to define us. To the contrary, race is inextricably intertwined with America and all of the issues that comprise who we are. In my view, the platform of democracy was the most powerful place to stand for change against all inequities, especially inequity relating to race, gender, and motherhood.

And as I worked on issues that were near and dear to the Jamestown Project's heart, as I wrote and thought much about how to inspire people to become agents of change in their own lives, I knew instinctively that I needed to take this message to children. My daughter, like I, was a Montessori child. Maria Montessori believed strongly in children as natural learners who under the right conditions would inspire and teach each other to master the most complex ideas. As a children's speaker, author, and a Montessori mom, I had seen this myself over and over. So when the Jamestown Project was asked to co-author *The Covenant in Action*—the action companion to the *New York Times* best-selling *The Covenant with Black America*—I was inspired to pen a companion for children. As we thought and wrote about how to operationalize the agenda that was set forth in *The Covenant with Black America*, it was crucial that we also consider how to translate this action agenda to children. After all, children may be less than 50 percent of our population, but they are 100 percent of our future. The Jamestown Project believed in my vision, and with their support, I was able to publish my second children's book, *I Dream for You a World: A Covenant for Our Children*. The book is a message to children imploring them to see themselves as agents of change to make this world a better place, starting with their own actions in their homes, in their schools, and in their community.

These experiences made me the person I am today. I am strong, Black, and proud. I am woman, I am mother, I am love. I am a wife to my husband. I live to inspire. I believe in God, myself, my children, my family. I believe in all families. I believe that families are at the center of our success as an African American community, as a nation, and as a human race. Strong families and healthy children feed and nurture democracy. Children are our future; we ignore them at our peril. Though I'll never forget my father's adage, "What's fair? Is life fair? Is anything fair?," I know that injustice eats away at our humanity. I believe that America has a special challenge to overcome racial injustice, and that sexual injustice is just as pervasive. I believe that if America has any chance at overcoming the challenges that lie before it, then we must actively seek change. But I also believe in the words of my law school friend Barack Obama. It is not enough to simply seek change; we must *be* the change that we seek. And if change begins with me, how do I put my values into action in my own life first and then ultimately in the world?

This brings me, full circle, to my long-standing challenge to reject my father's admonition to "do as I say, not as I do," to live, like my friend Andrea did, walking my talk. For it is easy to make audacious pronouncements about principles and values. But the real question for all of us is, how are you living every day? We must live our values and inspire our children, families, communities, and country to do the same.

Alas, this is a lot easier said than done. Five years ago, I had my first realization that I was not exactly walking my talk. It actually happened on the same day that I have already described—after the three-hour session "taming" my daughter's hair. In the midst of my "bright idea" to compare the strength of her hair to the strength of Black women in history, I mentioned Harriet Tubman, and received from her a blank stare. "Um, well, what about Mary McLeod Bethune?" Again, I got a blank stare. "Rosa Parks?" I hoped my child, the offspring of such a strong, proud Black woman like myself, knew about Rosa Parks. She shook her head blankly again. "Well, have you heard of George Bush?" I asked, and she nodded with familiarity. "It's okay," I consoled my Black spirit, "she's only three." But truly it was not okay. She knew George Bush and George Washington. And she definitely knew Dora the Explorer and Barney. I'd unwittingly taken the first steps along a road of letting the popular culture rear my child. I was embarrassed (at least in front of myself). I was not walking my talk.

Life is about the choices we make. And even more than the difficult choices, it is the everyday choices that truly comprise our character. Should I remain at work an extra hour, steal an hour at the gym, or get home in time for dinner? And when I come home in time for dinner (exhausted), do I lie on the couch in recovery, or do I play on the floor with my three-year-old? When the dinner hour arrives, do I let the TV remain on—just this once? Do I listen out for a report on the latest election standings, or do I listen out for my daughter's report on the latest happenings in her classroom? Do I check my email, make that phone call, clean up the kitchen, or unclutter the dining room? Or do I read an extra few pages in the latest chapter book about fairies? On Sunday morning do I send my children to Sunday school, or do I bring them along with me and stay for the adult class? Do I take on the extra project from the sorority, church, or political organization? Do I drop my daughter at Girl Scouts, or lead her troop in their quest for an achievement badge? Do I pursue my own quest for my own achievement badges in life?

And then there is the challenge of marriage. If I honor God and my role as a wife, am I doing my best to make my husband a priority? If I believe strong families are the underpinnings of the democratic ideals I purport to admire, can I name three things I did yesterday to truly strengthen my marriage? If I believe love is at the center of the family, do I make sure that every word I speak to mine is with love? My husband asked me yesterday to name one positive thing I'd spoken to him (and about him) that day. While I rose to the challenge, I was deeply troubled by how long it took my mind to churn through the debris of my everyday "speak." I am troubled by these questions and not always comfortable that my decisions reflect my life's goal to walk my talk. On some days I think I get the answers right, but on others I fear they are all wrong. On these "wrong" days, my spirit cries for clarity, and all is certainly not well with my soul. So what's a mother to do?

Recently I realized that I had unwittingly developed a three-step process for resolving my spirit when I feel like motherhood, wifedom, and the troubles of the world have it spinning out of control. I use this process to try to make real my goal to walk my talk. And while it doesn't always work, and I sometimes still tell my kids to do as I say, not as I do, the failure is usually because I got so caught up in life that I forgot to apply my rule. When I keep my wits about me, it works. Andrea would be proud. There is a method to my ability to stave off madness by consciously striving to embody the person I know I am.

My methodology is grounded in a lesson I learned from the Kennedy School at Harvard. For all of the tuition payments, student loans, studying, and clamoring for class position, the most insightful thing I learned there can be summed up in three simple words: "Fire, ready, aim." This simple but ingenious axiom is something I learned in one of my public administration classes after working through a case study that was fraught with impossible problems. It did not take me long to relate it to my life, which believe it or not, was sometimes with problems even more insurmountable than a Harvard case study.

The process, by definition, pokes fun at my "supermom" inclination to be prepared before I act. In and of itself the three-step rule turns the old adage "ready, aim, fire" on its head. Indeed, I think the new version struck me as truth so soundly because the original version makes little sense—ready, aim, fire? How can I possibly get ready and aim when I am not even sure that I am targeting in the vicinity of a solution to my woes? In my mind Stevie Wonder might have a better chance at landing a 747. The truth is that sometimes in life things get so complicated that in order to figure out your best next steps, you must first "do something"; you must "fire," or you will have no chance of learning where to aim. In my life, I am always firing. In fact, I live in a perpetual state of "doing something." What the three-step rule has taught me is to stop beating myself up about being in action, and to recognize how blessed I am to have so many opportunities to learn from my actions and refine my aim.

After firing, the second step is to get "ready." Here is where you must exit the perpetual state of "doing something," where so many of us mothers live. You must stop and recalibrate by taking in what you learned from your actions. Now this is a whole lot easier said than done. I've already noted that as mothers, we do too much. So when we enter the "ready" stage of the analysis, we end up with way too much data to process. I find it difficult to remember what I ate for breakfast this morning. How is it that I can be expected to sort out the lessons learned from my actions in a way that will give me intelligence about where to take my next steps?

The ready stage, however, is supremely important, so I actually developed a tool to help me sort through all of the information. In developing my sorting tool the first thing I had to do was to throw out the *b*-word. No, I don't mean the word that rhymes with *itch* that is now supposedly suitable for my eight-year-old to hear on prime-time TV. I mean the other *b*-word: *balance*. Whoever came up with the concept of "work-life balance" in my view needs a swift kick in the rear. I believe that a mother's life is all about harsh priorities. And while "work-life-self prioritization" doesn't sound so "nicey-nice," it is a far better description of the realities of mothers today, whether they work outside the home or not.

Prioritization is a crucial part of the "ready" stage of my three-step rule. I use it to help me organize my thoughts about all of my actions. In this "ready" stage, I often meditate and pray about my priorities. But I have also learned that I need something more concrete—a prioritization tool—to help me sort through the noise of my everyday life. I am so multifaceted that what was necessary (for me) was to divide my life into four quadrants. Each quadrant was allowed no more than three priorities, and similarly each quadrant had its own prioritized ranking.

When I retreat into my "ready" stage I use this tool to remind myself that I must come first. Top priority. If mom does not have inner peace and health, then our life will be little more stable than a house of cards. Secondly, (and in this order) comes the whole health and wellness of my marriage, my children, and my extended family (which includes my friends). For most mothers the next prioritized quadrant would be about income and financial health, though for me it tends to be my social, cultural, and political activities. This is probably due to my innate need to express myself. Admitting this has led to a deeper understanding of where I need to aim along my quest for happiness and satisfaction in life.

I place dotted lines between my quadrants because I've learned that prioritizing is easier when a potential activity satisfies priorities that might otherwise be competing. For example, I have limited some of my past social and cultural activities in favor of good works that simultaneously satisfy other priorities, such as my publishing company, which allows me a side-gig where I can satisfy my need for self-expression about all of the social issues that move me. This concept also helped me to choose canvassing with my children as my preferred way of political participation in the 2008 presidential election, as opposed to phone calling or participating on countless grown folks' committees. I may have compromised a bit of the impact I might have had on the process, but the much-needed lesson in civic engagement to feed the whole development of my three-year-old and eight-year-old was far more important, and allowed me to cross quadrants and maintain my priorities.

And finally, my handy little four-quadrant prioritizing tool leads me squarely to the final stage of my three-step process—to aim. Aiming is a whole lot easier with the wisdom of firing first and the reflective forethought brought about by an appropriate readiness stage guided by a thoughtful analytical tool. Aiming is easier when you know your priorities and which actions you should take to keep this complicated symphony called life in harmony. If I am successful, the symphony of motherhood I sing about in my first book will ring harmonious. If I am successful, my dear friend Andrea will be singing with me from beyond, where she too can feel the melody flow. And finally, if I am successful, I will have achieved a deeper understanding of myself, my multifaceted nature and the multitude of movements in my song, and the instruments I need to play to keep my symphony in tune. And that is not only walking my talk, triumphantly, it is dancing my song.

★ **CHARISSE CARNEY-NUNES**, freelance writer, attorney, and social entrepreneur, is the author of two children's books, *I Dream for You a World: A Covenant for Our Children* (2007) and *Nappy* (2006), as well as *Songs of a Sistermom: Motherhood Poems* (2004). She is a senior officer of The Jamestown Project, an action-oriented think tank focusing on democracy, and a graduate of the Harvard Law School, Harvard's JFK School of Government, and Lincoln University in Pennsylvania.

Sounds Like a Plan

REBECCA O'CONNELL

Dr. O., my ob-gyn, called to say that the plan was illegal in Pennsylvania, but it was legal elsewhere. Not only that, but it was also the very best source of organs for sick babies, since the organs would be new and strong and free of disease. He was expecting a call back from a transplant specialist; the specialist would find out where we could implement the plan.

I thanked him. It was his idea, but I was completely on board. I wasn't so sure about my husband, but I figured I could convince him.

I was carrying a twelve-week-old fetus with anencephaly: no skull. I'd seen the ultrasound the day before. It was very clear. There were its little legs, its arms, its bright-white spinal cord, and there was its brain: exposed, naked, all the whorls and swirls plainly visible.

Well, I thought, *we can make him a helmet. I'll knit him a nice, wooly hat to cover it up. We'll replace it as he grows. We'll manage. He'll be fine.*

But I was telling myself a story. The truth of the matter dawned on me, even as I visualized the cap I would knit my baby: No one can live without a skull.

The doctor performing the ultrasound confirmed it. No, the baby could not live outside the womb. No, the pregnancy was not likely to end spontaneously.

"Well, then, what am I supposed to do? What do people do?" I asked. Screamed, kind of.

The doctor patted my shoulder. The ultrasound tech gave me a Kleenex. "The counselor will be in to speak with you," she murmured.

I'm sure the counselor was warm and responsive, but I have no idea what she said. I think her main job at that point was to hand me things—a box of tissues, a paperback book called *Empty Arms: Coping with Miscarriage, Stillbirth and Infant Death*, another box of tissues when I'd used up the first one, a four-by-three-inch glossy print of my ultrasound. This last item she procured for me after repeated requests. "I don't want to seem morbid," I explained over and over. "I just want to have something to show my husband."

My husband was at work that morning. He'd already taken time off to go with me to the ultrasound at five weeks, the one I'd had after some scary early bleeding and a blood test indicating low hCG. He'd been there for the one at six weeks, at which they'd seen a heartbeat after all, and after which we'd gone out to Ritter's Diner for a huge waffles-and-sausage-and-eggs-and-orange-juice break-fast. He'd come to the one at ten weeks, when I was supposed to get the CVS test, but didn't. (A CVS—chorionic villus sampling—test can detect the same fetal abnormalities as an amniocentesis, only earlier.) The doctor had postponed it because the fetus was too small.

Small, but still within normal range, so I wasn't worried. I'd seen the heartbeat. I'd seen the fetus whirling around on the ultrasound screen. I'd had a little bit of morning sickness, and my jeans were tight at the waist. Things were fine. I could go in on my own at twelve weeks for the CVS. I could drive myself home afterwards. My husband had missed enough work. There was no need for him to come with me to this appointment.

The counselor gave me the picture, along with what I perceived to be a look of incomprehension. Was it weird that I wanted a picture of my doomed baby? The Victorians did that all the time. But my memento mori was an ultrasound, printed in a medical complex offering some of the most up-to-the-minute healthcare in the country. My request must have seemed incongruously nineteenth century in that technologically advanced setting.

I left the office with the picture, the book, a half a box of tissues, and instructions to call Dr. O.

But first, I toted everything over to my husband's workplace. There was no privacy in his office, and it was too cold to stand outside, so we had a brief, surreal conversation in the car. We agreed: It didn't make sense to us to carry to term a baby with no chance of survival. We'd have to terminate the pregnancy.

My husband and I are both pro-choice. We give money to Planned Parenthood and support NARAL-endorsed candidates, but my husband was raised in an anti-choice culture. In fact, I'd briefly considered breaking up with him in college, when we'd been talking about a pro-choice rally on campus, and he'd said, "I'm not sure how I feel about that issue." He'd come around, though, had married himself a feminist, and gotten her knocked up. But I thought he'd still been a little squeamish when I'd insisted on having the CVS.

"I'm pretty unconflicted about this," I'd told him. "I don't want to raise a child who has a severe disability. If the test comes back abnormal, I'll terminate the pregnancy." He'd agreed, but the conversation had left him looking like he needed to throw up.

Now our worst-case scenario had come true.

But that was before we'd ever heard of the plan.

I went home and called Dr. O.

"Can you come in? Right away?"

It had taken me months to get an initial appointment for my pre-trying-to-conceive physical exam, so the prospect of getting to see Dr. O. immediately, right now, that very afternoon, was intoxicating. Even though I thought all he was going to do was give me the name of the doctor who would terminate the pregnancy, I hurried right over.

"Now I bring this up not to try to influence you in any way, but just to give you another perspective," said Dr. O when I arrived for my spur-of-the-moment appointment.

If I carried the pregnancy to term, the baby would not live long, but its organs would be healthy and strong. Dr. O. counted out the list of strong and healthy organs:

A heart

A liver

Two kidneys

Two lungs

That's six organs, six lives that could be saved if I carried this baby to term. My baby could save six lives; my baby could be a hero.

That could-be-a-hero phrase might seem a little bit manipulative, but I don't think that's how he meant it, and at the time, I barely heard it. All I heard was a plan. There was an out. There was a way I could stay pregnant. I could grow organs for harvest.

Dr. O. wasn't sure that the local transplant program did this sort of operation. He gave them a call, while I watched and listened and blew my nose. He got the answering machine.

We discussed logistics while we waited for a call back. I wondered how they would get the organs out of my anencephalic baby in time to transplant them. They couldn't take the organs until my baby was dead, but once my baby had died, the organs wouldn't be good anymore.

"Could I have a scheduled C-section? Could they do the C-section in the transplant hospital, so that the minute my baby was done with them, the organs could be put right into the recipients, without wasting any time?"

Yes, Dr. O. assured me, that could be done. He could even give me steroids to speed up my baby's growth, so instead of waiting another twenty-six to twenty-eight weeks to have the C-section, we could possibly have it in as little as twenty-four.

But what about my son, the one who was four years old, almost five? How could I explain it to him? He would be sure to notice my growing belly. He would know something was up. What could I say?

Yes, Mommy is going to have a baby, but the baby is going to die. It's very sad, but there's a happy part, too. Your little brother or sister's heart, lungs, kidneys, and liver will go on living in other babies' bodies.

My son didn't know I was pregnant. Except for my husband and my friend Cathy, no one did. I was thirty-seven years old. This pregnancy had been planned; this baby had been wanted, but I was cautious, too. I knew that, elderly woman that I was, my chances of having a baby with a genetic abnormality were pretty good: one in one hundred, or something like that.

We had decided not to mention the pregnancy to anyone until the CVS results were in. The bleeding, the early ultrasound showing an empty gestational sac, and other reminders of my advanced maternal age reinforced our decision to keep mum, and by twelve weeks in, we still hadn't told anyone else.

But I'd picked out some names, and I'd found a really cute pickles-and-ice-cream pattern I was going to use on the email announcement once we were ready to share our joyous news. I'd been reading my son lots of picture books about new siblings or the miracle of reproduction, starring litters of kittens, puppies, and bunnies.

"Well," said Dr. O., "how much do you remember from when you were five?"

A lot. I remember my kindergarten. I remember my cats. I remember my sister very clearly. I remember that I wasn't crazy about her, but I don't have any trouble remembering her existence. I remember my mother going away to the hospital, my grandmother coming to stay, my newborn sister coming home and sleeping on my lap on the big orange sofa. And when all that happened, I was much younger than five. If my son found out about the baby and the plan, there was no way he wouldn't remember it.

"And once he's old enough to understand, think how proud he'll be of you," said Dr. O.

"I'll ask my husband," I told him. I thought my husband would probably go for it. I knew, deep down, my husband thought abortion was murder. He would be as thrilled as I was to find out we didn't have to have one.

"Are you religious?" Dr. O. asked. My name is O'Connell, but my face is more like Abrams, Levine, Rabinowitz. You don't need very sensitive Jewdar to pick up on my Hebraic ancestry, and Dr. O.'s Jewdar was state-of-the-art. "Because there is such a thing as *shalom bais*, a peaceful home." He gave me a minilecture about Judaism and the domestic sphere, the essence of which I took to be that while it would be preferable for me not to have an abortion, it was not worth wrecking my marriage over. If my husband was dead-set against the plan, we shouldn't do it.

He was.

My husband and I have been married for fourteen years, about twelve of them in couples therapy. Okay, well, maybe not twelve, but a lot. We've been on the brink of divorce more than once, sometimes for years at a time, which is not to say it is an unhealthy relationship. Rather, it's a relationship between people who have had a lot of practice having discussions.

Once Dr. O. and I realized the transplant hospital might be a long time calling back, I went home.

I had just finished debriefing my husband when Dr. O. called back. I told Dr. O. my husband was still on the fence.

"No, I'm on the other side of the fence," my husband said.

I told Dr. O. I'd call him back.

I presented my husband with my case. "Either way, our baby is going to die," I argued. "If I carry the pregnancy to term, at least its organs can help other babies live."

I imagined another mother, somewhere, holding her newborn, knowing that, without a donor, her baby would die. We could prevent that. All I had to do was carry my baby to term.

"And have a C-section," my husband pointed out. It was major abdominal surgery, not without risk, not easy to recover from.

"I know what a C-section is like." I'd had one with my son. It was miserable, but the whole thing was miserable. A little more misery on top would hardly even be noticeable. And if it resulted in something good, some baby getting a heart or a lung or a kidney or a liver, it would be worth it.

"You don't have to be a martyr."

This was from my mother. The conversation had gone from our kitchen to my parents' living room. My son watched TV down the hall while my family tried to talk me out of the plan.

My dad nodded in agreement with my mom. There is nothing my family loathes more than martyrs. My raised Catholic husband has a different understanding of the term *martyr*. To him, a martyr is holy, a person who gives of herself, who suffers for a higher purpose. To us, a martyr is someone who suffers for glory. *Oh, that's all right. Don't worry about me. You go ahead. I didn't want to go anyway. I'll just stay here and clean the grout around the bathtub.*

"I won't be a martyr," I explained. "I'll be really low-key. I'll wear baggy clothes. If anyone does notice I'm pregnant, I'll change the subject."

"But you would still have to travel at nine months pregnant to God-knows-where this scheme is legal, and leave your son for days and days, and have your baby only to watch it die. You're my little girl. I don't want to see you go through that."

I had answers to all their objections. As in my helmet-beneath-the-knitted-cap story, everything in the transplant-plan story would work out fine. Sure, I'd be uncomfortable; sure, it would be hard on my young son. But it would be worth it.

Anyway, I didn't have a choice. I was obligated. If you have a chance to save a life, isn't it your moral responsibility to do so? I had to carry this baby to term so its organs could be transplanted. It was the only reasonable, responsible thing to do.

And besides, I'd never even gotten to feel the baby move yet. Four more weeks, maybe five, and I'd be feeling the baby kicking in there, flipping like a fish. Each little flip would remind me of all those other babies, the potential organ recipients who would take my baby's organs and keep them alive for years and years.

Why didn't my family get that? Didn't they love this baby as much as I did?

I looked at their faces one by one—my husband, my mother, my father. They didn't look like abortion-promoters. They looked like sad, shocked, compassionate old people who regretfully acknowledged that terminating this pregnancy was the right thing to do.

My husband was against the plan. My parents were against the plan. Maybe they knew something I didn't. And even if they didn't, even if they were wrong, at least they were resolute.

Dr. O. referred me to Dr. T., another ob-gyn. Dr. T. explained about anencephaly. Somehow I'd thought it meant that my baby was normal and healthy in every way, just without the skull. That's not what it means. Anencephalic babies are missing the top parts of their brains. If I did carry my baby to term, it might be hours or days before brain stem activity and respiration ceased. By that time, the organs would likely have deteriorated; they would no longer be useful for transplant.

That's why the plan was illegal in Pennsylvania—and most other places. For the transplant plan to work, the organs need to be harvested before respiration ceases. This is theoretically possible because anencephalics are born in a vegetative state. But practically speaking, there are many ethical and medical obstacles to transplanting the organs of anencephalics.

Dr. O. may have exaggerated the plan's viability and minimized its liabilities, but if he had planted false hope, I had tended and watered it.

I had the abortion in the same hospital where I'd seen the ultrasound, the same hospital where I'd had my little boy. It didn't hurt. I was asleep throughout the procedure. When I woke up, the nurses brought me cranberry juice and crackers. They told me my hair looked nice. Nobody called me a baby-killer. No one even implied it. One nurse told me she had had the same operation. Another gave me information about a support group, Unexpected Choices, for people who had decided to terminate a pregnancy when they found out it was genetically abnormal.

Anencephaly isn't caused by a genetic abnormality. It is a form of spina bifida, something supplemental folic acid has been shown to reduce.

"I took my folic acid. I took it even before I was pregnant," I told my husband. I told Dr. O. I told the nurses, and Dr. T., and the counselor, and my parents, and my friend Cathy. But maybe I had missed a day. I'd taken the folic acid, but not the multivitamin. I'd had coffee. I'd stood near the microwave. I'd had a sinus infection and fever around week five.

"It's not your fault," they told me.

And, "I'm here if you need anything."

And, "It will get better. Just take it day by day."

My husband doesn't want to try for another baby. He never wants to go through anything like this ever again. And besides, we already have a beautiful, healthy, smart, funny, wonderful little boy. Our family is complete.

I can't disagree.

But I'm taking my folic acid every day. Just in case.

★ **REBECCA O'CONNELL** is a registered donor with the National Marrow Donor Program, www.marrow.org. She is the author of several books for babies, children, and teens. Her essay first appeared in the Winter, 2006 issue of *Brain, Child*. Visit Rebecca online at www.rebeccaoconnell.com

The Mother
I Always Wanted

ROBIN TEMPLETON

When I was six months pregnant with my son, I broke up with my mother. We were standing in her kitchen on Thanksgiving Day. It was almost nine o'clock in the morning. It was almost my third trimester.

Up until two days earlier, when Michael, the father-to-be, and I left our home in Brooklyn for my hometown in Louisiana, I'd been in a state of bliss—since the moment I passed the pregnancy test. I never left home without my ultrasound pictures, like a Jehovah's Witness wielding Bible scripture, proclaiming proof of God in our midst. No one was exempt—not colleagues, ex-boyfriends, near strangers—from blow-by-blow reports on the baby's every move, my every craving, graphic details of my birth plan. My elation was incorrigible, invincible, I thought. But I hadn't yet seen my mother, and she and happiness don't much abide one another.

The closer we got to Pineville, Louisiana, the more my glow was overshadowed by old emotions: regret that I was going to see her; guilt that I hadn't seen her in so long; shame that I reverted to a conflicted little girl in her presence; remorse that my child, in utero, would be exposed to her alternating fits of anger and contaminating gloom; resentment that going home for the holidays meant walking into a land mine; and most treacherous of all, fear.

What if my joy supreme had been a passing side effect of the pregnancy hormones? What if all this love and light, this elation and confidence was just a phase, wouldn't be mine to sustain and shower on my baby for his lifetime? What if, ultimately, I followed in the footsteps and recriminations of my mother who often said she never should have married my father or had children when she did?

I broke into a cold sweat on our flight from JFK to Houston. Michael and I were seated in front of the emergency exit row. The seats didn't recline and my protruding stomach blocked the food tray from folding down. For three hours I held on to Michael with one hand and a ginger ale in the other, with the complimentary vomit bag tucked under my arm. I broke into a hot sweat on the prop plane from Houston to the airport nearest Pineville. This plane's ventilation system was inoperable. Through non-recirculating air, the barely twenty-something flight attendant assured us that, otherwise, the aircraft's electrical system was fine. I fanned myself with the laminated safety instructions, closed my eyes and a neon warning scrolled behind them like an interruption from the Emergency Broadcast System: *Beep. This is a test. Beep. You are your mother's child. Beep. Your baby will be raised by a woman raised by your mother.*

What would I do in the event that this was a real emergency? What if one's capacity to mother is genetically predetermined? What if embedded in my DNA were not just my mother's height and the color and texture of her hair, but her maternal traits as well? What if it was already spelled out in X chromosomes, that I would be a mother like my mother? What if my nature and nurture—or the ways in which she failed to nurture me—made the case closed, that I did not deserve the miracle growing inside me?

On Thanksgiving morning I woke up to traditional smells, cornbread and turkey in the oven. And familiar sounds: my mother slamming cabinet doors, the percussive banging of pots and pans and run-on invective, the soundtrack of my adolescence. "I tried to raise you girls right but none of you thinks about anyone but yourself."

It didn't matter that no one else was in the room. Or that my two sisters and I hadn't lived in the house with her for a decade. "None of y'all ever listen to a word I say. Look at all these dirty dishes in the sink. Next year you can all go to goddamn Piccadilly and Christmas is cancelled." The rest of the family, including Michael and my sisters and their husbands, stayed in bed in various states of denial, staying out of her way as long as possible.

Mom's outbursts were becoming increasingly explosive and irrational over the years. She'd recently threatened to kill my father—not in a figure-of-speech kind of way—and had gradually cut off all her friends. Her hostility was plastered in sticky notes all over the house and spilled out of it, painted in irate acrylic warnings on garbage cans at the end of the driveway, thrown out on to the carport with random appliances that pissed her off, furniture she'd grown to hate, art projects she'd pulled all-nighters to finish, then discarded.

What had not changed was my family's response. We stuck to our routine of duck, cover, and wait for the storm to pass, the hurricane drill. In Louisiana you're taught young what to do in case of this kind of emergency. You learn that a hurricane is not a fire. It can't be extinguished or out run. Once the storm is imminent, there are no viable escapes. Just get as far away as possible from glass that might shatter, shield yourself from the roof that might cave in, seek higher ground.

We also never talked about it, each catering to her out of an emotion, I could never name or understand, a clumsy amalgam of obligation, guilt, abiding love, and sympathy. Mom's emotional instability is compounded by health problems that could fill a medical encyclopedia. She has chronic fatigue syndrome and fibromyalgia and, for as long as I can remember, suffered through a continuum of viruses, migraines, muscle spasms, and insomnia. She's also never met a doctor she didn't hate, who she did not insist was condescending and incompetent; stuck to a serious treatment plan; maintained proper nutrition; stopped smoking; or cut back on her drinking.

Reaching out over the years had only backfired. My suggestions—a relevant book or article, a new homeopathic or medical approach—were summarily dismissed: "I've already read that. We can't afford it. It would never work. That's not the real problem. You just think I'm a hypochondriac. Don't worry about me. It only makes it worse."

I too wanted to stay in bed that morning, ducked and covering, but the baby kicked and grumbled for breakfast; we were starving. I approached the kitchen, hugging my belly protectively, trying not to inhale the secondhand smoke of her Benson & Hedges menthol ultra light smoldering near the pantry. I offered a timid "good morning," smiled, pretended nothing was wrong, approached to give her a hug, went through the motions: "Is there something wrong, Mom? How can I help? Why don't you go rest for a minute and I'll clean up?"

"There's nothing you can do. If you wanted to help you should've thought of that yesterday when you used all the milk. I've peeled all these goddamn sweet potatoes and now I can't make the casserole. And you didn't wash the pan you used to make those lemon bars that no one's going to eat anyway. I had to spend ten minutes scrubbing it clean for the cornbread and now look at my hands."

I apologized. Said I'd go buy milk right away. "Gee, I hadn't thought of that, Robin," she shot back. "It's Thanksgiving Day and this is Pineville. There's nothing open." But it was a chance to get out of the house. I pocketed the keys to her Plymouth van as I backed out of the kitchen, went upstairs and fetched Michael, for whom I'd made the lemon bars, his favorite dessert, tiptoed with him back down the stairs, and snuck out the front door.

We drove down Pinehurst Drive, a narrow, potholed fray of blacktop, the only way to or from the house I grew up in. No yellow line marks its two lanes, if you can call them that. Vehicles going in both directions stay in the middle, careening out of the way of cars coming in the opposite direction at the last possible moment. Except for old people and Avon ladies who never surpass twenty miles an hour, everyone drives Pinehurst at freeway speed, especially trucks hauling fishing boats and tractors that tilt into the ditches that border the road, which, when they flood, are called creeks and facilitate craw fishing.

About five miles down Pinehurst, a gas station was open. We

scored a gallon of milk, and Michael tried to conceal the cigarettes he'd also purchased. I went into my antismoking, you're-going-to-be-a-father-you-have-to-be-more-responsible-and-quit lecture. He joked that I sounded just like my mother and did a hysterically accurate imitation of her. I cracked up and tried my own, and laughed the way home. It was a levity I'd never known.

My mother's first suicide attempt occurred just before my eighteenth birthday. I remember sitting beside her on her bed when she came home from the hospital, trying to play the grown-up. I asked her why, told her I wanted to understand. "You don't really want to know," she told me. When I insisted that I did, she said that the first time she remembered wanting to die was when she was pregnant with me. That was when my dad was diagnosed with Lou Gehrig's disease and told he wouldn't live to see thirty. (It turned out to be muscular dystrophy.) I was born prematurely, then sick all the time with routine bouts of pneumonia and asthma. But it was my adolescence that took the most out of her. I was so difficult and angry, she said, so she knew that what I needed was someone safe to fight against so I didn't really rebel and get into real trouble. And that's what finally did it. Getting through my difficult preteen years had taken her last bit of strength, she said, after that, she didn't have anything left to give. She didn't know how else to explain it: I had exhausted her will to live, back when I was in seventh grade, and she'd held on as long as she could, then just caved in.

I played the scene back and saw how ludicrous it was. My mother's depiction of me as responsible for her misery was a lie. It occurred to me that I could write myself out of the script, out of her tragedy. Maybe this dynamic with my mother, painful as it was, was all drama with no plot, much less a genetic blueprint, concluding that I would become her or live on her fault line.

I drove the Plymouth back to the house, pulled under the tin white overhang and parked the van in its oil-stained spot, iridescent in the late autumn, late morning light. Before I could unfasten my seatbelt, Michael told me not to move, then ran around to the driver's side of the van, opened the door, and tilted the steering wheel up as far as it would go, giving clearance to my belly. I felt the sticky morning, the clingy dampness, neither hot nor cold, that is fall in Louisiana. Michael pushed back the seat, helped hoist me down from the van, kissed my forehead, then my stomach, then the palm of each of my hands, and told me it was going to be okay, that we'd be home soon.

And then I saw the lemon bars. Mom had dumped them out of that pan she needed for the cornbread on to a plastic platter and put them outside on the barbecue pit where she stored the cat food. A veneer of Saran Wrap was ripped open. The cats had feasted.

Armed with the milk and what was left of Michael's lemon bars, I faced off with her in the kitchen, adult to adult, not daughter to mother. I told her she was mean, unfair, and made holidays miserable. I told her that her unhappiness didn't give her the right to blame and make everyone else unhappy. I told her I would not, ever, expose my child to her bitterness and temper. Then I sobbed out how much I loved her and that I was sick and tired of being treated like her enemy.

I don't remember what happened next, only the realization that she wasn't going to take me in her arms and tell me how much she loved me back and how much she would love her grandbaby. I remember the acceptance that saturated and settled into my skin. She was not, never had been, and never would be, the mother I'd always wanted. I had to stop wanting otherwise.

The rest was anticlimactic. It was one of those breakups that just happens, as random as it is necessary, painful as it is redemptive, unplanned but not an accident. Mom stormed out of the kitchen and locked herself in her bedroom. Two hours later she slammed out of her room, then without a word got her keys and walked out the back door. From the carport I heard her curse about someone changing the adjustments on the driver's seat and steering wheel. My sisters made mimosas and we finished all the cooking. We ate when the meal was ready, without her. Generously, no one blamed me for ruining Thanksgiving.

Washing the dishes, I considered my new relationship to Mom. I tried to see her for who she is: the woman who gave me life, cared for me through childhood sickness, gave me important parts of who I am. A woman who suffered abuse as a child, then continued the cycle of abuse with me, who sometimes approached mothering like a suicide bomber, like her pain entitled her to take it out on others.

And I also remembered something she gave me, a legend. It was the story of a woman who lived with us in the Carondelet apartment buildings when I was a toddler, who saved a baby from drowning. One muggy, lazy summer afternoon, the story went, the woman, from her fourth floor living room window, saw another child fall into the apartment complex's swimming pool when his mother had dozed off. Seeing the child in danger, the woman sprinted down four flights of stairs, scaled a chain link fence, dove into the far end of the pool, swam to the near end, and scooped up the baby, who never even cried, the story went. The woman splashed around in the pool with the child until he was calm, laughed, splashed back, and trusted the water.

I remembered clinging to this story as a child, imagining that the rescuer was my mother. As I remembered it and had recounted it to myself countless times, Mom was not a witness to but the hero of the story, not the mother who fell asleep, but the woman who came to the rescue.

Drying the dishes and putting them away, I drew an emotional curtain between my mother and myself. I felt the fear and doubt recede and I replaced them with what I knew: I would define motherhood for myself. I might make it up as I go along, as I've learned most mothers do, but I would revel in it. I would love my baby up and down and all the way through. I knew I already did; I knew I always would.

The only evidence I have of how I'm doing as a mother, making it up as I go along, is in the splendor of my son, in the delight he takes in the world, in the songs he makes up in the bathtub, in the self-portraits he paints before bedtime. The only point of reference I have for what constitutes a "good mother" is the mommies to whom I've borne witness. Mommies like my best friend, whose baby's first word, uttered between visits to her father in prison, was "happy." Mommies who've shown me what it is to be a good mother, whose standards I bear. Who've held my baby and whose babies I've held, who have entrusted me with their children and with whom I've entrusted mine. Mommies who lift me up and hold it down, who hold it all, many of them as single parents, all the way down, triumphantly. Mommies who are heroes and survivors. Mommies who have survived mothers that scorned them, fathers that fingered them, dates that raped them. Mommies who did not succumb to professors who refused to accept a paper late because their baby was sick, who suggested that maybe law school wasn't the best place for a mother. Mommies who graduated on time, with honors, anyway. Mommies who met deadlines, made homes out of next to nothing. Mommies whose children experienced being evacuated from Hurricane Katrina as a great adventure. Mommies whose children will never know that all the sleepovers they had that summer was because the restraining order had failed. Mommies who healed. Who write books, file lawsuits, make films, get to work on time, get their kids to school on time, make sure their children eat the USDA-recommended allotment of fruits and vegetables, who pay the bills, and, more often than not, manage to look fabulous, and who keep telling their stories, however ugly, scary, or beautiful.

On my altar in Brooklyn there's a portrait of my mother taken when she was pregnant with me. Everyone who's ever noticed it among the shells, stones, statues, and saints remark how much the two of us look alike, identical, even. Many friends have said that at first glance they thought the woman in the picture was me. And it doesn't make me cringe. In the photo I don't see her protégé. I see my cheekbones and the shape of my eyes. No less and no more.

★ **ROBIN TEMPLETON** has worked within the nonprofit and youth development fields as an organizer, writer, and researcher for the past fifteen years. Currently she is a Chancellor's Fellow and PhD candidate at the Graduate Center of the City University of New York and works as a consultant to organizations and foundations. She was the founding executive director of Right to Vote, the national campaign to end felony disenfranchisement. Robin was communications director at the acclaimed Ella Baker Center for Human Rights; worked with Pacific News Service's *The Beat Within*, the nationally recognized writing program for youth in detention; and worked with the national, online news alternative Alternet.org. She has a Master's in Education from Harvard University. She serves on the board of the Youth Justice Funding Collaborative and has been published on juvenile and criminal justice issues in such publications as the *Nation*, Salon.com, and *The Fire This Time* (Anchor, 2004), an anthology of young women's writing. She is the mother of a three-year-old son, Truth.

An Unnatural Woman

MARTHA SOUTHGATE

I am standing by the sink, chopping parsley, and putting butter into pasta. Behind me, my son, Nate, sits writing a story; he asks me to carefully spell out each word. He is almost eight. My daughter, Ruby, who is four, plays with a few small plastic dinosaurs on the rug in the dining room talking to herself in a quiet voice. My husband is not home from work yet. My voice is patient and even as I spell. I haven't worked on my new novel in a month and a half—haven't worked on it continuously and thoughtfully in six months. As I move the knife over the parsley, I think, briefly, of turning the knife to my wrist, a messy end. Or maybe I'll walk out the door and never return, seamlessly gone, leaving behind the children, the cold pasta, and chopped parsley. For a moment, I am tantalized by the idea that my disappearance from this scene would be easier than trying to keep going as an artist, a mother, and a wife.

You may ask: How could you think such a thing? You have two beautiful children, a loving husband and family, a home, two published books. How could you think of leaving them? How could you think you'd be happier without them? At one time, I would have asked those questions myself. I'm less judgmental now. I know how even the simplest request from the most beautiful children, the most patient husband, can feel like an imposition when you never feel like you have enough money, time, or ease.

In his essay, "Fires," Raymond Carver writes about being a young parent and a writer: "There were good times back there of course; certain grown-up pleasures and satisfactions that only parents have access to. But I'd take poison before I'd go through that time again." When I read those words in a bookstore, I sagged against the shelf, my eyes filled with tears. *That's exactly how I feel*. I thought. That the person who had articulated my feelings was a White man, a brilliant writer who revolutionized the short story form, and a recovering alcoholic who left his first wife, were not lost on me. Only a White man whose place was established, and who had nothing to lose, could write with such brutal honesty. For a woman, to talk so is almost unimaginable. I sweat even as I type these words.

A woman loves her children. That is a given in our society, reinforced at every conceivable turn. And a black woman is the mother to the world. Look at our history—all the babies we've raised. Our own and other people's. By necessity or by choice. A black mother's love is supposed to be uncomplicated. Aretha Franklin-like, it moves mountains. Some of us have always known the picture to be more nuanced than that—as in the scene in Toni Morrison's *Sula* when Hannah Peace asks her mother if she ever loved them and is met with an angry tirade that ends, " . . . what you talkin' 'bout did I love you girl I stayed alive for you can't you get that through your thick head or what is that between your ears, heifer?" That's a kind of love—but not the kind we talk about or celebrate.

Gradually, I have realized that I have to write to live. I'm like Sula—or would be if I hadn't found my way to words. "Had she paints, or clay, or knew the discipline of the dance, or strings; had she anything to engage her tremendous curiosity and gift for metaphor, she might have exchanged the restlessness and preoccupation with whim for and activity that provided her with all she yearned for. And like any artist with no art form, she became dangerous."

I am a writer, but I also have chosen to have children. And there's the rub. I'm 41 years old and I love my children, enormously. I'm a fairly good parent, but it's not easy for me. It's not easy for anyone, but I find it harder than most. Family life—taking care of others, the bump and rub of a group—I've never been comfortable with it. My children's needs intrude on my need for solitude, reflection, selfishness, time to be. I resent it. I try not to let my resentment affect my parenting, but I must be honest. As I become more serious about my work as an artist, I am less patient with chauffeuring and PTA meetings and all the minutiae that fragment a mother's day.

Carver wrote about that, too, how the little things can seem like torture, how the laundromat can be a kind of hell, how all the chat about how you should enjoy these years crumbles to nothing in the face of them. That seems like another thing that only a man would have stated so baldly; so without remorse. But there's something to that—getting to the nut of it, the ugly truth of how children intrude on an artist's life, how all writers are profoundly selfish in our consuming search for transcendence. Why do you think we can't stay married? Why do you think we drink so much?

Well. That's a cliché. In fact, I don't drink to excess (people in my family did but that's another story) and I love my husband. But we writers are scarred, and searching. Our search isn't compatible with family life, but we must pursue it in the end.

I didn't always imagine myself a mother or a writer. Both things came to me rather late in life, a surprise. I was always told I wrote well but never considered fiction writing as a career until I was thirty and found myself truly interested in some characters I was making up. Interested enough to tell their story even though no one else might want to hear it. I remember, before I had children, sitting at me keyboard, writing what would later turn out to be a novel, but was then, frankly, a mess. I loved it. I was possessed by a desire to know where my characters' lives would lead. I needed silence to do it.

Kids are loud. I am constantly shocked by the din my two small children make, their brown bodies colliding, shouting, shrieking, embracing each other. And the fighting. More often than I'd like,

I use a sharp tone with them, or I sound exasperated. Sometimes I'm not sure what they've done to frustrate me so. I only know that I feel overwhelmed, and fatigued by their persistent needs and desires, their mere existence.

I have had a few stays at artist's colonies, the Virginia Center for the Creative Arts (VCCA) and the MacDowell Colony in New Hampshire. They are bastions of calm where writers and visual artists can get away from the demands of daily life and be pampered and free to concentrate on their work. The first time I went away to VCCA, Nate was just two, Ruby not even conceived. I didn't miss Nate much. I thought sometimes of his soft, café au lait skin, the fuzziness of his hair. I knew I wouldn't want to be away forever. But I was in a fever of creating and no one could stop me. At VCCA, I was the only parent of a young child. The other artists looked befuddled as I explained why I could stay only two weeks instead of the customary month.

"Wow, you have a two-year-old," people would say, astonished. I, too, was astonished; astonished that I could leave and have such a good time; astonished that my husband and son could manage and even thrive without me. Other mothers who've visited artists' colonies talk of loneliness, missing their children so much that they couldn't work. I worked like a demon, made some dear friends, and went out one night to a feed-cap bar in the rural Virginia town, drank too much and came home giggling like a teen caught out after curfew. At the end of my stay, I returned to Brooklyn, reluctant but restored with 50 new pages. Being away was a gift, an invaluable jewel. I envied all those childless artists and their freedom.

The best part of my stay at MacDowell was the night I went with a fellow writer to see a movie with no negotiation, no discussion, no need for a sitter. Just free to go. The way single people are. Boy, that felt good.

Those memories should make the moments by the pasta bowl more memorable, but still the knife entices, the door beckons. But freedom is not all there is, in anyone's life. People without children struggle just as mightily to create as parents. In some ways, I've been forced into a kind of efficiency, a seriousness that I might never have achieved without becoming a mother. I know that writers can find every way under the sun to avoid writing and I can't blame my kids for every day I piddle away. My suicidal dreams, my fantasies of self-obliteration have everything to do with parts of my heart I hope my children will never know—and nothing to do with them.

They have given me great gifts, even as they constrain me. Labor was a gift with both of them—18 hours into a 30-hour-long labor with my son Nate, I realized that there was nothing I could do—it wouldn't be done until it was done. I couldn't type it into a Palm Pilot, to be rescheduled at my convenience. I just had to ride the wave until it was finished—a highly useful lesson for a novelist to learn.

From Nate, I have learned the virtue of attentiveness. On the subway or the bus, during any emotional encounter, he is all eyes and ears, silent and watchful, like a deer by a creek. It is all internal—he does not always share his thoughts, but he misses nothing. All of life fascinates him.

From Ruby, I learn language anew. Once, when I commented on something her assistant teacher did, she misheard me and responded indignantly, "Jackie's not the singing teacher, she's the washing teacher." The one who helps with handwashing and lunch and nap, these fine arts. One day, when I chased her around the playground, she scooted up the jungle gym, laughing and shouting to me, "Climb inside the poetry!" Who knows what she thought she was saying, but she offered me some words to live by.

Truth to tell, hard though it is, there is a certain usefulness to being forced to stop thinking of oneself all the time, to have to stop living in one's head. There is a certain usefulness in having to take care of someone else, to love and be loved so thoroughly, to learn how to hang onto oneself and one's work in the face of constant pressure not to. When I think of leaving, I think of the doorknob cool inside my hand, the comforting swing of the door towards me. I never think of the moments, days, years after—the devastation I would feel, the ache of not being able to feel those hard little heads under my hands. I suppose that's why my leaving remains a fantasy—it never goes beyond imagining. And I suppose that's how I know I have become a mother for good.

The best writing, the best art, shows us the world—either a character's inner world or the world as the writer sees it. My children force me, not as often as I should, sometimes resentfully or with exasperation, to look at the world. "Look, Mommy," calls Ruby, "there's music in the bench." We are coming from my son's flute lesson at the local music school. She points out a brick, embedded in a park bench, too low for me to see without crouching, in which someone has painstakingly carved a staff of tiny musical notes. Music resides in strange places. Music I might never have heard had I not had children.

★ **MARTHA SOUTHGATE** is the author of *Third Girl from the Left*, which was published in paperback by Houghton Mifflin in September 2006. It won the Best Novel of the year award from the Black Caucus of the American Library Association. It was shortlisted for the PEN/Beyond Margins Award and the Hurston/Wright Legacy award. Her previous novel, *The Fall of Rome*, received the 2003 Alex Award from the American Library Association and was named one of the best novels of 2002 by Jonathan Yardley of the *Washington Post*. She is also the author of *Another Way to Dance*, which won the Coretta Scott King Genesis Award for Best First Novel. Her non-fiction articles have appeared in *The New York Times Magazine*, *O*, *Premiere*, and *Essence*. She was the Associate Chair of the Writing Department at Eugene Lang College at New School University and has taught there as well. She now teaches in the Brooklyn College MFA program. She lives in Brooklyn, New York with her husband and two children.

Growing into a Woman and a Mommy
How I Came to Be a Mother

HEATHER MCCARY

Being a mother has coincided with the hardest and most enlightening time in my life. Not because of the motherhood itself or my child, but mostly because of my age. I am twenty-five years old with a ten-month-old daughter. I was twenty-four when I became pregnant with her. Not particularly young, not particularly old, just in between. Anyone who has been this age in the past or presently can tell you that it is a time marked by self-identification. Just after the age of figuring out who you are, this is the age of trying to implement who you are to be able to create a life. In American society, it seems that we are allowed to stay children longer, so instead of being made to take on responsibility at a young age, a lot of people wait until their twenties to kind of figure it out all at once; this is how my mama raised me. Though I was not quite ready for responsibility, I did the whole college thing and I actually loved it. I left Cincinnati, where I grew up, to go to Atlanta and attend Clark Atlanta University. I graduated within four years with a bachelor's degree in education just to ask myself, now what? I was twenty-two and supposedly about to begin my life as an independent, educated woman with goals and a future. It didn't quite fit together like that for me.

In my generation, women seem to be self-starters who now understand that a man is not necessary for a career or even a family. The women of my generation know that they can go to school, work, and succeed just as a man can, and there are many examples out there to prove it. But by the same token, women in this generation are also told to be trendy, sexy, and flawlessly beautiful. In the era of inhuman expectations of perfection and debilitating convenience, you must also have the perfect body, the perfect wardrobe with all the designer labels, the newest gadgets, hold down a career and a home, *and* be a full-time mom. All of these expectations are a tall order for women (and it would also be for men if they were expected to fulfill all of that). This leads to a woman who either takes that pressure and tries to be all she can be to everyone including herself, or to a woman who rejects all of it. I am mostly the latter.

I am not the kind of person you can tell to do anything. I've always been a rebel. I hate societal labels and expectations. The expectations imposed on the women of my generation are unrealistic and cause the anxiety and fear that a lot of women deal with every day from trying to be perfect. We are told that we *have* to be equal to men, so that seems to mean that in order to be equal, we have to do all of the things that they do *and* do the things that women were traditionally brought up to do.

I do not believe that I am unequal to a man just because I choose to stay at home and raise my daughter and keep a nice home. I think men and women are inherently equal, but are also inherently different. What a woman contributes to society is no less than what a man contributes. Just because you can work outside of the home, doesn't mean you have to. This doesn't mean that I do not ever want to work outside of the home, but I do believe that I have a choice and I am no less a woman for choosing either. I don't have to compete with a man to feel as if we are the same. We are not the same, and I like being respected as a woman, because I am just that.

So, back to my rebellion: I graduated college and I floundered. I loved my major, education, because I love children and teaching and learning. I am a nerd at heart. I absorb information, I love to read and learn new things. I love research and enriching my mind. But I was not interested in working, not just yet anyway. The free spirit inside of me felt that it was more important to experience the world. I had been with my boyfriend for about two years and we were planning to move to L.A. from Atlanta to pursue his acting career.

In August of 2005, eight months after I graduated, we packed up the car and drove over two thousand miles west with a few dollars, high hopes, and a pipe dream. The struggle began. We quickly realized that the $3,000 we had went quickly and we just did not have enough to stay in L.A., so we moved to Las Vegas, where my boyfriend's best friend lived. We spent time living in hotels and for a few weeks were homeless and living in my car while he worked as a salesman, trying to get enough money to move into a weekly hotel. We finally moved into a weekly hotel, and my boyfriend started making more money. But along with the money he made, the hours he spent at work multiplied. He usually spent sixty to eighty hours every week at work. This left me feeling very lonely in a new city where I had no friends or social life. Also the stress of him working and the remnants of the stress from living in the car and having to struggle from the moment we arrived in Las Vegas caused us to fight, a lot more viciously than we ever had before.

We transitioned from a loving couple with occasional issues to one living with trust and distance issues. My boyfriend still wanted to pursue the relationship and I spent the first half of 2006 trying to find any reason to run back to Atlanta. In fact, I packed up the car twice and drove an hour to three hours in that direction before he called and begged me to come back and work on the relationship. I was so unhappy in Las Vegas. My boyfriend didn't trust me. I had no other friends.

By June of that year, our union had broken down almost completely, and I was working and planning another escape back to Atlanta. I was finished and he seemed to be also. The fighting was getting worse and we were both unhappy. The last day of the month, an off day from work, I received my check from work and I was thinking over my plans to leave. I had informed my boyfriend and this time he had no objections. On that day I also realized that my period had not come all month, so I went to buy a pregnancy test, no big deal. No big deal only because during my time on earth, this had happened before: I missed my period, believed I was pregnant, bought a test only to find out I wasn't, and then my period would start right after. I always believed that your psychological state effected your physical state, so basically if you believe in any way that you are pregnant, you body will respond to the stress and thus you will miss your period. You may only get it back after confirming that you are not pregnant so that your mind will instruct your body to go on as usual. I have no proof behind that theory, I just always believed it.

So I took the test. And it said pregnant. It was one of those digital kinds that actually said the word to add to the drama of it all. My jaw almost dropped off the hinges when I saw that. I did not expect it to say that. I don't believe in abortion as an option for my person, so I pretty much was going to be a mommy.

I left the test sitting next to the toilet so that my boyfriend could see it when he went in the bathroom. The shock was almost too much. *Well, I guess I'm not going to Atlanta*, was all I was thinking. My boyfriend came home and I told him to go to the bathroom. He came out smiling. I knew it was not because of happiness but more because of total surprise. He didn't have much to say about it that night, so we kind of just discussed the day and the test in general, but didn't get into anything specific. The next day came and he was worried. He mentioned not being all too pleased with the pregnancy, and I lost it! Blame it on the hormones, but I started yelling about how he needed to be happy and that he knew that if I got pregnant I would keep it, and I threw a remote control at him. We had a pretty rough fight and I decided that I was going to Atlanta after all, if not for anything but to clear my head. So I bought a close friend a ticket to Las Vegas so that I wouldn't have to drive all the way across the country alone. And within three days, I was back in Atlanta.

I spent two months in Atlanta, not doing anything particularly special. I stayed with a friend, got prenatal care, and tried to decide what to do with me and my baby's life. In the meanwhile, my boyfriend called me every day begging me to come back to Vegas and trying to influence me to get an abortion. I said no, no, no, stop asking. My mind was made up. I was having my daughter. I just knew she would be a girl. That was what I wanted, and that was what I was going to get. I was excited about the prospect of being a mother. I was never sad or upset, just anxious. I wanted to make the right decisions from then on. So I made sure I stopped drinking alcohol and smoking weed and did everything my doctor told me. My baby girl needed a fresh start.

The Birth of Motherhood and the Stress

I came back to Las Vegas in September, four months pregnant. I was happy to see my boyfriend, since I missed him, but I was also slightly worried because of our unresolved issues. We spent the rest of my pregnancy fighting.

I worked and saved up until a few days before my daughter was born. I didn't have a lot of money, but I used what I did have. During the holiday season, while everyone else was buying for friends and family, I was buying for my daughter. I built up my excitement about my upcoming motherhood by buying all (or most) of the things that my pregnancy books and motherhood magazines said were absolutely necessary for a good mother to have. I even bought the best digital camera I could afford so that I could capture every living moment on film.

On February 20, 2007, around four in the morning, I began having labor pains. It was a week before I was expected to go into labor and just two days after I began my maternity leave. I walked around my living room and denied that this was the actual event until about eight in the morning when the pain became too unbearable to stand any longer. I woke my boyfriend and told him that it was time to head to the hospital. This was supposed to be his first day of work at a new job and he was pissed to have to get up so early and drive me to the hospital, especially when he did not believe that I was in real labor. I bitched, threatening to drive myself, until he got his behind up and got dressed.

The labor went quicker than I could have ever imagined. I was four centimeters dilated when I arrived, and the hospital assured me this was the real thing. I was put in bed and strapped up to the machines, and I spent the next few hours on the phone with my family, who thought they would be there to witness this in person. My boyfriend and I just kept looking at each other in shock: *Is this the real thing?*

Kameryn Chanel arrived at 2:13 PM while I experienced none of the pain that is usually associated with labor and delivery. True, I was on an epidural since I had dilated six centimeters, but there was no screaming, no cursing, no yelling. Just push, push, here's your baby! I looked at my child and did not have a clue as to what to name her. After a couple of hours, we decided on Cameron, with the middle name Chanel. I changed the spelling to fit my own preference and that was it. She took his last name, even though we were not married, because it looked better with Kameryn than my last name. And with the first major decision down, we were parents.

The first week with my baby girl was hard since I had no real clue how to be a mother. But I tried. I stayed up what felt like all night long and nursed my baby, held her, and tried to learn her cues. It was hard, to say the least. I felt like those days would never end, but I did my best. Our family came eventually and stayed for a few weeks. My mother was the biggest help I could have asked for. She cooked, cleaned, overlooked my handling of the baby, and did what a mother is expected to do for her daughter and grandchild, and I was grateful. My boyfriend and I were getting along okay while we tried to get used to this parenting thing.

I decided from the beginning that I would be an attachment parent, meaning that my child would be breastfed, would co-sleep, and would never have to cry for very long to get my attention. I bought a sling so that I could strap her to me while I cooked and cleaned the house so that she would not have to worry where I was when I was busy. I also decided that I would be a stay-at-home mom for as long as possible so I could be her first teacher. I wanted to raise the most well-adjusted, secure child that I could.

Eventually, the family left and real life set back in. We were still fighting. Over everything. Kameryn would be very quiet and very still when we fought. She was very aware that something was wrong, even in her early days, and her way of handling it seemed to be to try to be invisible. It hurt to see her act this way while we yelled, cursed, threw things, and destroyed our home.

When she was two and a half months old, we realized that his job and my savings were not enough to pay the rent. The landlord had raised it from $600 a month to $1,000 right when our child was born and we did not have enough for April and May. So we left before we were evicted, en route to L.A., to find out if the City of Angels would be kinder to us this time around. This time we had about $500 and a baby to take care of. We drove the four hours in the dark of night in the middle of May just so that we could park our car behind an apartment complex and sleep there for the next few weeks.

My boyfriend found a job and we stayed in the car until we had enough to pay for a hotel for a week. When we finally had enough, we moved from the car into a halfway decent hotel, where we spent $380 a week to live in one room. The cycle felt endless. He worked everyday and made enough each week for us to pay for the room, eat, and put gas in the car. Never enough to save. I applied for public assistance and diligently followed up until I got something, anything, since we had what felt like absolutely nothing. I did all I could to keep from getting depressed since I knew that depression only makes you sink deeper in the hole.

The fighting had decreased, partly because of how our child reacted when we behaved that way and partly because we realized that when we fought and destroyed our things and each other, it only set us back. Our relationship strengthened and we were absolutely in love with our daughter. So we kept on a happy face, tried to make the best of the little we had, and worked to get ourselves out of the hole we created.

I finally was able to get some assistance, just enough to move us out of the hotel we were in and into another one, one that was about $500 cheaper on a monthly basis. We were so excited, since we believed that struggling was starting to pay off. We felt that we were finally getting somewhere. With the assistance and his job we could finally begin to save for an apartment, and then we could start on what we came here for: his acting career.

Learning to Be a Mother

While my boyfriend works daily to keep us in the hotel and out of the car, I continue to stay home with our daughter. I stay home for a couple of reasons: One reason is that I am still determined to be my daughter's first influence for as long as I possibly can, and the other reason is that with childcare costing around $1,000 a month in L.A., and with the huge spike in gas prices that the West usually faces to a greater degree than the rest of the country, it wouldn't make sense for me to work, since my money would go only to childcare and gas.

Staying home, while being one of the most boring times in my life, is also one of the most fun; it is a weird paradox. I play with, read to, and care for my daughter all day, everyday. I chase her around the room, making sure she doesn't put anything in her mouth or pull something dangerous off the table and onto her head. Between those activities, I watch television and surf the Internet a lot of the day since I am too broke and do not have the car necessary to take me and my daughter out of the room most days.

Kameryn is very well developed. By the time she was three months, she was babbling endlessly and following the conversations being had by adults. She would watch people and look them in the eyes as they addressed her. She was called alert more times than I could count. I always attribute that to the fact that all day it is just me and her, and I always include her in my day and talk to her like she is an adult herself (sprinkled with occasional baby babble just to make her smile). She sat up and crawled at five to six months old, and suddenly at eight months old, she began walking. She started by cruising the furniture and then pulling off to take one or two steps until she finally got it down. Everyday she is getting faster and smarter, and I do what I can to keep up. I still breastfeed her in addition to giving her solid food, and her diet is pretty well maintained, considering my lack of a kitchen.

But the time I spend with her to make sure she is well-adjusted, secure, and alert comes with a price. My job is more than full-time, it is all the time. People do not usually believe that being a stay-at-home mom is really work, but it is. It is much different than having a job, since you do get a lot of down time, but your job never ends. My boyfriend loves being a father and loves playing with his daughter, but when it comes to changing diapers, feedings, bathing, and giving the needed medications, those are just my jobs. He feels that since he works every day at a job and has to get up in the morning, even weekends are his extended break, without noticing that I don't get an extended break, ever. No matter how many times I explain it to him, it just doesn't sink in. And since I feel more comfortable doing these things myself since I always do them, I don't really push him to help out at home. I think most stay-at-home moms can relate. I have heard the term "married single mom" many times. My daughter also expects me to be her primary caregiver. While she accepts her father's help when he offers it, she comes to me when she needs something done or just wants attention. She is very used to having all of my attention, so a lot of times she can be found on my lap.

So far I have learned the biggest lesson about motherhood sacrifice. As a mother, your time is no longer just your time. I think this is what mothers of all generations can relate to. When your child needs you, no matter when you were born, how you were raised, or how you make a living, you are there for your child. The child's needs supersede your own every time. I think that my generation may be a little more surprised and taken aback by the demands of motherhood, since my generation was taught to value independence and was not given many lessons on how to cultivate or nurture a family unit.

I am getting used to not being able to come and go as I please. I have an obligation to my daughter, which overrides anything that I have planned. I used to be the clubbing, party girl who went out at least twice a week before I was pregnant. Now I have yet to go anywhere that doesn't involve my daughter or family. Part of me misses the freedom I had before motherhood, but a huge part of me loves being a mother so much that it doesn't matter what I used to do.

The unfortunate part of life that has coincided with the birth of my daughter, but was not necessarily because of her, was the slight loss of a part of my identity. Since I moved out West, I do not do many of the things that I used to do that made me happy. I used to immerse my life in music, poetry, candles, alcohol, and weed-smoking and now I don't have the time or means to do those things anymore. I used to party and I used to live in the moment and never think much of consequences, just the excitement and fun of spontaneity. I had friends and could do activities outside of the home. I was more of an individual.

But the fortunate part of my life has been a gaining of a new type of identity. I do not live the way that used to make me happy, but a lot of the struggles that I have faced—living in a car and a hotel, becoming a mother—have made me stronger and more self-aware. Growing up, I was not made to take much responsibility because my mother would run in and save me before things got too hard. As an adult, I financially removed myself from my mother in an effort to learn to rely on myself and my own strength. Life is not nearly as comfortable as it used to be, but this discomfort was and is necessary because I am learning what I can handle. I have learned how resourceful I can be when my back is against the wall. I have learned to love and value myself because of who I am, not what I have. I have learned that no matter what, I have choices. I do not have to be what society expects of me. I don't have to be perfect, beautiful, or even rich because as long as I have the love of myself and my family I am okay. I am more than okay; I am happy. I have learned to look inside instead of outside for fulfillment. And I have learned to give these positive traits to my daughter in every way I can imagine. I do not have much, but I am happy.

I don't know where my life with my boyfriend will end up. I love him as he does me. I don't know if marriage is for me. Marriage is an outdated concept in my mind. I think it was a necessary institution when women depended solely on men for their income and financial livelihood, and men depended on women to make a home comfortable for them and raise children. Gender identification roles have been traded, reversed, and embraced by both sexes on many levels, where individuals are more self-sufficient and thus no longer *need* to be married, but are married more out of love than obligation.

This is the reason I am not married yet and I don't know when or if I ever will be. I think that as long as my boyfriend and I want to be together, we will; it is our choice, and we are not obligated to each other or owe each other anything. I want our life together to be a choice, not a chore or responsibility. We have grown together in our almost five years together and we have been through the ups and downs. He was and still is my best friend. We know each other very well and trust each other. I want him here for his daughter, and he wants to be here.

Teaching My Daughter to Be a Woman

The biggest challenge that I have had so far and that I think that I will have is teaching my daughter how to be a woman. I have never been traditional in my way of doing things and that includes being a mom. I have never liked labels and boxes and have always strived to stay true to myself. I spend a lot of time thinking and trying to identify what is best for me regardless of what others say or think or the ways that others try to define me. I will not marry just because it is expected of a mother to be married. I have practiced extended breastfeeding when the world says a woman's breasts should be sexual, rather than maternal objects. I breastfeed in a society that actually thinks and behaves as if the act is unnatural. I do not vaccinate my child because I am not completely convinced that the health benefits outweigh the liabilities. I hold my child and give her extra attention when she needs it in a society that says you should push your child toward independence as early as possible. I stay at home with my child to teach her and guide her when society says I should be working if I am a real woman. I believe that it is the role of the mother to guide and teach her child first, instead of leaving the child to figure it out from the television and the Internet.

I want my daughter to be educated. Not just the traditional idea of education, but truly educated. I want my child to enrich her mind with relevant information and to question things that do not make sense. I want my daughter to think independently and to do what is right for her, no matter what anyone thinks.

I want my daughter to feel loved and secure. I believe that self-esteem and self-worth are the most important values that I can give her, more than money, more than possessions, more than mindless traditions. I want her to know her worth, no matter what she looks like or what she owns, and to know that she is capable and can succeed.

I want to be honest with her. I want to be not only her authority and teacher but also her confidant. I do not want her to be too afraid to talk to me about anything, and I want her to know that I love her no matter what decisions she makes or what happens to her. I have no particular dreams for her life; I want her to be able to dream for her own life. I have no particular idea about how she should look or act; I want her to be true to herself. The only things I want is that she is well-adjusted, open-minded, gracious, loving, and happy. However she gets to those things are her choice. I want her to have choices.

I am a new mother, so I understand that maybe all will not be perfect just because I plan to strive for excellence, but I will try. I owe my daughter that. I will do everything I can to provide her with choices for her own future. The things that I want for her are the things I want for myself. I am her first teacher, and I plan to not only talk, lecture, and teach but also to model a woman for her. I want her to see her mother happy and fulfilled, so that she knows that she can be so too. I expect her to try and that is all. As long as she tries and doesn't give up on *whatever* it is that she wants, I will be happy.

★ **HEATHER MCCARY** is twenty-five years old and lives in Glendale, California. She is originally from Cincinnati, Ohio, where she graduated from high school. Heather attended college at the historically black university Clark Atlanta University, where she majored in middle-grades education with a concentration in language arts and social science. She is the stay-at-home mother of a ten-month-old daughter named Kameryn Chanel Clark. Heather plans to teach in the upcoming 2008–2009 school year at a local elementary school. She likes listening to music, reading, and writing and aspires to become a published author and to develop an after-school program.

The Sex Goddess and the Mama

LORRAINE RICE

Sometimes I think what I really need to do is get the Sex Goddess and the Mama to sit down together, maybe over tea, and have a little chat. Nothing too heavy, just a little light conversation.

"How are you doing today? You look a little flushed," the Mama would say sweetly, pouring out the tea.

"Oh, I'm just thinking about how I intend to get off later," the Sex Goddess would answer mischievously, peering over the teacup in her hand and running her tongue around its rim.

This would make the Mama uncomfortable, but she would pretend that she hadn't heard it, determined not to encourage the behavior, then point towards the window. "Look at that, a cardinal!"

I just can't get these two together, these two identities, aspects of myself. The more I struggle to integrate them, the more separate they seem. Sometimes the distance is so great that I can't believe there is no real physical separation. Don't they know each other by now?

When I was pregnant with my second child I read an article in a magazine about the sexuality of motherhood. The author encouraged women to embrace the Hot Mama within. A naked, round-bellied woman, looking fiercely seductive, taunted me from the pages of the magazine. I was not as far along in my pregnancy as she was, but I did not feel much like a "Hot Mama," and was doubtful that would change. What I did feel was a mixture of a surge of empowerment and a festering resentment. I liked the *idea* of being regarded as a Sex Goddess, but my reality was more one of a sex hobbyist. Something fun to do in my spare time, like knitting or hiking, minus the accessories and practical footwear.

There was something so sad and disappointing about this revelation; this demotion of my Sex Goddess to a lesser deity. I used to adore sex. There was one summer—the summer my husband and I started dating—when I practically subsisted on a diet of sex alone. Sex and ice cream. I fondly remember that as the "summer of overindulgence."

Even before then I took my sex life very seriously. I was no stranger to masturbation; actually, we were very good friends. I delighted in exploring every nuance of my body like a musician with a new piece of music. My fingertips knew just what chords to play, and yet were intrigued by the reverberations that followed. The solo rhythm of my breathing the backbeat to a song that looped in one tight little circle, from me, back to me, back to me, back to me.

Of course, it didn't start out that way. There was that guilt-laden time of adolescence, a period marked by the implicit, if not explicit, message that good girls do not have sex. Nor, so it seemed, did they play with themselves. No one ever talked to me about masturbating. No one ever showed me how. No one ever suggested it as an alternative to doing anything else which might result in pregnancy, disease, or lowered self-esteem. I had to figure that one out on my own. I remember lying on my stomach in bed, in the dark of my room, rocking my hips, and rubbing my pelvis against a pillow folded in half and propped between my legs. My immense sense of pleasure was always punctuated by pangs of guilt. When I got a little older I graduated to the bathtub and detachable shower head, and reveled, weak-kneed, in the power of a precisely aimed jet of water. I was convinced it was a discovery on the level of fire.

It was not until my college days that I ever actually touched myself. By that time I had realized that the warmth filling me to the point of seeping through my pores was a reason *to* do it, and not a reason *not* to do it. I entered a kind of sexual awakening, which included how-to workshops, the discovery of erotic stories that put my mother's Danielle Steele novels to shame, and battery-operated toys that never would have made it under the Christmas tree. In truth, I preferred these solo acts to the serial hook-ups that defined college social life. I was never good at that game; always falling in love, or at least imagining I had. Sex was just not easy for me—fun, but not easy.

I'm the type of person who leaves a movie with all kinds of questions like, what happened next? (as in, after the final credits have rolled) and, what was going on before? (as in before the title screen). I am obsessed with the story of things, the whole story or as much of it as I can get. The same was always true with me and sex. All the stories—mine, his, ours—which converged into that one experience, that one encounter, left my head spinning. The weight and work that were the price of sharing something, however carnal, however brief, with another soul, made me long for the unencumbered bliss of sleeping alone.

I don't sleep alone these days. There is always someone in my bed; a child or a man-child, someone determined to claim me as their own. Maybe this is the reason that I hardly masturbate anymore. Maybe it's this feeling that I don't belong entirely to myself that shifts pleasuring myself to the bottom of the never-ending, ever-growing to do list. There is something about motherhood that is not entirely conducive to a healthy dose of masturbation. The words "mother" and "masturbation" don't even look right in such close proximity to one another. It's like an embarrassing misprint or the unfortunate punch line to a very bad joke. As a daughter, I am a little disturbed by the combination. As a mother, on the other hand, I'm open to some further discussion on the matter.

When I became pregnant with my first child, I unwittingly signed some ethereal contract that promised the rights to my body to him and to any future siblings for some yet to be determined length of time. I watched the transformation with a dazed, sleep-deprived awe. My breasts were no longer erogenous zones, but feedbags, albeit somewhat attractive ones, and a twist of the nipple brought on a steady leak of wasted milk. My back was sore from countless nights of carrying my son up and down our narrow hallway, and my brain was numb from singing "The Itsy, Bitsy Spider" over and over again. There was no room in my life for sex. No room, no time, no energy.

My children are a little older now, but still clamber for me in the night, attaching themselves to me in some body-nostalgic way, as if deep down they remember when I was their home. Their sense of entitlement is great. My lap, my arms, my back: in their mind these things belong to them, in the same way that my attention, my gaze, my time belongs to them. It is enough that they have to share me with each other. It does not occur to them that they share me with myself. So I try to slip, unnoticed, into and out of these identities, but it isn't as easy as changing my clothes. I need time to reacquaint myself with each role upon donning it. And time is one thing I don't have in abundance; laundry, yes, but not time.

As a mother I am always on, and that makes it difficult for me to get off. It does not seem to be the same for my husband. He has a less complicated relationship with his sexual side. I don't want to use the word "simple," because that just seems mean, but if he were any less complex when it came to sex he might be a dog. At any given moment he is ready for it; no identities to navigate, no stories to tell himself. I don't know if this ability is something particular to being male or specific to his personality, but he sure does have that "Be Here Now" thing going. Or should that be "Get Some Now?"

And therein lies the double standard. His messages have been so different from mine. Men are expected to be sexual beings. They are encouraged to masturbate. There's that wink-wink, complicit approval to get as much as they can, as long as they don't get anyone pregnant, and even when that does happen, there is little expectation for anything to change. I've heard that theory that sex is all about emotion for women and for men it is all about the act, but I have known enough women just looking to get off and enough men requiring an emotional connection before they can do anything to challenge that.

Of course, a lifetime of conditioning has done wonders for me, and I often fall into the trap, buy into this idea that men have certain needs. (Even now my husband points me to scientific evidence that a regular release of semen reduces the risk of prostate cancer.) I allow this to distort the picture of my own sexual identity by becoming fixated on his so-called needs at the expense of my wants. This never does either of us any good.

In reality, what we both want and need is the same, to connect. It is when I remember this, when I weigh our desires equally, or better yet, when I leave all my weighing and judgments at the foot of the bed, tangled in our discarded clothing, that I enjoy myself the most, step fully into my Sex Goddess.

She laughs, and asks, "What took you so long?"

And I know she's talking to me because ultimately I'm the one who gets in my own way. I worry about how to bring my different identities together, when they were never really apart. Where would the Sex Goddess be without the nurturance and inspiration of the Mama? And wasn't it my sexual identity that got me into this motherhood thing in the first place? They aren't really strangers after all, at least not complete strangers. Whether they realize it or not, they exist in a symbiotic state, one feeding off of and into the other. One of these days I'll go to introduce them and they'll smile politely and remind me, "We've already met."

★ LORRAINE RICE is a writer and unschooler living in Philadelphia with her husband, Adam, and their two children, Ian Sol (seven) and Zahra Luna (four). She writes about motherhood, sexuality, education, and more on her blog at blueperiod.blogs.com.

Immaculate Conception

LYRICS BY RHA GODDESS

Open the well,

inner reservoir to ya soul

unleash the trueness . . .

shines like gold, (*um-um-um*)

Bolder than a million suns,

orbiting the universe in one . . .

Harmonious plan, brother shed his blood

on distant land . . . (*da-dump-da-dump*)

So far from home,

everywhere is sinking sand! (*sand-sand-sand!*)

Outstretch a hand if ya hear me! (*Outstretch . . .*)

Outcast a lie if ya feel meee! (*Outcast . . .*)

We seem to be choking on our own insanity . . .

We keep on perpetratin' . . . (*um-hum*)

They keep on regulatin' . . . (*um-hum*)

And now we're re-creatin' . . .

Our own devastation!

Imagine this . . . (*Imagine this . . .*)

You and I livin' in a world . . .
 (*You and I livin' in a world . . .*)

Picture this . . .

That embraces every boy and girl . . .

Dream on this . . .

Infinite rain-bows, and multicolored melodies,

Blend in harmony, (*in harmony*) gonna blend in harmony . . .
 (*gonna blend in harmony . . .*)

Mastabatin' you for the catch

Snatch this wisdom piece upside ya head . . .

Elvis is dead and so is your soul (*whooooooo*)

When ya got no control!

We put the 9mm to the temple, (*um-hum*)

Got poverty in the mental . . .

What will it take to break these . . .

Psychological chains? (*chains-chains-chains . . .*)

Raise up ya hands if ya hear me! (*Raise up . . .*)

Stand up and fight if ya feel me!! (*Stand up . . .*)

We seem too lost inside our own identity . . .

They keep insinuatin' . . .

We keep perpetuatin' . . . (*um-hum*)

And now they're isolatin' . . .

This whole generation! (*generation . . .*)

Imagine this . . . (*Imagine this . . .*)

You and I livin' in a world . . . (*Hmmmmmm*)

Picture this . . .

That embraces every boy and girl . . .

Dream on this . . .

INFINITE rain-BOWs, and multicolored melodies

Blend in harmony, (*blend in harmony . . .*) gonna blend in
harmony (*gonna blend in harmony . . .*)

Ah ha ha ah ah whoooooooooo (whooooay)

Uh huh huh ah huh huh huh (ay-ha-ha-ha-ay)

Ah ha ha ah ah ha whooooooo (whoooay)

Uh huh huh ah huh huh (ay-ha-ha-ha-ay)

Ay, ay ay ay Iy, yay Iy yay (ay-ha-ha-ha-ay)

Iy Iy Iy Iy Iy yay yay yay Iyyay

(*AYYYYYY-AAAAAYYYYY-AYYYYYYYYY*)

Imagine this . . .

Picture this . . .

Dream on this . . .

INFINITE RAIN-BOWS, and multicolored melodies

Blend in harmony, (*blend in harmony . . .*) gonna blend
in harmony (*gonna blend in harmony . . .*)

We're all family . . . (*We're all family*)

We're all family . . .

All family . . . (*We're all Family . . .*)

We're all family . . .

All Fami-eeeee-ly

Printed in the United States
by Baker & Taylor Publisher Services